HENRY FIELDING

A Biography

Henry Fielding, from the sketch by Hogarth published in *Works* (1762)

HENRY FIELDING

A Biography

PAT ROGERS

Charles Scribner's Sons
NEW YORK

for Doone and Peter Mitchell

1 3 5 7 9 11 13 15 17 19 I/C 20 18 16 14 12 10 8 6 4 2

Printed in Great Britain
Library of Congress Catalog Card Number 79-84177
SBN 0-684-16264-4

Contents

Illustrations

Pages 57–60

Southwark Fair by Hogarth, 1733 (Mansell Collection)
Grub Street (Museum of London)
Kitty Clive (Mansell Collection)
Charlotte Charke (Mansell Collection)
Strolling Actresses Dressing in a Barn by Hogarth, 1738 (Mansell Collection)
A riot in Covent Garden theatre in 1763 (courtesy of the Victoria and Albert Museum)
Theophilus Cibber, dressed as Pistol, confronts the Drury Lane management led by John Highmore (reproduced in Mary Nash, *The Provoked Wife*, Little, Brown and Hutchinson, © Mary Nash 1977; original in the Harvard Theatre Collection)
Plate 1 of *The Harlot's Progress* by Hogarth, 1732 (Mansell Collection)
Plate 3 of *Marriage à la Mode* by Hogarth, 1745 (Mansell Collection)

Pages 81–84

The house at East Stour, Dorset where Fielding grew up: engraving by James Basire the younger after a sketch by Thomas Rackett (reproduced in Wilbur L. Cross, *The History of Henry Fielding*, copyright, 1918, by Yale University Press)
The Thames at Twickenham: oil by Richard Wilson, 1762 (Mansell Collection)
Plate 2 of *The Election* by Hogarth, 1755 (Paul Elek Ltd)
Robert Walpole in the House of Commons: engraving by Sir James Thornhill after Hogarth, 1730 (Mansell Collection)
A benefit ticket for Fielding's *Pasquin* by Hogarth, *c.* 1736 (Mansell Collection)
'The Festival of the Golden Rump': a satirical print (reproduced by courtesy of the Trustees of the British Museum)
Fountain Court, Middle Temple (Society of Antiquaries of London)
A view of the Thames in the late 1740s by Canaletto (Mansell Collection)

Pages 117–20

Samuel Richardson (Mansell Collection)
Prior Park, outside Bath: engraving by Anthony Walker (reproduced in *The History of Henry Fielding*, copyright, 1918, by Yale University Press)
Illustrations to *Joseph Andrews*, 1743 (Mansell Collection)
Title-page of *Joseph Andrews*, seventh edition, 1764 (Mansell Collection)

Preface

Any admirer of Henry Fielding finds two causes for enduring regret. The first is his death at forty-seven, an age when neither Defoe nor Richardson had begun his career as a novelist, and when Sterne was only just getting *Tristram Shandy* under way. The second is the paucity of Fielding's surviving correspondence. Until 1978 only twenty-one letters were in the public domain. The largest single collection, written to the eccentric philosopher James Harris, has been unearthed in the course of extensive research on which Professor Martin C. Battestin is now engaged. (At present the 'standard' life is still that of W. L. Cross, published sixty years ago.) Meanwhile Professor Battestin has almost doubled the tally of published Fielding letters: early in 1978 he printed for the first time fourteen completely new items which illuminate Fielding's relations with his most important patron, the Duke of Bedford. A letter from his widow Mary Fielding to the Duke and new letters from his half-brother John Fielding add to the value of this discovery. I had completed the original draft of this life when the correspondence was published, and must acknowledge my good fortune in being able to use materials not available to previous biographers.

I have attempted to present in a short compass the major incidents and concerns in Fielding's career. I have not discussed his major works at length, since there is a substantial body of literary analysis in this area. Naturally I have profited from recent scholarship although—details aside— my narrative follows much the same course as that taken by Austin Dobson, Cross or F. Homes Dudden. But general attitudes to the eighteenth century have been transformed in the last generation. I have sought to reflect this new awareness, and to present Fielding in a guise more credible to modern readers. My debt to the writings of M. C. Battestin, W. B. Coley, Henry Knight Miller, Ronald Paulson and C. J. Rawson will be evident to all students of the novelist. The more lavish illustration now possible is an aid which I much appreciate. I am grateful to Antony Wood of Paul Elek Ltd for his agreeable invitation to write this book. Above all I owe thanks to Henry Fielding, in whose company I have passed so many pleasant hours: if the book induces others to enter the convivial society of this great man, its aim will have been achieved.

Prestleigh, Somerset   *May 1978*

A Note on Quotations

I have normally brought spelling and typography into line with modern usage, except where some special flavour would be lost. Punctuation is kept as in the original, unless this produces actual obscurity. I follow the Wesleyan edition for Fielding's own works, where this exists; otherwise I use Murphy's text. Old Style dates are silently modified to accord with later practice: thus 23 January 1749 or 1749/50 is given as 1750. To simplify the story I have generally referred to Kitty Clive or Charlotte Charke under these names, by which they are best known today, even though they bore other surnames for a time.

'I am just got up from a very amazing entertainment; to use a metaphor in "The Foundling", I have been these four or five days last past a fellow traveller of Harry Fielding's, and a very agreeable journey I have had . . . If my design had been to propagate virtue by appearing publicly in its defence, I should rather have been the author of *Tom Jones* than of five folio volumes of sermons . . .'

Captain Lewis Thomas
letter dated April 1749

ERRATUM

The last four words of the last line on page 13 should read:

'again after a generation'

ONE

A Distant Prospect

1707-28

I

Henry Fielding's greatest work was the story of a foundling, and this is apt because the early novel was generally regarded as a bastard among literary forms. Fielding, too, with his 'comic epic in prose', had presided over the strangest act of miscegenation—there was an air of daring paradox to that phrase which modern readers find hard to recapture. How neatly, then, it falls out that the writer was himself a kind of genetic sport, the product of a complex series of mixed marriages.

On his mother's side he came from comfortable Somerset gentry who lived decorous lives through a century of revolution. His maternal grandfather had been headstrong enough to go into the law, and ended up as the eminent Sir Henry Gould, justice of the King's Bench. The grandson of this luminary, Fielding's first cousin, was also named Henry; in time he also became a judge and attained a knighthood. Three years junior to the novelist, he lived on into the last decade of the eighteenth century.

Against this sober meritocratic achievement, there was an unpredictable streak on the other side of the family. The yeast of intemperance went back several generations. At least as far, anyway, as William Feilding, killed at Nottingham in 1643; he had volunteered for the service of Prince Rupert, after being given an earldom for his loyal principles. His elder son fought on the parliamentary side, but was accused of shirking his duties and found himself replaced in his command. Gradually he lost faith in the Roundheads and by the time of his death in 1674 he had made his peace with Charles II. A younger son was granted an Irish peerage and himself sired two sons who engaged in a savage brawl, recorded by Pepys under the year 1667—one was killed and the other sent to Newgate. Their brother John was given to less destructive pastimes. He became an archdeacon and a royal chaplain, and married into the Somerset squirarchy. There were six children of this marriage, including Edmund Fielding (as the name came to be spelt), father of the novelist.

In Edmund, all the wild Feilding blood welled up agaian f a neraintoegrte of repressed conformity. He enlisted in the Foot Guards, to fight with gallantry under the Duke of Marlborough; soon after his son Henry was born he bought a colonelcy and went off to the unpopular Spanish sector of the war. His military fortunes there are unrecorded, and by 1716 we find him gambling in the coffee-houses of London, bilking his opponents, and generally sitting for the portrait of a Hanoverian rake. (Perhaps the character of Captain Bilkum, in his son's *Covent-Garden Tragedy*, borrows a few of his lineaments.) The Goulds understandably did not think him a suitable parent, especially when his wife died and left him with a young family. There was another distant relative, called Beau Feilding, noted for duels and bigamy; people shook their heads and predicted that Edmund would go the same way. Somehow he survived, in a harumscarum fashion, and even reached the rank of Lieutenant-General—an outcome as little to be anticipated as the escape of Tom Jones from the gallows.

It was this muddled inheritance which gave Fielding his peculiar combination of qualities. On the one side, there was thrift, industry, learning, prudence, a talent for being inconspicuous. On the other, a kind of heroic unworldliness: an aristocratic swagger (why not, with English and Irish earldoms in one family?), a taste for adventure, a relish for the fight, an incapacity to go about the world unobserved. All his life Henry enacted in his own person, a struggle between these opposite qualities, January and May, Apollo and Dionysus. It did not help that the Fielding side had convinced themselves they were descended from the Habsburgs, a myth devised by creative genealogists in the seventeenth century but no doubt devoutly impressed on young Henry. To this lineage would be attributed all his characteristics, from the Roman nose to the tall muscular frame and impressive bearing. As we follow Fielding's career we shall witness the contest between a roué and a scholar, a reformer and a prodigal, a classicist and a show-business huckster, an athlete and an aesthete. There was a split in Fielding's nature, and genealogy goes a long way to explain it.

2

Sharpham Park lies on the edge of reclaimed marshland in the middle of Somerset, as the first gentle ascent begins towards the blue lias ridge of the Polden Hills. Just across the high ground, the levels return with the King's Sedgmoor, where the last major battle was fought on English soil when Fielding's father was a boy. Sharpham itself had been a residence of the Benedictine abbots of Glastonbury, and their chapel survived after the erection of a house on the site in early Tudor times. The last abbot, Richard Whiting, was executed on Glastonbury Tor in 1539 for resisting Henry

VIII: three centuries later, he was beatified for his courage. The estate was granted to the Dyer family, and here Sir Edward Dyer, poet and courtier in Elizabethan England, had his home. After the Civil War it passed to the Goulds, and it was almost certainly here that Henry Fielding was born on 22 April 1707.

He spent little time in legendary Avalon. The family moved to Dorset by the time he was three, and there can have been no more than intermittent visits to Henry's maternal uncle Davidge Gould at Sharpham. But we have one strong indication that the landscape left its impression on Fielding. At the start of *Tom Jones*, he describes the pleasant situation of Mr Allworthy's Gothick house, and in particular the superb view. Some details fit Prior Park, the home of his patron Ralph Allen, though this was a fashionably Palladian mansion. Much of the scenery relates instead to Glastonbury Tor, which stands in dramatic solitude three miles to the north-east of Sharpham. Exactly the same silhouette is visible from the top of the house in which I am writing, though my view is from the other side, 180 degrees around from Fielding's vantage-point. It is certain that the young man must have gazed up towards that remarkable profile, and almost as sure that he would in his formative years have witnessed 'the charming prospect of the valley beneath' as seen from the summit of the Tor.

Sharpham is today a farm, and not much of the old mansion survives intact—a fine Georgian staircase dated 1726 has been moved to the Victoria and Albert Museum. The room in which Fielding is supposed to have been born (it is unsupported but plausible tradition) is upstairs, looking out west towards the Bristol Channel. If this Harlequin Chamber, so called from a carving in the wall, was indeed the family's nursery, then Henry cannot have spent many months there. Inside two and a half years he was joined by two sisters, each christened in St John's, Glastonbury, a Perpendicular church with an almost top-heavy tower. The countryside around is relatively little changed. Willows and alders grow in the dark rich soil; the Mendips stretch away to the north, whilst on the other side of Street rows of wooded hills lead towards the southern fringe of Somerset.

That was the direction in which the Fieldings moved about 1710. Just before he died in March of that year, old Sir Henry Gould bought for his daughter an estate in the north spur of Dorset. Today the village of East Stour is so small that the holiday traffic on a busy A road scarcely notices its existence. It lies in the Vale of Blackmoor, not far from Marnhull where Tess of the D'Urbervilles was born. From here the River Stour meanders thirty miles past Cranborne Chase and Blandford to the sea at Christchurch Bay. The Fielding home was a converted rectory, and hundreds of acres of farmland adjoined it, angling away to the river almost a mile off. Here young Henry spent his childhood among scenes that he recalled later with some fondness. The family was growing: three more girls and a boy had arrived before Henry was ten, the most notable of whom was his sister Sarah, the future author of *David Simple*. Meanwhile Henry's education began under a local curate named Oliver, who may bear some responsibility for the character of the parson so called in *Shamela*. Edmund Fielding was by now a half-pay colonel, but with the War of Spanish Succession drawing to an end his role was redefined as that of a country squire. All the signs are that the elder Fielding found this way of life too dull by half; but at least it was a peaceful and happy spot for Henry to grow up in.

His birth had taken place in the middle of Anne's reign, and he was only seven when the last Stuart succumbed to dropsy, fever and contemporary medicine (bleeding, vomiting, blisters and garlic applied to her feet). Early on a Sunday morning, 1 August 1714, the Hanoverian dynasty came into its succession. 'Dead?', said one crusty Oxford don of the Queen, 'she is as dead as Julius Caesar.' But the years of stability, of calm Hanoverian torpor, were still some way off. Within a year the first great Jacobite rising had begun, and with sensible management it could perhaps have succeeded. Half-hearted attempts continued to be made every so often, until in 1745/46 there occurred the great rebellion that concerned Fielding so deeply. Even after that, the charade of a Jacobite court in exile went on for several decades, until in 1807 the Cardinal of York died at Frascati near Rome, never to become Henry IX of England and Henry I of Scotland. The Stuart cause had finally sunk beneath the horizon, an outcome Fielding must have ardently desired back in 1746.

These convulsions of state would seem very distant to the family in East Stour, though the West Country had its share of Jacobites like the Somerset baronet Sir William Wyndham. About the time of the move to Dorset, London was in tumult over the case of the incendiary preacher Dr Henry Sacheverell. The exciting years up to 1720, when the South Sea Bubble produced a national crisis of conscience, were witnessed by Swift, Pope and Gay, by Defoe and Richardson, even by William Hogarth as he approached adulthood. Fielding was just too young to know anything of this period at first hand. He came to maturity as Robert Walpole took control of political life, and he can have had few memories of the old England. (Unlike Samuel Johnson, two years his junior, he had no occasion to visit London to be 'touched' for scrofula by the monarch.) His was a tranquil provincial upbringing, exactly the right recipe for a wild spell up in town when he reached manhood.

And of course his father had never attuned himself to a peaceful rural existence. From time to time Edmund pops up in London, his old habits unaffected by his family responsibilities or approaching middle age. In 1716, when his fourth daughter died at the age of three, he got into trouble among the London gamesters; he lost a large sum of money playing faro (which was illegal anyway). He borrowed money from the Gould side of the family, and spent it without compunction. Without some luck, elaborate legal manoeuvring, and wealthy in-laws, he would certainly have found himself in the debtors' gaol, and given his son an early insight into those wretched places.

3

Events, however, took a different turn. In April 1718, when Henry was almost eleven, his mother suddenly died. The colonel took possession of the estate, which had been prudently left in his wife's hands while she was alive. He left his wife's aunt to look after the children at East Stour, and went back to his round of diversions in the metropolis. After a year he married again. His new wife was herself a widow with two daughters, regarded by the Gould side as socially dubious, and worst of all a Catholic—this when papists were proscribed by law from many ordinary rights of citizenship. Tactlessly he took her back to Dorset in the summer of 1719, when the children were adjusted to the guardianship of their great-aunt. It sounds like the scenario for a Victorian novel, and sure enough the household was quickly reduced to chaos. Doubtless the new Mrs Fielding was not wholly to blame for her unpopularity; the Goulds alleged that she locked the English Bible away and left the Romish prayer book around in its place, which is most likely an invention. But she was clearly not a good domestic manager, despite (or because of) the fact that she had supposedly kept an eating-house in London. There was a terrible family quarrel; Henry took the Gould side and was beaten for his intransigence. The idyll had emphatically come to an end.

Neither of the contending parties could happily leave matters in this state. Edmund Fielding acted first, by sending his four surviving daughters to a boarding-school in Salisbury. They were supposed to learn both needlework and how to behave themselves, which must have been much the same thing. The younger son (also an Edmund, now three) was packed off to live with old Lady Gould, also in Salisbury. Henry, rising twelve, received the most draconian punishment, as it seemed to him. He was dispatched to Eton College.

Not long afterwards Lady Gould got in her counter-blow. She brought an action in Chancery to gain custody of the children and to take control of the estate at East Stour. The colonel made his reply and the affair went on in best Chancery fashion for an unconscionable time. Side-suits were brought just in case some of the family's dirty linen should avoid exposure.

Eventually, when Henry had reached his mid-teens, the legal battles were over, and his grandmother had won virtually every point. His father was ousted from all real control of children or estate. From this date forwards he became a figure of marginal importance in Henry's life, quoted as a dreadful warning by the female Goulds. The second Mrs Fielding bore the colonel six sons before she died in 1727; the only one who concerns us is John, in adult life totally blind but later to become a distinguished magistrate. The colonel was transformed into a brigadier and then a general. He had one more wife or maybe two, nobody knows for sure. Edmund lasted out until 1741, which says much for his constitution; by then Henry was on the brink of his greatest achievements.

In 1719 he was a lonely twelve-year-old from a suddenly broken home, cast out from a large and close-knit family living in rural seclusion. There are some parallels here with Tom Jones, although the details are different. The boy Henry had to face not the open road (which he might have done cheerfully enough) but the rigours of Eton. Almost the only features of the great Victorian public school, modelled on Dr Arnold's Rugby, which were present at this time were intense study of the classics and spartan living, by which I mean everything from primitive sanitary arrangements to the undeniable prevalence of bullying. Among his schoolfellows he was to become closest to George Lyttelton, later the dedicatee of *Tom Jones*, a high-minded politician and rather low-talented poet. Others at Eton in his time were William Pitt, destined to play his most momentous role as a statesman in the years following Fielding's death; Henry Fox, later the Earl of Holland, and like Pitt the father of an equally famous son; and Thomas Augustine Arne, the outstanding British composer of his age. In this company Fielding construed Ovid and Homer, declaimed on the model of Cicero and Demosthenes, and wrote Greek verses. Hardly anything else happened within the school environment; there was no music or art, no mathematics or science, not even compulsory games. Like all writers prior to the twentieth century, the budding author did not read a page of English literature in his student days. It is a formula we have abandoned without obvious benefit to our store of creative talent.

Fielding stayed at Eton until 1724 or 1725. In the latter year a new boy came to the school, by name Thomas Gray. He was to form with Horace Walpole and others a kind of aesthetic movement within the college. Eight years after leaving Eton, at the age of twenty-five, Gray composed one of his finest poems which looks back across time and space to his boyhood at the school. The *Ode on a Distant Prospect of Eton College* presents what has been termed 'a stark contrast between the joys of childhood and the evils which maturity will bring'. Gray pictures the innocent boys 'disporting' themselves on the banks of the Thames—some 'enthralling' the captive linnet, in a phrase which prefigures Master Blifil. He recalls his own days at school, 'A stranger yet to pain'. It seems likely that Fielding won more battles than did Gray on the playing-fields of Eton: his muscular frame would have ensured that. But, like Gray, he imbibed far more than our facile idea of the philistine public school permits us to anticipate. His deep love of the classics was founded upon the solid training he received at Eton. In adult years he lost a smaller portion of the 'lively cheer of vigour born' than Gray; nevertheless, he must sometimes have thought back to these impressionable years, and recalled his first social experience among gifted, ambitious and well-connected young men. There is no evidence that he had been spoilt at home; still, his readiness to oppose his father after the remarriage suggests that he had got to like the role of senior male among a group of elderly female relatives and admiring younger sisters. Eton gave him his initial glimpse of a wider world, and provided the first satisfactory (not to add, fully present) male tutelage he had known.

Around his fourteenth birthday he is supposed to have run away from school and found his way to Lady Gould's house in Salisbury. Unfortunately the source of this information is none other than the colonel, and typically he gives two inconsistent versions. If Henry did 'elope' from Eton, it was probably not to escape the regime there but to allay his anxieties concerning matters at home. He was ordinarily allowed to pass his holidays at Christmas and Whitsun with his great-aunt, when he rejoiced to have the companionship of his sisters once again. Lady Gould had set up home in St Martin's Church Street, near the centre of the town. It was a bustling little place, for though the cathedral dominated the physical surroundings there was more commerce and less sleepy Barset about it than Trollope was to evoke when he set his novels there in the 1850s. Defoe wrote a description, published in 1725 but drawing on visits earlier in the century, in which he emphasises the prosperity of Salisbury:

As the city of Winchester is a city without trade, that is to say, without any particular manufactures; so this city of Salisbury, and all the county of Wilts, of which it is the capital, are full of a great variety of manufactures . . . The people of Salisbury are gay and rich, and have a flourishing trade; and there is a good deal of good manners and good company among them; I mean, among the citizens, besides what is found among the gentlemen.

Fielding's 'natural' companions would have been found among young persons from the gentry, and male ones at that. It is hard to imagine that he kept aloof from the citizens or that he clung by preference to single-sex pastimes.

The next projected elopement, at all events, not long after Henry left Eton, was a more serious affair than his brief interlude from schooling. His intended bride (a distant relative) was a girl of fifteen, and even though Lord Hardwicke's marriage act was still nearly thirty years off, runaway marriages with heiresses were not widely encouraged. (The 'Fleet' parsons of London were the great specialists in clandestine marriage ceremonies, but you could find an unfrocked clergyman for the purpose in most localities: a man who called himself the Reverend Sweetapple was the head of his profession in Nottinghamshire.) Sarah Andrew was the daughter of a Dorset mercantile family, with a country house near Blandford, a town Fielding must have got to know just before the disastrous fire which consumed it in 1731 and led to its rebuilding as a Georgian showpiece. It is thought that Sarah's mother was the sister-in-law of Davidge Gould. What is certain is that Fielding pursued the young lady to Lyme Regis around September 1725, and there his first known amorous adventure had its comic enactment.

Fielding went down to Lyme with a manservant to play Partridge to his Jones. He was, we must remember, eighteen years old. Lyme Regis is still a picturesque resort, with steep paths and overhanging arches. It makes a fitter setting for lovers' antics than for great doings of state, and one can understand why Macaulay wished to be shown, not the spot where the Duke of Monmouth landed, but rather the exact location of Henrietta Musgrave's fall in *Persuasion*.

Less propitious to the course of true love than the local topography was a certain Andrew Tucker, Sarah's uncle and her joint-trustee after the death of her father. This respectable burgher took steps to discourage her suitor, notably that of hiring a yokel to beat up Fielding, some time in September. Fielding made an official complaint and then tried to waylay Sarah on the way to church. He failed, and let slip his intention of mugging Councillor Tucker in return. Thereupon Tucker, with traditional aldermanic dignity, had Fielding and his servant hauled before the Mayor of Lyme, who bound them over to keep the peace. The disappointed lover promptly pinned to a prominent door in the town his own solemn articles of faith: 'This is to give notice to all the world that Andrew Tucker and his son John Tucker are clowns and cowards. Witness my hand, Henry Fielding.' Sarah meanwhile had been spirited away to the home of her other trustee in Devon. This gentleman next year married her to *his* son, thus forestalling a plan of Tucker's to give her to his son John. Fielding had been no more than a pawn in the entire game, and he had to depart a lot sadder and a little wiser. So far as we know, he made only a couple of references to the episode in his earliest works; at eighteen, his spirits were resilient. Sarah lived on until 1783 in dull respectability; what she made of Henry's later fame, we do not know.

An irritating blank now appears in the record. What Fielding was up to in 1726 and 1727 is a total mystery. This is doubly disappointing: we should naturally be interested to pursue the career at nineteen and twenty of a young man who had made such a bold entrance into the world, and beyond this they were intriguing years in which to launch upon society. Fielding very likely came up to London for the first time just as Swift made his first visit from Ireland since the old Queen had died, bringing some explosive luggage—the manuscript of *Gulliver's Travels*. Swift came back the following year, which also saw the death of Sir Isaac Newton, a fight on stage between the rival female stars of the opera Faustina and Cuzzoni, and finally the death of George I. In the autumn of 1727 George II and Caroline were formally installed at Westminster Abbey to the sound of the noble coronation anthems written by Handel, those we still use. There had been lighter events too: a woman from Godalming in Surrey had claimed to give birth to rabbits, which created a tremendous stir (she turns up again as late as 1762 in a print by Hogarth). Eventually she admitted the imposture, but until then she gained a wide measure of credence, notably from the Swiss doctor, Nathaniel St André, anatomist to the royal household. No wonder that people kept away from the medical profession until their case was already hopeless.

Fielding does not emerge into full light once more until the end of January in 1728, when he was rising twenty-one. At that date a leading publisher, James Roberts, issued his verse satire *The Masquerade*. This sixpenny pamphlet is addressed to 'C–t H–d–g–r' and signed as the work of Lemuel Gulliver, 'Poet Laureat to the King of Lilliput'. The allusion is to John James Heidegger, another Swiss who had reached England in uncertain circumstances. His grandfather had come from Nuremberg and, stranded in Zurich, had decided to settle there. John James had travelled through Germany as a valet, had attempted a little espionage, and on reaching Britain had joined the Life Guards. Somehow he slithered up the rungs of society, and became first librettist, then opera manager. After the Hanoverian accession he started to put on 'masquerades' at the Opera House when no performance was being held (normally operas went on twice a week only). By 1724 the popularity and scandal associated with these gatherings had grown to such a pitch that the Bishop of London preached to the Society for the Reformation of Manners on their iniquities, and attempts were made to suppress them.

A chapter in Fielding's last novel *Amelia* is called 'What happened at the masquerade', and that remains a good question. It was basically a fancy-dress ball; masks were allowed but not apparently essential. Gaming may sometimes have taken place, and for that matter lotteries were drawn on the Opera House stage as well. Heidegger's evenings were held in the Long Room on the west side of the theatre, lasting from 9 p.m. till 7 a.m. and attracting a matter of 700 people. Costumes could be hired on the premises; a bizarre fondness for the habits of religious personages (such as abbesses and nuns) vied with devils, savages and jesters. Dogs, parrots and monkeys were sometimes brought along. It remains a mystery why moralists thought *quite* so badly of the masquerade, bearing in mind some of the other ways then available of spending time in London. Somehow people were made anxious by the possibility of indiscriminate social mixing which the wearing of dominoes permitted. The occasions were seen as threatening a disastrous loss of identity. In later years Fielding wrote of them as 'rather a silly, than a vicious, entertainment', but many disagreed.

Why Heidegger should have attained notoriety is much easier to explain. He was in the first place astoundingly unpleasant in appearance, or so contemporaries thought: his surviving portrait does not bear out quite so dramatic a judgment. Fielding was to dub him Count Ugly, whilst Hogarth had only to sketch in a couple of features in his *Masquerades and Operas* (1724) to gain the desired effect. A pamphlet claimed that earlier generations of women (unlike the present shameless hussies) would have swooned at the thought of a masquerade, whilst 'the sight of Heidegger would have terrified them as much as one of their churchyard-spirits'. Secondly, Heidegger had made it with a vengeance. By 1727 he was appointed to take charge of the illuminations in Westminster Hall for the coronation. He became Master of the Revels to George II, with a regular royal bounty; he was perhaps the most effective of all the entrepreneurs to work with Handel. He survived until 1749; obituaries put him at ninety years of age, but they would always over-estimate in such cases. However, Heidegger had one of the features which marked him out for a place in Augustan satire. He was indestructible, that is shameless, and eternally ripe in new projects. An ugly man who became a social leader, he belongs with Beau Nash (a low-born and clumsy figure who ended up arbiter of all things elegant) and Colley Cibber (a foppish player who was made royal laureate and theatrical controller). They went on living for ever, and none of the satirists could ever resist a dig at them.

As one would expect from a beginner, Fielding works in the conventional manner. He versifies the Hogarth print *Masquerades and Operas*; there is a vague hint that Heidegger, 'first minister of masquerade', stands for Robert Walpole, first minister of state—and that is all part of the agreed scheme. The poem makes some good thrusts at ruling amusements, and catches one or two of the targets Pope was to assail more powerfully in *The Dunciad*, published four months later.

The theme of masks appears more glancingly in a play which Fielding now had ready, and which went on the stage at Drury Lane on 16 February, just two weeks later. It was a considerable achievement for a young man of twenty to get *Love in Several Masques* accepted by the Theatre Royal. The managers, Colley Cibber and Robert Wilks, had long stood at the top of

Above Fielding's birthplace, Sharpham Park, Somerset

Below Old Sarum and Salisbury in 1723

Overleaf London in 1720: from John Strype's edition of Stow's *Survey*

Top left John James Heidegger, the impresario who figures in Fielding's early works

Top right Colley Cibber, theatrical manager, dramatist, actor and poet laureate

Above left Anne Oldfield, the great actress who starred in Fielding's first play

Above right Lady Mary Wortley Montagu, Fielding's second cousin, who encouraged him as a young writer

their profession; the house itself, which was the second on this site, had been erected in 1674 to a design by Sir Christopher Wren. It was regarded as superior acoustically to its rivals, especially after alterations made during the 1690s. (The shell remained, retouched by the Adams and others, until 1792.) Here the London theatre had its headquarters, though not always its most commercially successful company. The ease of Fielding's *entrée* doubtless had a lot to do with his second cousin Lady Mary Wortley Montagu, who read the manuscript, attended two performances, and duly received the dedication when the play was published a week after its opening night. Another midwife of his muse was the celebrated actress Anne Oldfield. Both ladies are impressive enough to compel a brief pause in the narrative.

Mrs Oldfield* was the senior of the two: in fact, at forty-five she had only two more years to live. She had made her début at Drury Lane as far back as 1692 and appeared as a young girl in plays by all the leading dramatists. But it was as Lady Betty Modish in Cibber's *Careless Husband* (1704) that she made her real mark. Later triumphs included her roles as heroine of the 'she-tragedies' by Rowe, *Lady Jane Grey* and *Jane Shore*. She was still at the top in 1728 and indeed no other actress dare attempt to portray Lady Betty. In a period when actresses were expected to acquire wealthy protectors, Anne Oldfield—once apprenticed to a seamstress— fared particularly well. She was distinctly well off by the time of her death, and arranged to have herself buried, contrary to statute, in an outfit of rich lace. This provoked Pope to picture her demise in grisly terms:

> 'Odious! in woollen! 'twould a saint provoke,'
> (Were the last words that poor Narcissa spoke)
> 'No, let a charming chintz, and Brussels lace
> Wrap my cold limbs, and shade my lifeless face:
> One would not, sure, be frightful when one's dead—
> And—Betty—give this cheek a little red.'

Narcissa, incidentally, comes from another starring role which Cibber wrote for Mrs Oldfield. She was a major theatrical figure and her performance as Lady Matchless in Henry's new play must have been a source of great encouragement for him.

An altogether different kind of great lady was represented by Lady Mary Wortley Montagu (whose mother was a daughter of the third Earl of Denbigh, the brother of Archdeacon Fielding, Henry's grandfather). Now reaching the delicate age of thirty-nine, she was still formally tied in glum and loveless marriage to her mean husband. She had quarrelled with Pope

---

*We should say 'Miss Oldfield'. *Mrs* was a courtesy title given to all adult ladies of standing; *Miss* referred to children and servants.

and was making one or two desperate efforts to find a worthy object for the passionate intellectual friendship she always desired. In years to come she was to try sexual *ambigus* like Lord Hervey and the cosmopolitan adventurer Algarotti (women would not do—they were too crushed by boring domestic routine and stifling convention). Only Voltaire would have matched up to her needs. Witty, ferociously intelligent, ambitious in an age when women were confined to drudgery or ornamentation, she tried to console herself with reading and travel. She eventually settled in the lake region of Lombardy, conducting a proud and courageous correspondence with her daughter and begging larger and larger parcels of novels to keep her going. Like other great ladies, Mary was No Lady. But she was a person of great literary discernment, whom few liked to cross: it was lucky for Henry Fielding that his cousin had taken to him. In these early days her opposition could have blocked all dramatic avenues.

As for the play, it is a comedy of intrigue drawing on odd recollections of the Lyme Regis episode. A brutish squire called Sir Positive Trap is generally supposed to be based on Andrew Tucker, though there were enough precedents in Restoration comedy for this sort of character. In the plot there is an heiress like Sarah Andrew, but she is a *fille mal gardée* compared to the real-life case, and a happily sentimental ending is made possible. Perhaps the most promising aspect of the play is the characterisation of Lord Formal, a languid fop—again the type is familiar, but the execution is highly amusing: his lordship has found that reading 'vastly impairs' the lustre of his eyes, and he quickly 'lost the direct ogle'. All in all, it was a fittingly precocious start: Fielding was always an adept learner.

4

We now come to an abrupt change of direction. Suddenly Fielding is to be found enrolling as a university student. These days we suppose sudden reversals of intent to belong to the private experience of modernist art. Stravinsky and Picasso are the exemplars of a stratified career, shifting rapidly through pink period or neoclassic phase according to the demands of a deep creative logic. As a matter of fact the homely old Augustans were already into such things. Daniel Defoe lived about six lives (as potential ordinee for the dissenting church; as protestant rebel fighting for Monmouth; as businessman and inventor; as spy and political agent; as journalist and pamphleteer, and much else) before he hit on the novel when almost sixty. Samuel Richardson was an industrious apprentice who became a master-printer and eventually turned to fiction, late in life, when he needed a sequel to *The Young Man's Pocket Companion*. In their various ways Swift,

Dr Johnson, and Sterne show considerable irresolution in their writing life. Let no one imagine that artists were sure of their way ahead until their confidence was spoilt for good by the Great War in 1914.

Fielding had just reached London, had seen his first play put on with fair success, and had published an effective satire on the taste of the town. About three years before he had elected not to proceed to Oxford or Cambridge, for what reason we do not know. It seems likely that there was less family pressure than personal whim behind the decision; one can hardly suppose that the Goulds considered existence as an idle young man in county society a preferable alternative to the moderate dissipations of university life. Admittance to Christ Church or King's might not have prevented an escapade like the Lyme Regis affair—nothing short of a major operation could have curtailed Fielding's energies—but he would have learnt to take his drink like a man, and would have made useful contacts. Instead of booby squires from Dorchester or clothiers' sons from Devizes he would have met scions of the great families. In any case young Fielding did escape to London pretty soon, which scarcely argues that his guardians had him on a tight leash. My own view is that Henry probably just changed his mind. At eighteen he wanted to get out in the world; by the age of twenty he had seen enough of its follies and its tedium to reconsider the matter. So he went to the university after all.

Not, however, to Oxford or Cambridge. On 16 March 1728, a bare month after his play had been premièred, he was registered in the faculty of letters at the University of Leyden. This notable centre of learning in the western Netherlands, founded in 1575, enjoyed a high reputation throughout Europe, more than anything else on account of its medical training. The great physician and teacher Hermann Boerhaave was turning out a steady flow of skilled pupils; such was his fame that a letter addressed 'To Boerhaave of Europe' was said to have reached him safely. There was also a well-known professor of civil law, 'the learned Vitrarius'. But we can now be sure that Fielding went there not to study law but to pursue his interest in humane letters, a sort of metonymy by which people really meant classical literature. The particular attraction would be Pieter Burmann (curiously the subject, as was Boerhaave, of an early biography by Samuel Johnson). This Latin grammarian was advancing the art of editing with a fierce technical attention to minutiae that would have gladdened the heart of A. E. Housman. In spite of the sneers of *The Dunciad*,

> Let standard-authors, thus, like trophies born,
> Appear more glorious as more hack'd and torn,
> And you, my critics! in the chequer'd shade,
> Admire new light thro' holes yourselves have made . . .

this was the way scholarship was to advance. (Burmann gets a brief rap from Pope later in the poem; and Fielding himself was to parody the methods of 'the great Professor *Burman*' in his joke-apparatus to *The Tragedy of Tragedies*.) Nevertheless, Fielding was doing more than stoke up his satiric furnaces; he was also learning the value of close and disciplined attention to a text, a lesson the Scriblerians never quite assimilated. He lived in lodgings, walked alongside the canals, attended an execution, and looked with some distaste on certain inhabitants, whom he identified with 'fat substance', aldermanic pomp, and plump femininity—the national stereotype, in fact. He worked on the draft of a play which was ultimately to become *Don Quixote in England*, but not until some years had elapsed and the managers had rejected a preliminary version.

In the late summer of 1728 Fielding came home for the summer vacation. He probably spent most of the break in Salisbury, but we know that he went to a village just off the London road named Upton Grey, not far from Basingstoke. His reaction was to write a poetic description of the village, which he rechristened New Hog's Norton in tribute to the high population of grunting pigs. Yet again he had a clear model, the common Augustan contrast between the sophisticated enjoyments of town life and the boorish inanity of country pursuits. Pope's lines to Teresa Blount after the coronation of George I in 1714 are the finest example of this genre. Fielding's poem went into his *Miscellanies* later on and makes agreeable reading. It does not tell us very much about his state of mind in that summer of 1728; his absent Roselinda may or may not be based on a real person, and either way Henry was capable of finding consolation pretty soon at the age of twenty-one. The work shows his literary urge still strong, and indicates that Dutch pedantry had not done anything to hebetate (as the phrase then was) his lively wit.

As it turned out, he had only one more session to get through. He went back to Leyden in October 1728 and remained until the next long vacation in the following August. Nobody is quite certain of the reasons which led him to cut short his studies: Arthur Murphy, his first biographer, puts it down to the withdrawal of an allowance he was receiving from home, and this is as likely an explanation as any. He would at last have ceased to be a ward of Chancery when he came of age, but his prospects were not good. His father had a second family, maybe a third wife, on his hands; the Goulds were understandably reluctant to trust any young Fielding with very much of their stolidly-earned fortune. Looking to the future, he could see few opportunities for advancement. Lady Mary Wortley Montagu wrote much later that 'he was to be pitied at his first entrance into the world, having no choice (as he said himself) but to be a hackney writer or a hackney coachman.' Perhaps the alternatives were not really as stark as that. But he could no longer identify himself with his boyhood friends and schoolfellows, Lyttelton, Pitt and Fox; they had moved on to Oxford or the Grand Tour, and were beginning to look for a likely constituency. The distant prospect of greatness that Fielding could have glimpsed when he was at Eton had now vanished, as the sharp eminence of Glastonbury Tor had been lost to his childhood gaze when the family moved from Sharpham.

TWO

The Scribbler

1729-33

I

When Fielding returned he was twenty-two, ready to be dissipated perhaps, eager for experience. London was the one place in England capable of satisfying such urges. Unlike Bath, it functioned all the year; it offered more than a round of amusements, with its political and legal centres, its commercial activity, and its varied cultural life. To a young man London seemed a lively city, flourishing anew after the extensive rebuilding which followed on the great fire. Queen Anne's ambitious church-building programme had fallen short of its original intentions, but inventive architects like Wren, Gibbs, and Hawksmoor had studded the landscape with beautiful and often fantastic steeples. 'Behold! Augusta's glittering spires increase, / And temples rise, the beauteous works of peace', Alexander Pope had written in 1713. Even Daniel Defoe, in his sour old age, had brought out in March 1728 a pamphlet called *Augusta Triumphans*, subtitled 'the way to make London the most flourishing city in the universe'. True to form, Defoe allotted most of his space to futuristic projects—the setting-up of a university in London (a good century before this became reality), the creation of a hospital for foundlings, the establishment of an academy for music, and the suppression of numerous abuses ranging from gaming and prostitution to gin and 'pretended mad-houses' where husbands locked up their wives. Defoe, at sixty-eight, could not keep out of his jeremiads a sense that London was the chosen home for modern civilisation. What chance, then, that a robust and confident young man like Fielding should resist its attractions?

London stretched only some four to five miles from Tyburn gallows in the west (near present-day Marble Arch) to the suburbs of Mile End and Stepney to the east. The historic areas of Westminster and Southwark extended the bounds southwards, but the main inhabited region ran no more than a mile north from the river. A combination of lordly entrepreneurs and shrewd speculative builders were developing the land around Mayfair and Oxford Street when Fielding arrived; within a decade the ladies and gentlemen of quality would have removed to this fashionable district in large numbers, distancing themselves not only from the City but also from the raffish corners of town Fielding knew best. But Marylebone Gardens were still right out in the country; you crossed some open heath-land to get to Islington; and Bethnal Green was a rural fastness. Special convoys of trippers came back from the gaming-house at Hampstead under escort, to avoid the attentions of highwaymen as they drove back to the metropolis. Montagu House, the home of the British Museum from its inception in 1759, looked out on to fields at the back. In Fielding's lifetime there were only a few buildings at the south end of Tottenham Court Road as it straggled off into grazing land and market-gardens.

The population of London (that is, the City together with Westminster and Southwark) was about 400,000; the growing 'out-parishes' on its borders added another 250,000. In all the capital contained something like a tenth of the nation's inhabitants; Bristol was still larger than Liverpool, Chester still almost as large as Leeds, and country towns well known to Fielding like Salisbury or Taunton maintained their dignity as regional centres with five or ten thousand residents. Of the assize towns Fielding was to visit when he rode on the Western Circuit, most were sleepy little settlements periodically awakened by a market or a fair. London, then, was wholly unique—not just in its size but in its truly urban character. As a magistrate later on, Fielding had to face social problems totally unknown to the mass of English men and women, who were living very much as their ancestors had done in agrarian occupations. The overcrowding and squalor in St Giles', the immigrant communities in Wapping or Southwark, the industrial disputes among Spitalfields weavers—these were problems un-matched anywhere else in Britain. A country JP around 1730 would rarely see any of the organised crime which the London justices were beginning to encounter. There were petty shoplifters everywhere but not the elaborate system of receiving established by Jonathan Wild.

It was only four years before, in 1725, that Wild had met his end at Tyburn. Eight times a year the procession made its grisly way from Newgate along Holborn and the Oxford road; near the gallows stood the place 'where soldiers are shot', as a contemporary map has it. Fielding, who had only just left Eton, must have been well aware of Wild's downfall, and stored many details in his mind for future use. By the time he came to London, there was another strong reminder. John Gay had brought out his *Beggar's Opera* in January 1728, and it enjoyed unprecedented success for two entire seasons. At the centre of the drama, pulling all the strings, is not the titular hero Macheath but the grubby Peachum, a satiric portrait blending features of Jonathan Wild with those of the prime minister Robert Walpole. The popularity of this play had changed the whole theatrical climate; ballad opera became the favourite form for years to come, and Fielding was to exploit this mode as profitably as anyone.

Another direct consequence was that John Rich, the impresario who had produced the *Opera*, was able to move his operations. He issued a subscription to pay for a new playhouse in Covent Garden, and enough money was raised to erect a theatre on the north-east side of the market, 'contiguous to Bow Street'. The builder in charge was Edward Shepherd, notable for his developments in Mayfair. The theatre was opened in 1732, and Rich duly abandoned his former base at Lincoln's Inn Fields. From this date Covent Garden became the home of entertainments such as pantomime and harlequinade, often performed as an afterpiece to tragedies by Shakespeare or comedies by Congreve. This remained through Fielding's lifetime the main rival to Drury Lane, which stood a quarter of a mile further east. The royal patent was still attached to this theatre, but with the death or departure of its former managers (Sir Richard Steele, Colley Cibber, Robert Wilks and Barton Booth) the house suffered all kinds of upheavals during the 1730s. Meanwhile the lofty and incommodious Opera House built by Vanbrugh endured statelier vicissitudes down on the west side of the Haymarket. Here prima donnas quarrelled and royalty joined rival factions while Handel fought a losing battle against lavish expenses and public indifference. Just across the road stood the Little Theatre, which since 1720 had subsisted on a diet of French dancing and native extravaganza; the management here sailed closer to the wind than any other house, and so the theatre was closed by the authorities at regular intervals. Here Fielding achieved his major success as a dramatist in the years to come.*

As well as the new Covent Garden, there was another extension to theatrical opportunities in October 1729. A playwright named Thomas Odell, who later became an official licenser or censor, opened a house in Ayliffe Street, Goodman's Fields, a little way outside the city walls north-east from the Tower. There was considerable opposition to siting a theatre in this previously undramatic quarter, where the straitlaced local community feared that other features of the hundred of Drury would appear—large-scale prostitution, mainly. However, the playhouse did open, with a performance of Farquhar's popular comedy, *The Recruiting Officer*, and no more than three months later a work by Fielding himself reached the boards there. Odell's theatre had a troubled existence and in 1731 he handed over the management to Henry Giffard, a leading actor in the resident company. Giffard played one more season and then raised money for a new theatre in Leman Street a few yards down towards the river. This second building survived a little longer, that is a decade. It subsequently became a dissenting

---

*The Opera House stood on the site of the modern Her Majesty's, whilst the Little (or 'New') Theatre occupied the position of today's Haymarket, a little higher up on the east side.

A masquerade ticket designed by Hogarth (1727). The lion and unicorn above the clock suggest royal patronage

A performance of *The Beggar's Opera*, by Hogarth (1729). John Gay and John Rich are among the spectators depicted

Top Rich's 'triumphant entry into Covent Garden', by Hogarth (1732); St Paul's, Covent Garden in the background

Above The interior of Drury Lane theatre in the 1770s

Top right Frontage of the Little Theatre in the Haymarket, where Fielding's greatest dramatic triumphs occurred

Right *The Laughing Audience* by Hogarth (1733)

Alexander Pope

Pope's house at Twickenham

meeting-house and then a warehouse.

Perhaps it is a cause for surprise that it should have lasted so long, in this distinctly unfashionable part of London: Defoe in his *Tour* of 1725 tells us that the area had only recently been built over, that is since 1680. The old-clothes market of Rag Fair lay immediately to the south of Goodman's Fields, and this was where Pope located the nerve-centre of Dulness in 1728. According to an early biographer of Dr Johnson, Sir John Hawkins, the expected blight duly set in: 'the adjacent houses became taverns, in name, but in truth they were houses of lewd resort; and the former occupiers of them, useful manufacturers and industrious artificers, were driven to seek elsewhere for a residence'. It is odd to think of that stern and upright (if humane) magistrate, Henry Fielding, assisting in what Hawkins terms the extension of 'allurements to vice and debauchery'. But we shall mistake the shape of his career if we forget that actors were still liable to prosecution as vagrants, and that Hogarth's feckless apprentice Tom Idle would have been expected to call in at the play on his way to ruin.

There was another locality where you could see plays in eighteenth-century London. This was amid the teeming life of the fairs held at set times of year. The two most important were St Bartholomew's and Southwark. Bartholomew Fair had its origins in the twelfth century, with the sale of cloth as its real reason for being. It came to be held annually in Smithfield Market from 23 to 25 August; it survived unscathed even during the joyless Commonwealth period and after the Restoration it was extended to fourteen days. Periodic orders were made in the eighteenth century to ensure that the allotted three-day term was observed, but without evident success. The civic authorities were engaged, too, in a perpetual effort to regulate the play-booths and the gaming tables: despite the appointment of special constables, disorders remained uncheckable. Various people attempted to get the fair suppressed, but it lingered on into the middle of the Victorian era. Here straight actors had their place alongside tight-rope walkers, contortionists, puppet shows, jugglers, waxwork models and other motley performers: naturally enough, 'legitimate' drama was not much in evidence, and a special brand of fairground 'droll' evolved. This often featured lavish scenery; sometimes a hit from the main theatres like Drury Lane would be put on at Smithfield in a suitably lurid version. Pope's *Dunciad* makes much of this easy transfer from fashionable Theatre Royal to low street hustings.

The other big fair was that held in Southwark since the reign of Edward IV. By 1720 it had become almost exclusively an occasion for amusement, with no real trading function. It took place from 7 to 9 September, though again the drolls tended to stretch on beyond the allotted period, much to the annoyance of the authorities. A few years after Fielding's death the Common Council heeded a petition from residents of the borough of Southwark and closed the fair down. This left Bartholomew with no serious rival, as May Fair (held in the first half of that month, in the vicinity of Shepherd Market) was also on its last legs. A lively account by the social observer Ned Ward shows us May Fair in 1699, with strolling companies, clowns luring the crowd by dint of much 'labour, sweat and nonsense', and an array of grisly freak shows. Finally the troupe of comedians got its audience trapped, until 'they turn'd their arses upon the players, and devoted themselves wholly to the monkeys, to the great vexation of . . . all the strutting train of imaginary lords and ladies'. The vivid animation of such events would be familiar to Fielding as to all Londoners in his time. Hogarth's great picture (1733) immortalised Southwark Fair not long before its demise.

The most striking figure in the London theatre, beyond a doubt, was Colley Cibber, now approaching the age of sixty. The son of the distinguished German-born sculptor, Caius Gabriel Cibber, he carried with him all his days a certain un-English lack of reserve: his 'uncommon vivacity' was seen by enemies as vacuous bonhomie. He had fought for William of Orange and entered the household service of a peer before embarking on his stage career. He was by no means the best actor in London, but he was a brilliant exponent of the idiotic beau, a role much exploited in recent comedy. He was far from the ablest dramatist, but he did have the capacity to strike the public taste with variations around the theme of *comédie larmoyante*. He was not the most obvious choice for a theatrical manager, but he clung on to this post when others were collapsing around him. Suddenly in 1730 this slightly absurd personage acquired new dignity, which he was well able to sustain: he became poet laureate in succession to the bibulous Eusden. Some of the other candidates had even less talent; but he was not the most natural man for the job. His feeble attempts at official verse brought on him the derision of Fielding and others, in years to come, and ultimately ensured him the position of King Dunce in the last version of Pope's satire. But he shrugged criticism off with commendable good humour; like Robert Walpole, the great impresario of state, he knew how to survive without being popular.

His motley collection of relatives we shall encounter from time to time as Fielding's career develops; but the main tree can be set out as shown at the top of the facing page. It is an eccentric array of misfits;what the more or less respectable Arne family were doing in this *galère*, along with bumptious little Theophilus and tragi-comic Charlotte, defies explanation.

Meanwhile the literary world at large was still dominated by the commanding presence of that group of Tory wits known as the Scriblerians. They included Jonathan Swift, Alexander Pope, John Gay and Dr John Arbuthnot; originally they had come together in the reign of Queen Anne, and some have accused them of clinging on to a 'politics of nostalgia' for the good old days. Most formidable of all was the great Dean of St Patrick's Cathedral,

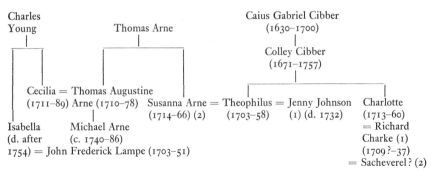

Charles
Young

Thomas Arne

Caius Gabriel Cibber
(1630–1700)

Colley Cibber
(1671–1757)

Cecilia = Thomas Augustine
(1711–89) Arne (1710–78)   Susanna Arne = Theophilus = Jenny Johnson   Charlotte
                           (1714–66) (2)   (1703–58) (1) (d. 1732)   (1713–60)

Isabella   Michael Arne   = Richard
(d. after   (c. 1740–86)   Charke (1)
1754) = John Frederick Lampe (1703–51)   (1709?–37)
                                                                      = Sacheverel? (2)

Dublin, Swift—absent in body (except for two trips at the time of *Gulliver*) but present in spirit through his coruscating wit and implacable hatred of the reigning establishment. People could never be certain that the Dean would not suddenly turn up again in their midst, carrying with him some lethal baggage like the manuscript of *Gulliver*. Modern critics and biographers sometimes tame Swift's unruly spirit: he was in truth a man of fearsome will and resource, almost a great dictator manqué. He ran the business of his deanery with immense efficiency and zeal, accounting for every halfpence as though it were his own. He was now over sixty but his fires had not burned out: *A Modest Proposal* (1729) showed his black comedy as unremitting as ever.

John Gay was at the peak of his success, after years of struggle and disappointment. A plump, easygoing man in his early forties, he was loved more than Swift, feared less than Pope. *The Beggar's Opera* would redeem the heavy losses he had incurred in the South Sea Bubble; but within a few years his pampered way of living was to undermine his health and lead him to the grave. Dr Arbuthnot was a learned, witty and sociable Scotsman, skilled in his own brand of pseudo-pedantic foolery. Attached to one or other of this group were lesser writers, among whom the most interesting was Pope's informant on Grub Street affairs, Richard Savage. Savage claimed to be the illegitimate son of a countess, and may have been right about it. In later years he came to know Samuel Johnson, and the first great work which Johnson produced was his superb biography of Savage (1744), describing such events as Savage's indictment for murder after a tavern brawl, and evoking the hectic world of this neurotic hack writer with amazing psychological insight.

But sooner or later all roads led to Twickenham and to Pope. He was still only forty, but thanks to his own efforts this dwarfish invalid, the member of a proscribed religious minority (the Catholics), had achieved fame, independence, security, and social position. He was now more prominent than ever, by reason of his wicked assault on the contemporary literary scene in *The Dunciad*. The old satiric idea of the bad writer, formerly imaged as one Scriblerus, had been extended to a wider corpus of hack composition, which Pope located in Grub Street, traditional home of needy authors.* A barrage of replies went up; howl after howl revealed the pain inflicted by Pope's vivid and resourceful poetry. Strangely enough, it was young Henry Fielding who put together one of the ablest retorts—though he, of course, had not yet made his mark and had escaped mention in *The Dunciad*.

What happened was this. Some years before Pope had quarrelled with Lady Mary Wortley Montagu, and a barbed reference in his great satire ensured that the breach would not be healed. When Fielding came back from Leyden in 1729, Lady Mary was staying in Twickenham (within buzzing distance of the wasp's nest), whilst her tedious husband toured in glum procession around the pleasure resorts of England. Fielding probably visited her there, and together they apparently concocted various replies to Pope. They were not, however, published; and it was not until the 1970s that much of this work saw the light. In particular, a long mock-epic by Fielding, portraying Pope as the son of his own Queen Dulness, lay unknown in the Harrowby family manuscripts. Together with a companion piece (a verse epistle to George Lyttelton, dating from 1733), it constitutes the only autograph manuscript we have for any of Fielding's works. In the poem he attacks Swift and Gay as well as the arch-enemy Pope (styled 'Codrus'), and turns back upon the satirist the whole machinery of Scriblerian comedy:

> The Bard then rubbing oft his Iron Scull
> Impenetrably hard supremely Dull
> Reflects with Pain, on what his Mother said
> Willing—but knows not how—to give her Aid
> In dreamy Slumbers pass'd the silent Night
> While visionary Glories court his Sight
> Sometimes the Lawrels on his Temples spring
> And Grubstreet Allies ecchoe to their King . . .
> Last, at one view his ravish'd Eyes behold
> Whole Rheams of Rhimeing Nonsense—Heaps of Gold . . .

*It is still not always realised that there was a real Grub Street in London, which underlay the use of this term to connote 'writers of small histories, dictionaries, and temporary poems' (Johnson's *Dictionary*). It ran north and south, just outside the old city wall, in the parish of St Giles', Cripplegate, for a distance of about two hundred yards. It was a district of ramshackle Tudor buildings that had escaped the fire, with narrow passages and surrounded by a thicket of courts, where Jonathan Wild was once a resident. It had gone down in the world socially in the seventeenth century; the 1720 edition of Stow's *Survey of London* glumly acknowledges, 'This street, taking in the whole, is but indifferent, as to its houses and inhabitants; and sufficiently pestered with courts and alleys.' Fielding's great predecessor, Daniel Defoe, was born near its southern end; he came home to die, like an animal at bay, in Ropemaker's Alley, running off eastwards from the top end. The entire site is now covered by the Barbican scheme.

As well as anti-Pope, this fragmentary poem seems to be pro-court, perhaps pro-Walpole, in a manner that is hard to reconcile with the Opposition tone of his early dramas. It is also a fact that Fielding came later to express a high admiration for Pope and the Scriblerians. Perhaps his satire on the little man, like his later assault on the great man Walpole, was a phase to be gone through; perhaps it was Lady Mary who put the words into his mouth. At all events, this early, suppressed poem shows Fielding using the dominant literary techniques of the day, and siding with the hard-done-by scribblers, whose ranks he had not yet properly joined.

When Fielding got back to England, *The Beggar's Opera* was still riding high. A peculiar hit early in 1729 was *Hurlothrumbo* at the Little Theatre, a farcical entertainment acted some thirty times with its author starring as comic dancer and stilt-walker. His name, incongruously enough, was Samuel Johnson—but he haled from Cheshire, not Staffordshire, and was never to be offered any doctoral degree by Oxford University. In the wider literary world Pope had followed his original *Dunciad* of 1728 with a 'Variorum' text the following April, its poetic malice newly surrounded by equally damaging notes and psuedo-scholarship. Fielding began his writing career very much under the influence of the Scriblerian group, and we should recall that *Gulliver's Travels* was no more than three years old at this date. Though his prospects were no brighter than those facing many a Dunce, Fielding boldly identified himself with the wits. From now on he began to range himself against Grub Street, despite many suggestions from the adverse party that he belonged—by reason of poverty and lack of talent —in the very grimiest of garrets.

Where he actually lived at this time, we do not know. His first certain location is not to be found until after he married, when he rented property off the Strand. It is overwhelmingly probable that he stuck to familiar quarters of London—perhaps the parish of St Martin in the Fields, which included much of theatre-land, and where Gibbs had completed his noble church in 1726. The neighbouring parish of St Paul's, Covent Garden, is another possibility. A resident of this part of the city was William Hogarth, who moved to Leicester Fields in 1733—Fielding got to know him soon afterwards, if he did not already. A man who was later to become Fielding's arch-rival among novelists, Samuel Richardson, was living over the printing business he ran in Salisbury Court, at the farther end of Fleet Street. The other great pioneer of English fiction, Daniel Defoe, had been settled in the village of Stoke Newington, three miles north of the city, for twenty years. But his last years were dogged by misfortune, and he died in shabby circumstances about eighteen months after Fielding reached London. If the capital offered promise and excitement, it could also deliver to an unsuccessful literary aspirant most forms of indignity and neglect. In 1729 Fielding stood on the brink of spectacular success or depressing failure. As it turned out, he was to experience something of both.

2

At this point a word of caution is in place. Accounts of Fielding's life here generally launch into a list of stage successes, with a full complement of performers and a detailed synopsis of obscure plot-lines. The effect is very much that of Hollywood biographies, with one item following another in a breathless parade of mammoth productions. Unless the reader is already well up on the subject, such recitals have a wearisome quality. The trouble is that we know far more about Fielding's dramatic output in the early 1730s than about his private life. He was bringing an average of three or four plays a year to the stage; we can set out the *dramatis personae*, the themes and the critical reception—we even have some idea of their box-office success. But what was going on in Fielding's daily existence is quite another matter. Only two letters survive, both addressed to his cousin Lady Mary Wortley Montagu.

Let us, then, look first at the plays, for there we have no need to rely on speculation. His first effort on returning from Leyden was a conventional comedy of manners entitled *The Temple Beau*. Having been refused by the managers at Drury Lane, the play was offered to the new theatre in Goodman's Fields and accepted by Henry Giffard. It was performed on 26 January 1730 and ran initially for nine nights, not a bad showing for a new play by eighteenth-century standards. Fielding got his benefit nights (the receipts on the third, sixth, and ninth evenings, after deduction of expenses, went to the author, who normally got no other payment from the theatre). There were sporadic revivals for some months, and the text was soon published. Fielding's biographer Cross thought it suitable that his dramatic career should 'really begin' out in the East End, 'among the tradespeople of Whitechapel'. Fielding certainly suggests that he wishes to correct the absurdities of fashionable West End taste; but this was conventional, and the impetus obviously derives from *The Dunciad*, which had rebuked Drury Lane for its willingness to adopt the poses of low fairground entertainment.

As for the play itself, it is a pleasant study in generation conflict, with the young law student Wilding enjoying the pleasures of the town until the arrival in London of his father, a foolish old country gentleman. Henry Giffard, who had recently come over from Ireland, himself starred as the wastrel son; the part of his gullible father was taken by a well-known comedian, William Penkethman the younger. By 28 April 1730, when opponents of the new theatre finally got it closed for a time, the piece had ichieved some degree of celebrity. In terms of Fielding's later career the most important aspect of the work was the prologue by James Ralph, who was quite likely responsible also for the epilogue 'by a friend'. Ralph was to remain one of Fielding's close associates for many years to come.

Born in Pennsylvania, he had come to England with Benjamin Franklin at the end of 1724. Franklin describes Ralph in his autobiography as 'ingenious, genteel in his manners, and extremely eloquent; I think I never knew a prettier talker'. Not everyone in England shared Franklin's high opinion of his inseparable companion. One of Ralph's motives in crossing the Atlantic was to rid himself of a disagreeable wife, and he had to borrow money from Franklin within a week of their arrival. He tried to get work as an actor and a journalist, but neither profession would open its doors. In July 1726 Franklin sailed back to Philadelphia, leaving behind Ralph, who had 'kept him poor' by failing to settle a debt of £27. Two years later Ralph finally attained prominence when he wrote a silly riposte to *The Dunciad* called *Sawney: An Heroic Poem*. It made a shilling pamphlet of forty-five pages, with a dedication 'to the gentlemen scandalised in *The Dunciad*', and mildly amusing attacks on the Scriblerian group—Sawney (Pope), Hounslow (Gay), and Shameless (Swift). This performance earned Ralph a tiny role in *The Dunciad Variorum* of 1729, which was probably the sort of notoriety he had been banking on. (Pope's phrase for *Sawney* is 'a swearing-piece'!) By this time he was in his middle twenties, maybe a year or two senior to Fielding; he was sometimes to prove an embarrassment to his friend, but Fielding stuck loyally to him for a decade.

It was at this juncture that the young dramatist turned his considerable talents to a new theatre, the Little Theatre in the Haymarket, and a new genre, ballad opera. The first of his eleven works of this kind, *The Author's Farce*, was put on to succeed *Hurlothrumbo* late in March 1730. It proved almost as much of a triumph as its weird predecessor, and, of course, it has stood the test of time far better. There were forty-one performances that season, excluding one occasion in April when the last act was tacked on to *Hurlothrumbo*. During the summer break actors from the Haymarket company staged a version of the puppet show in Act III at a booth in Tottenham Court, the first occasion of many in which Fielding's satire of popular culture itself emerged as a popular entertainment. When the new season started in October, the Little Theatre opened with *The Author's Farce*, and there were a dozen more performances before the next summer. A revival at Drury Lane in 1734 occasioned extensive revisions by Fielding. Meanwhile the original version received an occasional hearing in more or less truncated form; the puppet shows in fairground booths kept one portion of the text alive through the 1730s. Since it is a part of the play's effect to imply that leading show business personalities of the time were mere waxwork dummies, the transition to this mode of representation is apt enough.

Ballad opera is differentiated by one particular trick: the fitting of new words to existing music. Generally the words would be in some sense topical, as in *The Beggar's Opera*, which was the original and model. Music could be taken from any source provided it was sufficiently well known: art-songs by major composers like Handel occasionally found their way into the score. But more often folksongs, ballads and popular ditties provided the tunes used in ballad opera. There are twenty-eight airs in *The Author's Farce*, almost all of them in the final act. Some of them had actually been used in Gay's famous original, and others were exceedingly well-known pieces which every member of the audience would recognise. Incidentally, the dominance of the form at this juncture in theatrical history is indicated by the fact that another ballad opera opened at Drury Lane on the same evening (which was Easter Monday!) and two nights later Goodman's Fields saw the première of one by James Ralph.

In effect Fielding's play is two separate entertainments. Acts I and II provide a frame, in which the struggling author Luckless contends with an array of contemporary Grub Street types, including a publisher Bookweight, loosely based on the 'unspeakable' Edmund Curll. Act III consists of a rehearsal for Luckless's show called 'The Pleasures of the Town'. This play-within-a-play device was the stock mode of dramatic burlesque throughout the eighteenth century, but Fielding was probably the ablest practitioner. Here he reduces to the status of ghosts a whole gallery of contemporary stars. Leading figures from each branch of the theatre pass in review, seeking the favour of the goddess of nonsense. (Pope was to take some hints for a new book he added to *The Dunciad* in 1742.) In turn we are introduced to Don Tragedio (Lewis Theobald); Sir Farcical Comic (Cibber); Dr Orator (the mountebank preacher John 'Orator' Henley); Signior Opera (the castrato singer Senesino brought to England by Handel); Monsieur Panto-mime (John Rich); and Mrs Novel (Eliza Haywood, author of scandalous romances). The usual stage-army of conspicuous celebrities is present in addition: Cibber's scapegrace son Theophilus, the ubiquitous Heidegger—who figures as Count Ugly in the revised version—Samuel Johnson of Cheshire (author of *Hurlothrumbo*), and so on.

If Fielding's targets are predictable, then his weapons are unusually sharp and his wit extraordinarily fresh. It is a pity that so much topical allusion debars the play from performance today; in all other respects its exuberant comedy has all the qualifications for stage success. Bernard Shaw thought that Fielding was the best practising dramatist (Shakespeare always excepted) between the middle ages and the nineteenth century, i.e. himself. It would be fascinating to be able to witness the 1734 revival at Drury Lane, with Kitty Clive impersonating Mrs Novel and a relatively new actor from County Donegal, Charles Macklin, taking off Theophilus Cibber in the role of Marplay Jnr. Macklin, a former strolling player, was to gain his most spectacular success in tragedy, notably as the greatest Shylock of the century, a villainous extortioner rather than a martyr, who gave George II sleepless nights. Mrs Clive, on the other hand, was a specialist in musical parts: an outstanding Polly Peachum who could also sing in Handel's *Solomon*. Once more Fielding was lucky in the calibre of his cast. Few livelier theatrical occasions can ever have been seen than the original runs of *The Author's Farce*, with their mixture of broad comedy, personal satire, tuneful scenes and rapid action. Strangely the play was not published until 1750.

3

Before *The Author's Farce* had ended its first run, Fielding had an even bigger hit on his hands. *Tom Thumb* went into production at the Little Theatre less than a month after the *Farce*, on Friday 24 April. It played for 'upwards of forty nights, to the politest audiences', according to Fielding. Night after night pit, gallery, and boxes were all crowded out. The Prince of Wales came on the second night, which gave further cachet to the play. Sometimes it was performed as an after-piece to *The Author's Farce*, but though the latter could stand well enough on its own feet it was *Tom Thumb* which became the rage of London. An edition of the text was immediately published by James Roberts, and within a few weeks a revised version now in performance likewise went into print (this was reprinted twice in the course of 1730). Then, in March 1731, a completely rejigged play was presented at the Little Theatre under the title of *The Tragedy of Tragedies*: again Roberts brought this out in print and again several impressions were called for. The main feature of these revisions is an extended parody of scholarly editing, attributed to 'Scriblerus Secundus'. By this means Fielding announced his allegiance to the group headed by Swift and Pope. There are no signs that the Scriblerians were anxious to recognise Fielding as their heir apparent, and the compliment was not returned until the *New Dunciad* imitated features of Fielding's Haymarket farces. It is said that Swift saw the play and laughed when Tom Thomb's ghost was killed— one of two known occasions of laughter in his entire life. This can only have been in a Dublin performance, as he was never in England after 1727.

The immense popularity of *Tom Thumb*, in either guise, is explained first of all by the currency of heroic tragedy. The highfalutin' neoclassic dramas of men like Otway, Lee, and Dryden still held the stage, with their clashes of love and duty, their gestures of selfless renunciation and their grandiose verbal histrionics. It was a mode which stood up and begged to be parodied, yet Fielding was the first to move beyond travesty into a kind of surrealist fantasy. Even without the elaborate textual apparatus, by which the pedant Scriblerus directs our attention to absurd precedents for the even more absurd burlesque, the play has pace and point. Particular felicities are the queen of the giants, Glumdalca, who falls in love with tiny Tom; and the final cataclysm by which every character stabs the next until the stage is filled with bodies and no living soul is left. Here the courtier Noodle (who looks as if he might have a touch of Lord Hervey about him) announces the catastrophe to the king:

> NOODLE. Oh! monstrous, dreadful, terrible, Oh! Oh!
>   Deaf be my Ears, for ever blind my Eyes!
>   Dumb be my Tongue! Feet lame! All Senses lost!
>   Howl Wolves, grunt Bears, hiss Snakes, shriek all ye Ghosts!
> KING. What does the Blockhead mean?
> NOODLE. I mean, my Liege
>   Only to grace my Tale with decent Horror;
>   Whilst from my Garret, twice two Stories high,
>   I look'd abroad into the Streets below;
>   I saw *Tom Thumb* attended by the Mob,
>   Twice Twenty Shoe-Boys, twice two Dozen Links,
>   Chairmen and Porters, Hackney-Coachmen, Whores;
>   Aloft he bore the grizly Head of *Grizzle*;
>   When of a sudden thro' the Streets there came
>   A Cow, of larger than the usual Size,
>   And in a Moment—guess, Oh! guess the rest!
>   And in a Moment swallow'd up *Tom Thumb*.
> KING. Shut up again the Prisons, bid my Treasurer
>   Not give three Farthings out—hang all the *Culprits*,
>   Guilty or not—no matter—Ravish Virgins,
>   Go bid the Schoolmasters whip all their Boys;
>   Let Lawyers, Parsons, and Physicians loose,
>   To rob, impose on, and to kill the World.
> NOODLE. Her Majesty the Queen is in a Swoon.
> QUEEN. Not so much in a Swoon, but I have still
>   Strength to reward the Messenger of ill News.
>   *Kills* NOODLE.
> NOODLE. Oh! I am slain.
> CLEORA. My Lover's kill'd, I will revenge him so.
>   *Kills the* QUEEN.
> HUNCAMUNCA. My Mamma kill'd vile Murtheress, beware.
>   *Kills* CLEORA.

DOODLE. This for an old Grudge, to thy Heart.

Kills HUNCAMUNCA.

MUSTACHA. And this
I drive to thine, Oh *Doodle*! for a new one.

Kills DOODLE.

KING. Ha! Murtheress vile, take that.

Kills MUSTACHA.

And take thou this.

Kills himself, and falls.

Now and again a modern audience might be reminded of the parodies of Shakespearian histories in *Beyond the Fringe*: but Fielding has an entire pseudo-narrative to relate, not just a short sketch of incidental amusement. It should be added that a large ingredient of political commentary was secreted in the text—the character of 'Tom Thumb the Great' clearly alludes to Robert Walpole, the 'great man' as he was widely known. *Tom Thumb* is still actable, and acted from time to time with success. Despite its allusion to a mode of dramatic expression that went out with Fielding (nobody had quite the face to compose pure heroic tragedy again, not even Edward Young), *Tom Thumb* has spawned imitations and adaptations ever since. And even today, as well as 'the sheer sense of farce bustle and activity', as one writer puts it, 'the grand and pointless activity ... continues to be satiric because ... aimed at something we always have with us, theatrical pretension'.

Two hits in repertoire at the same theatre made something even Noel Coward or Alan Ayckbourn might have envied. For Fielding it was not enough: in his youthful exhilaration he brought the Little Theatre another play. *Rape upon Rape: or, The Justice Caught in his own Trap* went on at the Haymarket on 23 June, just as the 1729/30 season was drawing to a close. A farce in five acts, it revolves around a trading justice named Squeezum and a merchant called Mr Politic, obsessed with the tittletattle of the day. (Some aspects of the play were used in *Lock Up Your Daughters*, a 1960s success at the Mermaid Theatre in London and later a film.) There were eight performances before the season came to an end. In the autumn a revised version was presented with the less offensive title *The Coffee-House Politician*, this time at Lincoln's Inn Fields. It had also been seen in September at Southwark Fair, where Charles Macklin appeared nine times a day, amid the rope-dancers and performing apes, dressed 'in a fine lace coat and bag wig'—for which he got half a guinea per day. The play was published under both titles but enjoyed a far less spectacular success than its two predecessors. Perhaps its dramatic methods seemed old-fashioned to the audience. At the Little Theatre they were used to risqué political satires, whilst at Lincoln's Inn Fields sorcery, juggling and dogs on stilts were the expected fare.

In choosing his title, and now and then during the plot, Fielding certainly had in mind the most notorious libertine of the age, Colonel Francis Charteris. He had become known as 'Rapemaster General of Great Britain' by reason of his vicious conduct. Early in 1730 he had been convicted of sexual assault upon a maidservant, and imprisoned in Newgate. But by April he had been granted a royal pardon, which made even the least cynical believe that he had eminent friends at court. The Earl of Egmont called him 'one of the greatest and most known rogues in England'; Swift attacked him, and Dr Arbuthnot wrote a savage mock-epitaph beginning, 'Here continueth to rot the body of Francis Chartres . . .' Pope's note on his character fills out the details:

> . . . a man infamous for all manner of vices. When he was an ensign in the army, he was drumm'd out of the regiment for a cheat; he was next banish'd Brussels, and drumm'd out of Ghent on the same account. After a hundred tricks at the gaming-tables, he took to lending of money at exorbitant interest and on great penalties, accumulating premium, interest and capital into new capital, and seizing to a minute when the payments became due; in a word, by a constant attention to the vices, wants and follies of mankind, he acquired an immense fortune. His house was a perpetual bawdy-house. He was twice condemn'd for rapes, and pardoned; but the last time not without imprisonment in Newgate, and large confiscations.

Fielding does not bring Charteris directly onto the stage; perhaps he does not dare. What he attacks is corrupt screening of the guilty; Charteris was said to be 'one of the runners of Sir Robert Walpole', and it was believed that Walpole bent the law to get his minion released. A bitter comment on the operation of justice is made in lines like these (from Act II): 'The laws are turnpikes, only made to stop people who walk on foot, and not to interrupt those who drive through them in their coaches.' Here we have a faint hint of the novels to come, with their generous indignation against wealthy wrongdoers. Charteris earns only an occasional mention in Fielding's later work—he died, totally unlamented, in 1732—but his career prompted some of Fielding's first onslaughts on villainy in power.

By now Fielding had, of course, acquired both fame and notoriety Viscount Perceval, later the first Earl of Egmont, went along to see a double bill of *The Author's Farce* and *Tom Thumb* in April 1730. He found them 'exceedingly full of humour, with some wit', but in his journal he added 'The author is one of the sixteen children of Mr Fielding, and in a very low condition of purse.' By June of the same year the pro-Pope *Grub-street Journal* was beginning a campaign of hostility towards Fielding that lasted several years. In the early 1730s *Tom Thumb* became a byword in stuffy literary circles for cheap effects. One writer complained that some fortunate booksellers had acquired large estates by publishing '*Tom Thumb*, riddles, songs, fables, the *Pilgrim's Progress*, and such like common trumpery'. But Fielding's purse was perhaps a little less empty as time went on, and he could afford to laugh away such ill-natured attacks.

He had, besides, other works on the stocks. First came a bit of a failure, a three-act farce intended as an afterpiece to *The Tragedy of Tragedies* (rather oddly, because it is rather the longer of these two). *The Letter-Writers* went on at the Little Theatre in March 1731; its theme is Chaucerian, with two elderly Januaries trying to keep local Mays away from their youthful wives. But it did not please the town, and had to be taken off after the third night. For once Fielding was behindhand. A new play was required, and it took him all of three weeks to get his ballad opera written and rehearsed in time for its opening just after Easter. The title was *The Welsh Opera*. This was the most daring treatment of topical realities that Fielding had yet attempted, and marks his début as a direct political satirist. (The state of politics will be discussed in the next chapter.) It also saw a return to the popular appeal of his earlier musical plays. *The Welsh Opera* was performed ten or more times in a month, and so good were the box-office results that the managers put up the price of tickets for the pit to five shillings from three when Fielding had his benefit night.

Not satisfied with this indication of popular esteem, Fielding was already busy producing a revised and expanded version. This was given a more striking (if less accurate) title, *The Grub-Street Opera*, and supplied with an additional third act. The new play was due to go on at the Little Theatre first on 11 June, and then (after a transparent excuse of sudden illness in the cast) on 14 June. An advertisement in the *Daily Post* on that day announced that the company had been obliged to defer production until further notice. As far as we know, this version never reached the stage. Clearly the ministry had stepped in to apply pressure, how gently or otherwise we can only surmise. This would be a great disappointment to the 'persons of quality' who had been encouraging the company to go ahead—they were no doubt leading opposition politicians—as well as the garreteers who had been urged to attend a play 'calculated for the propogration' of their interests, as the sneering *Grub-street Journal* had suggested on 11 June.

Luckily the play did find its way into print. First came a pirate text of *The Welsh Opera* late in June. On 18 August what seems to have been a rehearsal copy was published 'for the benefit of the comedians', that is the Haymarket company, with yet another title, *The Genuine Grub-Street Opera*. Finally James Roberts brought out an authorised edition, taking the opportunity to bind in unsold sheets of *The Masquerade*, a three-year-old poem which had not yet exhausted its printing. This last text, *The Grub-Street Opera* pure and simple, is the play as it would have been performed in June but for ministerial intervention. Censorship was heavy that summer, with the Haymarket company (as usual) bearing the brunt. They were on the receiving end of a presentment by the Middlesex grand jury for another play attacking Walpole, and late in July their cast was actually raided by the constables during a performance—fortunately for the company, they managed to make their escape on this occasion. On 19 August the same thing happened during a showing of *Hurlothrumbo*, a play with about as much political content as Laurel and Hardy films. The explanation seems to be that the actors continued to show their intransigence, and the government took their reprisal by invoking vagrancy laws. The oily preacher 'Orator' Henley predicted that the players would make their next public appearance on the podium at Tyburn, and that was only just beyond the bounds of possibility. Meanwhile Fielding lay low, unwilling this time to risk his own freedom in the cause of theatrical liberty.

To tell the truth, *The Grub-Street Opera* does not look very seditious after two and a half centuries. There is not very much plot, and the point of all the contention lay in the easily identifiable characterisations. Robin the butler is, of course, Walpole; the coachman William, with whom he quarrels, is William Pulteney, a prominent figure in the Opposition. The groom John represents Lord Hervey, courtier and writer of superb political memoirs, who had earlier that year fought a duel in St James's Park against Pulteney. Thomas the gardener is the Duke of Newcastle, that busy and durable Whig grandee. The servant-girl Sweetissa is Walpole's mistress Molly Skerrett, whom he eventually married after his wife had died. (Poor Molly, beloved by Lady Mary Wortley Montagu, had retained the role of mistress for fifteen years or more, but died from a miscarriage after only three months as an acknowledged wife.) There are also roles for the King, Queen, and Prince of Wales. But there are no direct onslaughts upon any of these figures: the satire only strikes home if the audience makes an application to events they already know about. Again, much of the theatrical appeal must have been owing to the songs. This time there are over sixty airs: by far the most famous is 'The Roast Beef of Old England', sung by the cook Susan in the third act. It was set to an anonymous tune called 'The King's Old Courtier'. It soon became a rallying-call to patriotism (this was nine years before *Rule, Britannia* was composed); its title was borrowed for the print made of Hogarth's *Calais Gate*; and high-spirited audiences in the playhouse were always liable to break into the chorus when bored by a piffling monsieur or degenerate Latin performer. It had the great virtue in a hit song of suiting occasions other than its original dramatic setting.

4

The year 1731 opened with a new play performed on the night of 1 January. It saw an extraordinary burst of youthful energy on Fielding's part: five fresh works were seen at Drury Lane, where Fielding had migrated owing to the continued harassment of the Haymarket players. Perhaps the ministry were glad to see his move, as the Theatre Royal was easier to keep under check—though the managers were given reasonable artistic freedom, in the last resort they were creatures of the official will, and generally took care not to bite the hand that fed them. It was also in this year that Fielding first became the centre of critical controversy, with the *Grub-street Journal* setting the pace for other newspapers. It is difficult to recall that he was still only twenty-five.

The show seen on New Year's Day was yet another ballad opera, under the title of *The Lottery*. Described on publication one week later as a 'farce', this lively little piece contained about twenty songs. At Drury Lane, Fielding could supplement old ballads with original scores by the musical director, a mysterious figure called Mr Seedo. He may possibly have been a Prussian whose name should be 'Sidow'; his wife was an Italian singer. As well as arranging existing melodies he wrote new items for *The Lottery*, and he was conspicuous enough at this period to be given a one-line part in the revised *Author's Farce*. (Just possibly, he had been in charge of the music at the Little Theatre when the *Farce* was first put on.) At all events, he supplied some effective music for the cast of *The Lottery*, among whom Kitty Clive as the heroine Chloe again stood out. The plot does not matter very much: it is built around the draw for a state lottery, one of the many excellent institutions in Georgian England which we have permitted to emigrate to less prim surroundings. Fielding manages to satirise the abuses (mainly concerning the 'jobbers' like Mr Stocks in the play who buy up large allocations of tickets and sell—or lease—them at a profit). But he does not convince all of us that the lotteries were a bad thing in themselves. In any case, the social criticism is only a faint wisp of cloud on the horizon; the opera works by its gusto and amusing dialogue, plus, of course, the songs. Not surprisingly it proved to be one of Fielding's many huge successes. It continued to draw audiences throughout the century and was frequently reprinted.

Six weeks later Fielding had a full-length comedy ready for Drury Lane, called *The Modern Husband*. It had in fact been in preparation for a considerable period, perhaps as much as two years. In September 1730 he had sent the manuscript to Lady Mary Wortley Montagu, with some conventional-sounding appeals for critical guidance. (He later thanked her for reading three acts of a play, which may indicate that the draft was unfinished at this stage.) His modest tone reflects some anxiety concerning a new departure, that is a move into so-called 'sentimental comedy', a genre pioneered by Richard Steele, Colley Cibber and others. The hallmarks of the form are lachrymose situations, pathetic dilemmas for a virtuous heroine, pitiable family divisions, and the like. Fielding in fact takes a more robust line than most, although his theme was a sensitive one: a scheme to entrap a lascivious nobleman, mounted by a poverty-stricken married couple. Its direct treatment of sex and money made it a daringly 'frank' play for its time, and even the tough-minded Lady Mary seems to have grasped with relief its portrayal of the bright gadabout, Lady Charlotte Gaywit, who represents a more conventional brand of comedy. On the first night, 14 February, Fielding had the unusual experience, for him, of hearing the audience hiss the production. Its run lasted on and off till 18 March, and there were some admirers; but it never matched the success of Fielding's other plays in this period.

Most of the biographers have been a bit stuffy about *The Modern Husband*, and even in 1952 Dudden was writing in the purest Victorian accents about this 'sordid drama'. It might be supposed that a writer today would react by praising the unflinching gaze of Fielding's study of modern vice. I am bound to confess, however, that I would rather attend a second-rate performance of *The Lottery* than endure the five-act virtue-in-distress which constitutes *The Modern Husband*. As a final oddity, the play was dedicated, on its publication later in February, to none other than Robert Walpole. Nobody has ever satisfactorily explained this circumstance; it is scarcely possible to believe it a piece of ironic effrontery. Perhaps Lady Mary, who was on pretty good terms with the prime minister, was attempting a rapprochement.

Fielding, with the resilience of one sure of his purposes, did not allow this partial failure to impede his career. On 1 June he was back at Drury Lane with a double bill. The major item was a three-act comedy entitled *The Old Debauchees*. It was based on a sensational case in Toulon during 1731. A Jesuit father was charged with seducing a young and beautiful penitent by means of sorcery. Ultimately both principals fled from the area, to avoid persecution or notoriety. It is good rich material for popular journalism, but again Fielding's touch rather deserted him in the execution. There is a hint of Marlowe in some of the grim farce, with devils, visions, and disembodied voices; but the final effect is a little confused. Kitty Clive took the heroine's part, while Theophilus Cibber, whose father had created a famous Jesuit villain years before, played the part of the evil confessor. The play had a mixed reception on its first night; perhaps it would get a better hearing if revived today, when *Measure for Measure* is among the most admired of all Shakespeare's plays.

The afterpiece, called *The Covent-Garden Tragedy*, fared worse; it was greeted by the dreaded Drury Lane catcall, and had to be withdrawn after its opening performance. It seems to me the better play for all that. It is a burlesque again, but instead of the dispersed targets of *Tom Thumb*, Fielding has confined himself to a single object of satire—this was Ambrose Philips's popular tragic vehicle, *The Distrest Mother* (1712), a reworking of *Andromaque* to native taste. The place of Andromaque in the plot is taken by Mother Punchbowl, proprietor of a brothel in the red-light district of Covent Garden. This role was taken by a man, Roger Bridgwater; a clear indication that 'travesty' was intended, since the clown in petticoats was usual in such performances. (Glumdalca, the giantess in the revised *Tom Thumb*, was often played by a male actor.) Fielding undoubtedly had in mind Mrs Elizabeth Needham, the most notorious bawd of her day, who appears in the first plate of *The Harlot's Progress*. (Hogarth was clearly an influence on the play.) In 1725 Mrs Needham, alias Blewit, had been prosecuted for keeping a disorderly house in an alley off the top of New Bond Street— which *was* then a very new street. She was imprisoned and sentenced to the pillory. However, it was not until 1731 that she became particularly well-known as a procuress for the infamous Colonel Charteris, the most depraved of all rakes. Again she was tried, again pilloried, and there she suffered so badly at the hands of the mob that she died within a few days. These events were only a year old when *The Covent-Garden Tragedy* reached the stage, and would be in the recollection of every spectator. The bully Captain Bilkum is based on a guards officer named Edward Braddock, who later became commander-in-chief of the British forces in America, where he was killed in action some twenty years after this date. Kitty Clive played Kissinda, a prostitute; her protector Lovegirlo was taken by Theophilus Cibber.

Fielding took the opportunity, when the *Tragedy* was published towards the end of June, to hit back at some of the critics. (He was paid twenty guineas for the copyright of his two new plays.) He inserts a supposed letter from a gentleman in town to his friend in the country, asserting that '*The Modern Husband*, which we hissed the first night, had such success, that I began to think it a good play, till the *Grub-street Journal* assured me it was not.' But it was to no avail: the *Tragedy* was totally ousted from the Drury Lane repertoire, and indeed it appears that the next performance in a legitimate theatre was a revival by the National Theatre in 1968. This, too, was something of a flop. Fielding managed to score some hits against his enemies (a semi-literate porter is revealed at the start of the play as a contributor of dramatic notices to the *Grub-street Journal*), but he was quite unable to turn the tide of public disfavour.

Rebuffs were arriving thick and fast at this juncture. It is lucky that Fielding was robust and self-confident enough to withstand this flow of abuse. Less hostile criticism has silenced major talents before now. At the heart of the opposition to Fielding stood a rather curious organ which has been mentioned several times. This was the *Grub-street Journal*, founded in 1730 as a sort of serialised *Dunciad*. Its seven-year existence was marked by steady loyalty to the Scriblerians, and especially to Pope. Its editors were Richard Russel, a nonjuring clergyman, and John Martyn, a botanist who became a Fellow of the Royal Society at the age of twenty-five. The pretence was maintained that the journal issued from a tavern 'vulgarly called the Flying Horse' in Grub Street, that is a depraved Pegasus. There actually was such a tavern, a few yards up Grub Street, on the right hand side as you went up from the city. Early in its career of over four hundred issues, the *Journal* took against Fielding, as it did against his friend James Ralph (dubbed 'Vitruvius Grubeanus' for his writings on architecture). As we have seen, Fielding had set out on his literary career as an avowed disciple of the Scriblerian party. It may have been this assumption of *their* inheritance which irritated Pope, Richard Savage and others who set the tone for the *Journal*. Certainly by the summer of 1732 Fielding was a regular target in its columns.

Already in March of that year the editors had printed a cold appraisal of *The Modern Husband* by Dramaticus—he was long identified as one of the court placemen, Sir William Yonge, but this is probably incorrect. In June Dramaticus returned to the fray, taking into account the subsequently premièred pieces: he was now joined by Prosaicus and Publicus, maybe pseudonyms for the editorial team. A reply appeared in the pro-ministerial newspaper, the *Daily Post*, on 21 June, for which Theophilus Cibber is thought to have been responsible. But Fielding held his hand until 31 July, when he defended his work under the pen-name Philalethes. He concludes the article by asserting that greater indecency than appears in his own work will be found in the writings of 'a most witty, learned, and reverend writer of our own age', that is Swift. The *Journal* refused to let go, and in August printed a mock-defence of *The Covent-Garden Tragedy* amongst other anti-Fielding blasts. A sharp epigram by Maevius (Russel himself?) suggested that Fielding's plays consisted, 'Of good sense scarce an ounce, and of bawdy a pound.' He had an occasional voice on his side. Thus, a periodical called *The Comedian* replied to the attacks by observing,

> When Grubs and Grublings censure Fielding's scenes,
> He cannot answer that which nothing means.

But most of the press supported Maevius in this regard.

By this date the *Grub-street Journal* had one more offering in its sights. This was an adaptation of Molière's great comedy, *Le Médecin malgré lui*,

Southwark Fair by Hogarth (1733). Fielding's own plays were often performed in such a setting

Grub Street: the rickety old-fashioned dwellings of hack authors. The street lay near Moorfields, on the site now occupied by the Barbican

Top left Kitty Clive, the singer and actress who took the leading part in many of
Fielding's works for the stage

Top right Charlotte Charke (daughter of Colley Cibber), actress and adventuress, who
also worked with Fielding

Above Strolling Actresses Dressing in a Barn by Hogarth (1738)

Top A riot in Covent Garden theatre in 1763, during the performance of an opera by Thomas Arne

Above Theophilus Cibber, dressed as Pistol, confronts the Drury Lane management led by John Highmore (1733). Seated in the right foreground is Colley Cibber

Plate 1 of *The Harlot's Progress* by Hogarth (1732). The bawd is Mother Needham; Colonel Charteris is waiting in the doorway

Plate 3 of *Marriage à la Mode* by Hogarth (1745). The setting represents Dr Misaubin's consulting room

under the title of *The Mock Doctor,* which went on at Drury Lane late in June. It proved a far more successful afterpiece to *The Old Debauchees.* Once more cast in the form of a ballad opera, it contained ten musical numbers, including three original items by Mr Seedo, still in his post. The play enjoyed lasting success, indeed judged by the number of performances over time it must be about the most popular of all Fielding's dramatic works. Skilful theatrical craftsmanship is evident throughout, with the pace unrelenting and the observation sharp. It is not, of course, Molière; minor roles are severely curtailed, and a number of scenes omitted altogether. The mock-doctor's wife, Martine (now called Dorcas), was played by Kitty Clive, who naturally wanted the part expanded to fit her starring talents, and Fielding did this by writing in some new material. He was always a great admirer of Molière, and may even have taken a share in the translation which appeared in this very year as *The Select Comedies of Mr de Moliere.*

But the greatest factor as far as the contemporary audience went was the home-grown detail, notably a wicked portrayal in Gregory (the Sganarelle of the original) of a famous London figure, Dr John Misaubin. He was the most celebrated of quacks in an age when there was no shortage of them. Hogarth introduced him into both the *Harlot's Progress* and *Marriage à la Mode*; indeed the third scene of this latter series is thought to be set in Misaubin's house at 96 St Martin's Lane. He stands, short and crooked-legged, on the left of the scene, surrounded by the props of a charlatan, skeletons, skulls, jars, and strange machines. As the great commentator on Hogarth, Lichtenberg, remarks, 'the laboratory at the back seems to be a mere showpiece—a chemical kitchen in which no cooking is ever done'. The quack, Monsieur de la Pillule, he speculates, 'began as a barber, then became a urine-diviner, surreptitiously gained the doctor's hat . . . through his cures . . . and now even reckons upon a knighthood'. It was Fielding's genius to be able to bring such grotesque figures on the stage without blurring the lines of action: again young Cibber's performance must have helped. Like Hogarth, Fielding could blend caricature into a scene of everyday realism.

At thirty-four William Hogarth was just coming into his own. Three years earlier he had married the daughter of Sir James Thornhill, an artist who had succeeded to the tune of becoming serjeant-painter to the King and an MP. During 1731 the couple had moved into Thornhill's fine house in the Great Piazza of Covent Garden, immediately adjoining Rich's theatre, then in the process of construction. Hogarth stayed only a couple of years, before setting up his own establishment in Leicester Fields. By this time he had scored a real triumph with his first brilliant 'moral' series, *The Harlot's Progress.* Up till then he had produced mainly topical pictures on subjects like the South Sea Bubble. He had provided a wounding illustration of

Gulliver's Travels, aimed at Robert Walpole; had painted *The Beggar's Opera* in performance, and had designed twelve plates to accompany Samuel Butler's boisterous *Hudibras*. He was, consequently, well known to the literary world. Swift praised him, and to many contemporaries he seemed the graphic equivalent of Scriblerus.

Nevertheless, his most lasting alliance with any man of letters was to be with Fielding. Both men kept their London base around Covent Garden, in the district largely owned by the Russell family, headed by the Duke of Bedford. In time each was to set up a suburban ménage to the west of London, within convenient reach of one another. As for their art, Fielding and Hogarth independently sought to bring a new particularity and lifelike quality to comic portrayal. Their aims have been summarised by Ronald Paulson: they wished, he observes,

to replace the fantasy of traditional, emblematic, and Augustan satire with a more restrained delineation, closer to experience, and reliant on 'character' rather than 'caricature' ... Both, moreover, sought a more secure place in the classical hierarchy of kinds than satire, the grotesque, or even the comic by itself could command.

It took Fielding several more years to achieve the right formula, when he turned to the novel. Hogarth was already on course, with the *Harlot* series followed by *The Rake's Progress* (1735) and *Southwark Fair*. By 1742, when *Joseph Andrews* came out, Fielding would be saluting 'the ingenious Hogarth' as a brother and colleague. Other compliments were extended in later works. From the time of *Tom Thumb* (for which Hogarth designed a headpiece) to the day of Fielding's death they were unshakable allies.

It was around this time that Fielding returned to poetry in order to defend his patron Lady Mary. The occasion was a devastating couplet in Pope's most recent 'imitation of Horace', plainly recognisable as an allusion to Mary:

> From furious *Sappho* scarce a milder fate,
> Pox'd by her Love, or libell'd by her Hate.

Stung by this treatment of his cousin and benefactress, Fielding composed a verse epistle to vindicate her. It was addressed to George Lyttelton, his schoolfellow at Eton, now a friend of Pope and favourite of the Prince of Wales. It was around Lyttelton that day-to-day opposition to Walpole revolved: he was not an ideologue like Bolingbroke nor a parliamentary figure of weight like Pulteney, but he was much more of a campaign manager. His true role was as patron but he had pretensions enough as a writer to earn the last place in Johnson's *Lives of the Poets.* (Johnson had met him about 1725, when visiting Stourbridge, before Lyttelton had left Eton.) Fielding's epistle was never published, and the only copy to have survived turned up a few years ago among Lady Mary's papers: it was, after all, for her eyes that Fielding's message was intended. In the poem Fielding admits the merit of Pope's work, as he had not done in his mock-heroic fragment of 1729 (see page 42), but he condemns with the utmost vigour the 'libellous' character of personalised satire. It was an awkward posture for an opposition supporter to adopt, and indeed Lady Mary's continued loyalty to the ministry must have been one of the factors inhibiting Fielding's political expression. Only in the oblique form of drama does he risk assailing Walpole; and before too many years had passed, even that was given over for good.

In the new theatrical season, 1732/3, the pace slackened, as well it might. Fielding brought out only two new plays. One is another translation from Molière, while the other is lost. A mysterious ballad opera called *Deborah* was acted at Drury Lane on 6 April 1733. It cannot have been at all successful, and was never published. Efforts have been made to reconstruct its likely components, but we are largely in the realm of guesswork.* It is unlikely that we are missing very much. The other item was performed seven weeks earlier at the same theatre: *The Miser,* an adaptation from *L'Avare* which attempts more radical surgery than had been the case with *The Mock Doctor.* There was no music this time—Fielding concentrated on plot mechanics and characterisation. If not more believable than Harpagon, Fielding's anglicised Lovegold is equally funny and still more loathsome in some respects. The role of the chambermaid, Lappet, created for Mrs Clive once more, combines aspects of two minor personages in the original. As the play proceeds, Fielding departs further and further from Molière, and by extending the element of intrigue he achieves rather more of a well-made play—which is not to say a better play. *The Miser* was exceedingly successful, playing for twenty-six nights. It was taken by Theophilus Cibber to Bartholomew Fair during the theatre's summer break; it also reached Southwark Fair at just the moment Hogarth was painting his memorable picture. In the legitimate theatre it kept its hold on the public for many years to come. Lovegold was another of Charles Macklin's great parts, and the eccentric comedian Ned Shuter also scored in this role. Voltaire praised it for the beauties added to Molière's dialogue. The play was published within a month, with a dedication to a prominent young peer, the Duke of Richmond; thereafter many editions appeared into the nineteenth century.

Fielding had devoted his early twenties almost exclusively to the stage,

---

*There was probably some current of allusion to Handel's oratorio *Deborah*, then struggling for an audience at the Opera House: Handel had unwisely put up the prices of admission.

where he had rapidly matured in skill and invention. He wrote a few prologues and epilogues, together with some occasional verse; but in general he could be said to have committed himself totally to the theatre. At twenty-six he was still by no means rich, but at least he was firmly launched on a career that promised a secure future in writing. It was not to work out like that.

THREE

Politics and Plays

1734-37

I

We can get some idea of what contemporary people thought about Fielding from a satiric paragraph published in July 1734. It appeared in the *Universal Spectator*, a weekly journal run chiefly by Henry Baker, Defoe's son-in-law, until about this time. The writer concentrates on Fielding's hasty and 'negligent' manner of composition: he draws up a mock-bequest in this form:

Item, I give and bequeath to my very negligent friend Henry Drama, esq., all my industry. And whereas the world may think this an unnecessary legacy, forasmuch as the said Henry Drama, esq., brings on the stage four pieces every season; yet as such pieces are always wrote with uncommon rapidity, and during such fatal intervals only as the stocks have been on the fall, this legacy will be of use to him to revise and correct his works. Furthermore, for fear the said Henry Drama should make an ill use of the said industry, and expend it all on a ballad farce, it's my will the said legacy should be paid to him by equal portions, and as his necessities may require.

Negligence meant principally the lack of artistic care, but it suits Fielding in that he was already cultivating his swagger and gentlemanly nonchalance. There is something cruelly appropriate in the way this article defines Fielding's limitations: in real life he was an impoverished sub-aristocrat, denied the inheritance which an elder son in his social world might reasonably have expected. Whether or not he was speculating in the funds, we do not know.

Around this period, in Dublin, Jonathan Swift was completing one of his most scathing reviews of the contemporary cultural scene. *On Poetry: A Rapsody* is a cynically accurate poem, rather than a rhapsodic one as we should use the term—it contains the famous lines on fleas with smaller fleas to bite 'em. Not much farther on in the poem, Swift considers the art of sinking in literary composition:

> In poetry the height we know;
> 'Tis only infinite below.
> For instance: when you rashly think,
> No rhymer can like Welsted sink.
> His merits balanced you shall find,
> That Fielding leaves him far behind.

Such references were a sign that Fielding was still seen by many as the genuine Grub Street article, lucky to have escaped a niche in *The Dunciad* through his late arrival on the scene. It is true that there is an alternative reading, replacing Fielding's name by the phrase 'The Laureate' (Colley Cibber), and that George Faulkner (Swift's Irish publisher) asserted that the Dean had 'a great esteem' for Fielding. Nevertheless someone, even if it was some malicious rival in London, believed that Fielding suited the context. To be aligned with Leonard Welsted (1688–1747), an effete and would-be genteel poetaster properly incarcerated in *The Dunciad*, was no great compliment.

In fact, the initial burst of energy was running down. During 1734 Fielding brought out three plays: but one was a revision and one a rehash of the play he had sketched out at Leyden. A new version of *The Author's Farce* came on at Drury Lane just after the new year; as we have seen, it incorporated new thrusts at men like Heidegger and Cibber, with an intensification of the satire against Italian opera. There were only six performances. Three months later Fielding returned to the Haymarket, after certain difficulties which we shall come to in a moment; in the Little Theatre, scene of his earliest triumphs, he saw the production of *Don Quixote in England*. This play, first sketched out six years before, is a good brisk comedy: closer in spirit to his later novels (and those of his successor Smollett) than anything else he had written for the stage. The thirteen airs are less important than the songs of his earlier ballad operas.

The Don stands for parliament and thus provides the dramatist with an opportunity to pillory the corruptions of a country borough, notoriously the most venal type of constituency. Fielding, I am sure, had some town or towns in mind, but they have not been identified. Salisbury, as it happened, was a notably uncorrupt borough, which liked to send independent local men to parliament. Old Sarum, nearby, was wholly irrelevant: it was just a ploughed field, more of an archaeological site than a place of human habitation, and since the Pitt family controlled all seven votes bribery was as pointless as any other mode of electioneering. On the other hand, Fielding must have known towns where contests were regularly fierce and well-subsidised: Hindon, Shaftesbury, and Milborne Port, which all lay close to East Stour; Stockbridge, Wootton Bassett, perhaps Chichester and Worcester.* There is a Hogarthian quality in the 'genial gusto' of this play, as one critic calls it; although Fielding was to tack on a sharply anti-ministerial dedication to the great Earl of Chesterfield when he published the play shortly after its production, the text itself is not an explicitly partisan rendering of topical affairs. Its great strength on the stage lay in the character of the boorish Squire Badger, and especially in the redoubtable Charles Macklin's performance of this amusing vulgarian.†

The one totally new play had been premièred at Drury Lane with the revised *Author's Farce* on 15 January. It was a two-act work, *The Intriguing Chambermaid*, based on a thirty-year-old French play. Like many ballad operas, it was commonly performed as an afterpiece. In this capacity it enjoyed worthwhile but not outstanding success. Kitty Clive yet again took the main part, as the resourceful intriguer, Lettice, a soubrette role with a hint now and then of Susanna in *Figaro*. Fielding in fact wrote a dedicatory epistle to the published play, praising Kitty for her loyalty and dramatic ability. Another reliable vocal performer (there were thirteen airs this time) was Michael Stopler, who had appeared in most of the earlier operas. It should be added here that Fielding's contribution to the musical stage had been augmented not long before when Mrs Haywood and others adapted *Tom Thumb* as *The Opera of Operas*, with music by Thomas Arne.

As usual, we are in the dark concerning the inner workings of Fielding's mind at this juncture. But creative spirits have to operate in a commercial world, and the whole of London theatrical life was set by the ears during the 1733/34 season. Walpole's hitherto stable command of national affairs also faced severe challenge during these years. Fielding was to make his most lasting mark as a dramatist within the next short period (1735–37), with works that brought him into a head-on collision with the ministry. To understand how this came about, we must look briefly both at the state of the theatre and the structure of politics. These two areas of life set up the lines of force that surround Fielding's achievement.

2

In the eighteenth century people went to the theatre earlier than we do

---

* Hindon was 'a notoriously venal borough'. In 1734 it was won by Stephen Fox and George Fox; when the former decided to sit for Shaftesbury instead, his brother Henry (Fielding's schoolfellow) was elected to take his place. More relevant is the previous contest in 1727, when a violent struggle took place in which, it is reasonable to deduce, the returning officer was bribed to declare a false result. As late as 1750 the constituency was tagged by one observer 'to be bought'. There are possible echoes in Fielding's plays and novels, including *Pasquin*.

† As late as 1772 Dr Arne presented a short opera called *Squire Badger* based on the play; but it did not catch the public fancy.

today: at the beginning of the century it was usual for the curtain to go up at six o'clock, following a brief segment of music. More accurately what happened in most cases was that an actor or actress stepped forward in front of the curtain and delivered a prologue, after which the scene opened for the play to start. The audience was divided between a number of locations, each with a social tone of its own: seats on the edge of the stage itself, boxes, the pit and the galleries. At the very back of the auditorium in the upper gallery there was often a collection of footmen, some of whom had come early to the theatre to reserve a place for their masters. The seating capacity of each house in the 1730s would be something of this order: Drury Lane, 1,000; Covent Garden, 1,400; the Opera House, 1,250 or more (on special occasions, such as a star singer's benefit night, the limit was stretched to near 2,000); the Little Theatre and Goodman's Fields, say 750 each. Of course a full house was by no means the rule. One theatrical historian has calculated that the attendance figures for a representative week in 1733 show some 15,000 or a little less. The Opera House was open on Tuesday and Saturday only, in the normal way; the Little Theatre tended to limit its performances to evenings when its rival across the street was 'dark'. But the other houses would play on six evenings. If they had all played to capacity a good 25,000 attendances per week would have been possible; in fact they averaged between 50 per cent and 60 per cent of that. The season ran from autumn to the following midsummer, after which the regular houses took a break.

The repertoire was divided also, between established favourites (Shakespeare, Dryden, Otway in tragedy; Congreve, Farquhar, and Vanbrugh in comedy) and newer writers. The managers were genuinely anxious to recruit fresh talent, though their taste was often conservative—at Drury Lane anyway—and they were under various political and economic pressures. Sentimental comedy afflicted most of the theatres, farce turned up everywhere, whilst the original home of harlequinades and pantomime (Lincoln's Inn, whence Rich migrated to Covent Garden) found the other houses copying its fare very quickly. It is curious that a period which saw rope-dancers invade the patent houses and nuggets from Purcell's *Dido and Aeneas* slipped in halfway through *Measure for Measure* should also see a major Shakespearian revival, but such is the case. *Hamlet*, *Macbeth* and *Othello* were the most popular items in Fielding's day, while some plays never got a look in (*Antony and Cleopatra*, for instance, was wholly supplanted by Dryden's *All for Love*.) There were horrific cases of Shakespeare improved beyond recognition, with a burlesque *Taming of the Shrew* almost outplaying the real thing; but there was also real interest and appreciation.

Even the largest theatres had a company of no more than twenty or thirty, including specialist singers and dancers; the ratio would be two men to one woman. As always, the opera was by far the most costly form of entertainment to run, and its finances make sorry reading for most of the 1730s. Elsewhere things were tending to expand. Long runs, once a rare phenomenon, were growing more common; apart from *The Beggar's Opera* and *Hurlothrumbo*, another smash-hit emerged in Henry Carey's *Dragon of Wantley* (1737), a 'burlesque opera' which enjoyed some apt music by John Frederick Lampe. It was to have been put on at the Little Theatre, but it soon transferred to Covent Garden, where it broke box-office records set by *The Beggar's Opera* eight years before. In addition the printed libretto had fourteen editions inside a year. One change in programming policy much evident at the time of Fielding's arrival in the theatre was the liking for a double bill. John Rich at Lincoln's Inn had been readier to accept this innovation than the stuffier Drury Lane management; but by 1730 it was a regular, if not universal, feature. Farce, burlesque or pantomime were common modes of afterpiece; music and lavish processions were occasionally substituted. Fielding's development of the afterpiece into a major vehicle of dramatic satire marked his ability to convert popular forms of expression to his own purposes.

The prevalence of rioting in the Augustan theatre has perhaps been exaggerated, but noisy affrays did take place from time to time. The occasion might be an increase in admission charges, a dislike of a play's political ideology, or hostility to foreign performers, especially at times of war or diplomatic crises. Organised claques were not unknown, whilst a leading part in any kind of audience participation was taken by the law students or 'templars'. Idle apprentices were suspected of fomenting trouble at Goodman's Fields, but this could have been a story put about by employers and aged puritans.

Quarrels, however, were not confined to the audience. There was keen rivalry among the companies, and though there existed official restraints on movement of the players, in practice a star might be wooed and 'transferred' like a modern footballer. The personnel of the various theatres had enjoyed a fair measure of stability for some time, thanks mainly to the orderly regime at Drury Lane. But soon after Fielding's entry, the world of the playhouses underwent drastic changes. The process was set off by a break-up at the Theatre Royal. Sir Richard Steele died in 1729, and though he was inactive by this date it was a significant event for Drury Lane: the royal patent would expire in a given term, now established as September 1732. A new patent was drawn up in favour of the ruling triumvirate of actor-managers, that is Colley Cibber, Robert Wilks and Barton Booth. This ageing team was more interested in making a profit from the new licence than in creating fresh dramatic glory for Drury Lane. Booth sold half his share to a rich young fribble, John Highmore, for an alleged £2,500: and by May 1733 Booth himself was dead. He had been preceded to the grave by

Wilks, whose widow sold half her reversionary interest to a painter called Ellys. Cibber first made over his share in the management on a temporary basis to his unstable son Theophilus. Then, when things continued to go badly, he decided to take his money and run. He sold his entire share to Highmore for the huge sum of 3,000 guineas—worth something like £50,000 or $90,000 at current prices. With the survival power that men of his robust outlook often command, he lived for another twenty-five years.

All this, of course, was a recipe for disaster. Drury Lane during the 1732/33 season was run by an inexperienced team made up of theatrical widows and untried outsiders, holding six separate shares. Highmore held the controlling interest, but he showed no capacity to lead. The ructions culminated in a lock-out of the actors by the management in May 1733. The players, led by Theophilus Cibber, were accused of seeking to take over the theatre themselves. A noisy public debate began, with strong feelings expressed on both sides of the dispute. Eventually young Cibber took his colleagues over to the Little Theatre in September, a declaration of unilateral independence, and risked prosecution for their unlicensed performances. Highmore tried to get them declared vagrants, but the suit was lost on a technicality. The wrangles went on, in and out of the playhouse. Highmore lost more and more money with his depleted complement at Drury Lane. Around February 1734, after a wretched season, he had had enough. His share was sold to a man of a rather similar stamp, Charles Fleetwood; but Fleetwood was willing to make terms with the seceded actors, and they returned in triumph on 8 March. Thereafter the theatre gradually found its feet under Fleetwood, who had appointed Charles Macklin to look after the artistic side. It had been a major upheaval, with the old guard vanishing rapidly from the scene, as well as the threat of player-power and the invocation of legal sanctions.

The convulsions were not restricted to Drury Lane. Handel's company were having a struggle of their own at the Opera House, despite (or because of) royal patronage. An opposition group of influential aristocrats, led by the Prince of Wales, organised a rival opera season at Lincoln's Inn. The Nobility Opera, as it was called, contrived in 1733 to steal most of the best singers. Handel had to make do with lesser performers. Attendance figures slumped disastrously: most of the company were 'scrubbs', said one lady after visiting 'a dull empty opera'. In the following season (1734/35) Handel relinquished the Opera House to his rivals, and moved to Covent Garden. Unable to find an attraction to match the great castrato Farinelli, he turned more and more to oratorio—a major step artistically, but a makeshift as far as Handel was concerned at this time.

Some of these upheavals affected Fielding directly, others did not; but he took the keenest interest in all that went on. On the Drury Lane issue, he took the side of Highmore; the satire on Theophilus Cibber as Marplay Jnr in the revised *Author's Farce* is one indication, and another is the tribute to Kitty Clive's loyalty which occurs in the dedication to *The Intriguing Chambermaid*. His stance on the operatic quarrel is more difficult to determine: the revisions to *The Author's Farce* focus the attack on Count Ugly—Heidegger, who was still locked in an edgy partnership with Handel. On the other hand Fielding may have resented the excessively partisan Nobility Opera, despite the fact that some of its leading lights were patrons of his own like the Duke of Richmond. At all events Fielding stayed at Drury Lane; even though Fleetwood could not find room for *Don Quixote in England* at the major house—while the return of Theophilus Cibber to the fold meant some awkward moments for his recent critic.

All in all, this troubled phase of theatrical history had the effect of impeding Fielding as a dramatist, but to no unfortunate end. If the Drury Lane management had gone on its accustomed way, he would very likely have continued to produce the mixture as before, with a special emphasis on the orthodox five-act comedies in which he obviously wished to excel. As things turned out, he found himself thrust willynilly into the live action; and he was best as a playwright when dealing with the events and personalities of contemporary England. In a quieter theatrical climate, he might have been pushed into academic modes and conventional themes.

3

Two figures stood at the centre of the political life of the nation during this period, of whom one is well-known and the other astoundingly obscure: the premier and the king. The chief minister, Robert Walpole, is familiar to most people as a resilient and shrewd manager of the country's affairs. We look at the portraits by Jervas, Van Loo, Wootton and Kneller, and see a bluff figure whose solid bulk is set off by a glint of humour in the eyes; we think of him as capable, realistic, a shade coarse. This is a true impression but it is not the whole truth. His gaze could be cold enough when he chose, and he was a fearsome enemy. Pacific, it is true, in the sphere of diplomacy and foreign policy, he used his control of the administration at home to impose a ruthless and implacable dominance over every aspect of government. Those who crossed him could expect to be stripped of all influence sooner or later. And if we should not sentimentalise his character, neither should we underrate his intellectual qualities. He was a discerning collector of pictures and a connoisseur of beautiful things; his tastes included eating well and country sports, but these were then no disqualification for the man of feeling. The idea that persons of aesthetic sensibility should keep their complexion pale and their windows closed had still to be invented.

Yet Walpole was even in the eighteenth century primarily the king's minister. He was responsible to parliament and in some very remote fashion to the people at large; but he existed through the good offices of the king. Our textbooks tell us that the Bloodless Revolution of 1688 had introduced a system of limited monarchy; we are taught that the early Hanoverians had little interest in their adopted country. Neither assumption entirely squares with reality in the reign of George II. Though he was forty-four when he came to the throne, he had been in England throughout his father's reign, building up contacts and establishing a taste for many facets of English life. His command of the language was perfectly adequate; he knew his own mind, and whilst he could sometimes be talked out of his obstinacy the mere whim of politicians with a dubious power-base did not much impress him. That was one reason for his lasting respect for Walpole, who counted heads rather than composing hymns to liberty like the opposition ideologues. Both men were methodical and organised; Walpole had much the higher general intelligence, but the king possessed tenacity and, behind his tantrums, a sort of literal-minded honesty.

There was, too, the queen—Caroline of Anspach, fair, plump and comfortable in appearance, but restless and ambitious in spirit. She had long been on good terms with Walpole, since the days of the alternative court at Leicester Square during the time of George I. Whether she exercised as much power over the first minister as she liked to believe is open to question. Nevertheless, she gave Whitehall a spaciousness which the narrow, rather prim electorate of Hanover would never have brought it. She liked patronising intellectuals, and though the wits found her choices a matter for ridicule—as with the thresher poet, Stephen Duck, hauled up from the Wiltshire countryside to preside over the royal folly in Richmond Park—she imbued the court with a measure of cultural interest. (Her husband hated all art except music: at least his record as a patron of Handel is good.) Together the unlikely triangle of George, Caroline and Walpole remained immovable while critics, opponents and satirists came and went. Fielding was by no means the first person to find his sharpest volleys bounce back without inflicting the expected damage.

However, Walpole was in real trouble at last, when the so-called Excise Crisis came to a head in 1733. It centred on a seemingly rational plan to introduce increased taxes on tobacco and wine, both commodities which were intensively smuggled but also legally imported in great quantities. The Opposition stirred up a tremendous fuss over this proposal, depicting it as a threat to individual liberty (it is true that Walpole would not have been averse to giving fresh powers to inspectors and agents of the government: his own unchallenged authority rested on his control of a vast network of placemen who owed him or his nominees a favour.) In the end the bill was withdrawn and Walpole survived. But it was not without the attendant disadvantage of providing a cause on which his opponents could focus their grievances. Now there was a coherent body of opinion ranged against the prime minister. Its figure-head was the turkeycock Prince of Wales, 'poor Fred', who is remembered for having been alive and then being dead. The intellectual guru of the movement was Viscount Bolingbroke, the reformed rake and disillusioned Jacobite who devised what has been termed 'the politics of nostalgia'. It was a creed eminently appealing to idealist young men like Fielding, with lofty goals in life and no immediate prospects; the thesis was that a noble, organic, British system of government had been corrupted by Walpole's graft-laden political machine. The laureates of this party were legion, and unfortunately for the king almost all of them possessed greater poetic ability than the official incumbent, Colley Cibber, whose conspicuous talents did not extend to making verses. The parliamentary lead was taken by William Pulteney, and after the Excise Crisis had split the government he was aided by Lord Chesterfield amongst others.

Against this impressive force Walpole could only line up what appears an inadequate troop. There is Lord Hervey, a clever, self-consuming, androgynous person, unrivalled as a chronicler of court life but not always effective in day-to-day business. There is the Duke of Newcastle, anxious, befuddled in manner, a man with innumerable clients and dependents but scarcely any close friends. There is Hardwicke, the Lord Chancellor, an outstanding lawyer with limited political insight. Somehow Walpole managed to keep hold of power until the death of Queen Caroline in 1737 saw it slowly start to erode. Gradually his ability to win the crucial votes was sapped; the independent MPs who had supported him—mainly local worthies and backwoods gentry, suspicious of the highminded 'Patriot' ideas of the opposition—peeled away one by one. But that seemed remote and unattainable in 1734 to men like Fielding. Walpole had seemed within their grasp during the Excise Crisis, but he had escaped again. The struggle would have to be renewed.

4

Before Fielding could begin any campaigns against Walpole, he had more pressing private business to transact. For five years he had been living in the capital, no doubt within easy distance of the playhouses. He had certainly not become rich. James Miller, a clergyman and a distinctly able satirist, pictured him as living a chequered existence, depending on the fortunes which his plays met with:

Fielding who yesterday appeared so rough,
Clad in coarse frieze, and plastered down with snuff.
See how his instant gaudy trappings shine;
What playhouse bard was ever seen so fine!
But this, not from his humour flows, you'll say,
But mere necessity; for last night lay
In pawn, the velvet that he wears today.

All observers agree that he was generous to a fault with his money. Lady Mary Wortley Montagu compares him to the notoriously improvident Steele, whilst her grand-daughter wrote that 'if ever he possessed a score of pounds, nothing could keep him from lavishing it idly, or make him think of to-morrow.' This was all very well so long as he remained a bachelor, living in the bohemian company of actors and musicians; but that was not to last for ever.

As to the assertion of Arthur Murphy, his first biographer, that he conducted an active sex life, I can only say it seems entirely probable. Even if he had not been 'disposed to gallantry, by his strong animal spirits', his undoubted natural charm would have led him into temptations. He was over six feet tall when the average height for an adult male was only about five foot six; he would have stood out in any company. (Garrick, Richardson and Hogarth were inches shorter.) He can never have been remarkably good-looking; the Hogarth sketch shows him in his later years, and may not do him full justice, but his cast of features was strong rather than beautiful, with a jutting chin (so unlike that of the Habsburgs) a large nose and thick eyebrows. But women noted a determined and masculine aspect, which may well be more seductive than a face of pretty regularity. Fielding always writes as though he had enjoyed his share of female favours, and it would take a radically revisionist biographer to suggest that this was all based on fantasy.

From time to time he went back to the family home in Salisbury. Lady Gould died at an advanced age in June 1733 but his sisters stayed on in St Martin's Church Street, which ran through the south-east corner of the old town, up to the ancient church of that name. Nowadays the district is sliced in two by the A30 carrying heavy traffic bound for the coast; but St Ann Street, the route leading into the town centre, remains unspoilt, a pleasant mixture of commercial properties and amenities such as the county museum. The noble outline of the cathedral spire stands out ahead as sharply as it did when Fielding made his way along this route, more than two centuries ago.

Among the friends he made locally, the closest was certainly James Harris, two years his junior, who began life as an eccentric philosopher—interested in such futuristic schemes as a 'universal grammar'—and later shifted his talents into politics. At the age of over fifty, some time after

Fielding's death, he was offered a seat in parliament on the interest of a cousin; within two years he found himself a Lord of the Treasury. Not everybody admired his character or attainments: Samuel Johnson called him a prig, and many found his universal grammar universally opaque. Among the nabobs, generals, lawyers and bankers who crowded into Westminster, a philosopher was certainly something different. But he did his work effectively, and in time his son became the first Earl of Malmesbury. Fielding, we may assume, valued him above all for his knowledge of the classics.

Harris lived in an imposing house near St Ann's Gate, the picturesque archway which stands in the north-eastern corner of the cathedral close, opposite St Ann Street. The building survives, known today as Malmesbury House: it is built in a charming light-honey-coloured stone, remodelled during the early eighteenth century. A sundial erected in 1749 must have been proudly shown to the owner's friend Fielding; high up on the south wall, it bears the Shakespearian motto, 'Life's but a walking shadow'. Henry no doubt spent many happy hours in this delightful setting. A house in the close, just across the road, is traditionally said to be Fielding's own later residence, but the evidence is thin. As it happens, a large number of Georgian, and even earlier, buildings have been preserved around the spacious close, and we really do not know which if any was Henry's.

On the way from his mother's home to see Harris, Fielding would have had to pass the entrance to Friary Lane. At the near end of this, in the vicinity of an old Franciscan settlement, stood the Friary House, a substantial L-shaped house dating from the early seventeenth century. It is still there today, though the northern arm had been in time separated off as Cradock House. The occupants of this solid rather than beautiful residence, to put the matter from their point of view, would have passed the Goulds' home on their way to their parish church, which was St Martin's. They were a widow called Mrs Elizabeth Cradock, genteel perhaps but not particularly rich, .together with her two daughters, Charlotte and Catherine. I have announced the details in a fashion that makes only one outcome possible, and I need only identify the right girl. In fact it was Charlotte on whom Henry fixed his attentions, after the proper amount of vacillating between the two. Both young ladies were celebrated for their beauty in local society, and made the object of excruciating compliments in verse. The harbour master at Poole even got his lines, in English and Latin parallel texts, printed in the *London Magazine* years later; Catherine (or Kitty) is adjudged the more lively but Charlotte the prettier. There may have been a touch of the Dashwoods about them; Fielding, like Jane Austen's hero, put elegant sense above sprightly sensibility.

An eighteenth-century courtship and marriage are often hard to explore in detail. An age which was not reticent in many things did hold licit sexual activity to be a private matter; even the rakes and the brothel-creeps hung up a 'Do not Disturb' sign when they got anywhere near matrimony. However, Fielding wrote a number of verses addressed to 'Celia', a reigning beauty of Salisbury; and since these were published in the *Miscellanies* during his wife's lifetime, it is inconceivable that Fielding was tactless enough to write of some other Wiltshire maiden. The poems are standard amatory fancies which might be condescendingly dismissed as a young man's prentice work if we did not recall the calibre of the plays he was producing at the same period. We cannot say just when the couple first met, but it is likely to have been by the time Henry was twenty-one, if not a good deal earlier.

Charlotte's personal appearance is thought to be the model for Sophia in *Tom Jones*, where Fielding specifies the resemblance (IV, ii), and for the heroine of *Amelia*, where he does not. She seems then to have been dark, with an oval face and a firm chin; slightly above average height, which might then mean five foot five or thereabouts. According to Lady Louisa Stuart, Lady Mary Wortley Montagu's grand-daughter, the accident to Amelia's nose reflects a similar mishap undergone by Charlotte—a 'frightful overturn' of her carriage, which 'destroyed the gristle of her nose'. Henry did not marry her for her money, tempting as such a match may have been for this personable young man, in whom daydreams of success were accompanied by distinct competence in making friends and influencing people. Charlotte can have brought him only a moderate fortune, as her father was long dead and the widow had not remarried. Arthur Murphy states the dowry was £1,500 and there is always an even chance that anything Murphy says may be true.

The marriage for some reason took place over thirty miles from Salisbury, at Charlcombe near Bath. Odder still, Fielding was described in the register as resident (along with his bride) in St James's parish, Bath. He was later on to have important connections with the city, but none have been identified in time for the wedding, that is by 28 November 1734, which would fall on a Thursday. Biographers have speculated on how this situation came to arise, and I cannot claim to have any ready explanation.

St Mary's, Charlcombe, is perched high up on the Lansdown hills, five hundred feet above sea level. It is a small Norman church, with a tiny tower at the west end which is concealed from below by a yew tree that stands several feet higher. There is a fine view southwards across to Bathampton Down. A flowering cherry and a plum tree adorn the trim churchyard; between the church and the brow of the hill there is a coppice of mature trees. Even today it is a fairly secluded spot, and in that era it would have been just the place for a clandestine marriage. There is no means of confirming the story that the couple eloped in the face of opposition from Mrs

radock, but the circumstances do look exceedingly suspicious. A runaway
edding was the kind of thing everybody expected from the unstable
ieldings. Luckily Henry had a complicating strain in his heredity, and he
aade a prudent choice—it was a blissful match. The couple had no further
onnection with Charlcombe that we know of; but here Sarah Fielding was
uried in 1768. A tablet with marble surrounds commemorates her, high
p on the wall of the church at the west end.

Charlotte, a girl from the provinces who had grown up as the queen of
ae New Sarum assembly rooms, now found herself the wife of a high-living,
ard-drinking London gentleman, who was committed to an insecure
rofession and lacking the funds to keep up the way of life he wanted to lead.
ome young ladies would have taken refuge in tears and begged to be taken
ack to a tranquil country retreat. Charlotte, so far as we can tell, was
ltogether more mettlesome. She provided her husband with a security he
ad never known before, when fought over as a child by the squabbling
.mily factions. His character was lovable but his habits were probably
ritating in the extreme; he led not the calm and genteel existence of an
dwardian man of letters, but the hectic routine of a resident house-
ramatist. He would, perhaps, have liked to become a scholar instead, and
ae awful possibility is that in our days he would have had his way.

The couple set up home first in lodgings just off the Strand. To be more
recise, they lived in Buckingham Street, perhaps with a relative of
harlotte's as their landlord. The street runs southwards to the river, on the
te of York House, near the spot where the Adelphi was later to rise. It had
een erected by the great speculator Nicholas Barbon* late in the seventeenth
entury, and consisted of terraces of tall, narrow houses—a novelty in
ondon until this time. At the junction with the Strand were premises soon
) be occupied by the great map-maker John Rocque and then by a toyshop
un by the apprentice of William Deard, often mentioned in Fielding's
orks. Deard had his own establishment just round the corner in the Strand,
hile his daughter traded in Cockspur Street, right by the two theatres in
ae Haymarket. It was a prosperous area, with single-fronted properties of
our storeys each, the ground floor being normally occupied by a shop. Two
cars before the Fieldings settled there, the parish clerk of St Martin in the
'ields had drawn up a report on his district for a metropolitan survey. He
ad listed many 'remarkable places and things' in the parish, from Whitehall
) a French chapel; there was room for the playhouse 'on the west side of
ae *Hay-market*' (the Opera House) and for a part of Drury Lane (the rest
elonged to St Clement Dane's), but no mention of the Little Theatre.

Barbon had also been to Leyden University and, unlike Fielding, had taken his degree—in
sedicine.

As Charlotte accustomed herself to living in these unfamiliar surround-ings, Henry resumed his career as a playwright. A week into 1735 he saw the curtain go up at Drury Lane on a new 'farce'—actually a ballad opera—entitled *An Old Man Taught Wisdom*. It is the kind of romp we associate with untroubled Georgian England, full of well-marked and easily identifi-able 'characters'. The central figure is a country girl called Lucy, a part naturally taken by Kitty Clive. She is offered various desirable matches by her father; all are rejected in favour of the footman. The book was published soon afterwards with the music for no less than twenty songs, and there were many reprints. This has never been one of Fielding's better-known plays, and it is relatively unambitious: but the fact remains that, judged by the number of performances, it was among his most popular plays in the eighteenth century. Short enough to serve as an afterpiece, it was often played under the alternative title of *The Virgin Unmasked*.

Not long after this première, on 10 February 1735, Fielding had another play opening at Drury Lane. It was another attempt to pull off a full-length comedy success; there would certainly be more copy-money from a pub-lisher for a long work, and maybe more playhouse returns for a given length of run. In any case Fielding wanted desperately to make his mark in the more serious reaches of comedy; the poor reception accorded to *The Modern Husband* had only strengthened his resolve. Again he was unlucky. *The Universal Gallant* received a quite extraordinarily bad reception, and after three nights was taken off for good. The author complained in a preface to the published text that people had gone along to the playhouse with their minds made up against his work; but in a new theatrical journal the ex-perienced critic Aaron Hill rebutted this charge. Hill reports that on the first night the audiences 'sat very quiet' until the third act was almost over, 'in hopes it would mend, till finding it grew still *worse* and *worse*, they at length lost all patience'. It must have been a severe blow to Fielding's *amour-propre*. Not only did he have in the cast a major actor, James Quin, the great Falstaff who was making a much publicised return to Drury Lane: he also had a wife whom he was obliged to support and whom he wished to impress. His bitter series of preliminaries to the published text shows a new vein of disillusion with the theatre and with playgoers. This reaction on his part was understandable; *The Universal Gallant* is not such a bad comedy The taste of the town had previously been a jest with him. He was only twenty-seven but for the moment weariness had overcome him.

5

A long holiday in the country is the common prescription for such a state of health. The Fieldings soon got the opportunity, though as a result of a sad event. In February 1735, just about the time *The Universal Gallant* came on and off, the life of Mrs Cradock reached its close. Her will, proved on 25 February, is a surprising document (it survives at the Public Record Office); precisely one shilling is bequeathed to Catherine, and all the rest of her estate is left to her 'dearly beloved daughter Charlott Ffeilding wife of Henry Ffeilding of East Stour'. In addition Charlotte was appointed sole executrix. We have little idea of the size of this legacy, though Murphy's estimate of less than £1,500 puts a safe upper limit. Equally we do not know how Catherine had offended her mother. Biographers have related the bequest to the evil conduct of Amelia's sister in the later novel, but this is unsubstantiated guesswork. The kind treatment of Charlotte by no means squares with the story of a runaway marriage against Mrs Cradock's wishes, come to that. One certainty is that the Fieldings' most pressing financial worries would have been alleviated—'plate and jewels' mentioned in the will would have settled a good many small debts.

Henry's own income, outside what he earned by his writing, was still tiny. The family estate had been tied up as a result of the Chancery battles; it was held in trust until the youngest child, Edmund, should reach his majority, and that was not until 1737—when Henry, as the eldest of the six survivors, would already be thirty. The rents from East Stour were inconsiderable, and when further sliced into six shares more or less invisible—Henry could have got through an annual dole of his patrimony in four good nights out on the town. Nevertheless, he remained the master of East Stour, insofar as there was one, and had apparently made regular visits during the summer break at the theatres. Now the chance had arisen to make a more protracted stay. In the event he and Charlotte spent perhaps six months or so in Dorset; but it is a period around which a good deal of legend has accreted.

The blame belongs squarely with Arthur Murphy, who tells a colourful tale of Fielding as a would-be country gentleman, vainly attempting to stifle his urges towards folly and intemperance acquired during his London years. He was overcome, Murphy alleges, by 'a kind of family pride', which made him 'vie in splendour' with the neighbouring squires. With his small resources he insisted on encumbering himself 'with a large retinue of servants, all clad in costly yellow liveries'. The tragic dénouement is as inevitable as the last scene of a Hogarth progress-piece:

His chief pleasure consisting in society and convivial mirth, hospitality threw open his doors, and, in less than three years, entertainments, hounds, and horses entirely devoured a little patrimony, which, had it been managed with economy, might have secured to him a state of independence for the rest of his life.

Now Murphy's account is demonstrably inaccurate at several points—he puts the death of *Fielding's* mother about this time (rather than Charlotte's), and that of course had happened when Henry was ten. Moreover the couple cannot have spent anything like three years in uninterrupted occupation of East Stour; Fielding is constantly to be found in London during the following years, and if he was living beyond his means it must have been in the capital. Nevertheless the legend has gone on growing; a table presented to the Somerset Archaeological Society for their museum at Taunton Castle is claimed to derive from East Stour Farm where 'in three years [Fielding] dissipated his fortune keeping hounds'. Guidebooks to Dorset regularly mention this lavish bucolic existence.

The truth seems to be that the couple went down to East Stour after settling Mrs Cradock's affairs, say around March 1735. They passed the spring and summer there, possibly the autumn too. Henry being Henry, it is fair to assume that he gave some hours to vigorous sporting pastimes, and that he got through some of his wife's windfall. But everything we know about him suggests that he would also have taken the opportunity to extend his studies: to return to his favourite classical texts, to dabble in theology and history, to relax with some of the newfangled novels and perennially popular romances. He had satirised Mrs Haywood on the stage, but he would not have been above reading her latest effusion. There was Mrs Aubin, too, with her suspenseful narratives of Turkish captivity, wronged heiresses, brutal abduction and the like. Daniel Defoe may have been too plain a fellow for Fielding, with his flat recital of intense and purposeful lives; but any book with a powerful story-line and a clear moral might engage Henry's attention, for his literary tastes seem to have been orthodox and straightforward.

There were friends in the neighbourhood, too, with whom he could spend agreeable hours. Most congenial among these was the Reverend William Young, a thirty-three-year-old clergyman who held a curacy at the small town of Gillingham, a few miles north. He had been to Oxford and then taken orders; in 1731 he had moved to Dorset, where he had the parish of East Stour among his responsibilities. He possessed considerable knowledge of the classics along with astounding ignorance of the ways of the world. His homeric absence of mind is said on one occasion to have led him to wander deep beyond the enemies' lines while serving as a military chaplain on the continent, but the dates hardly seem to fit such an episode. It is certain, however, that he was to give up his curacy a few years later and attempt to live by his pen. Once he joined with Fielding in a translation of Aristophanes, but most of the time he fared very badly. Grub Street was a hard enough place for the shrewd and self-confident; it must have been purgatory for this shambling, ragged, unworldly man, with his odd gestures and simple

Top The house at East Stour in Dorset where Fielding grew up

Above The Thames at Twickenham: oil by Richard Wilson (1762)

Left Plate 2 of *The Election* by Hogarth (1755). Subtitled 'Canvassing for Votes'

Below left Robert Walpole (*left*) in the House of Commons

Right A benefit ticket for Fielding's *Pasquin* (c. 1736), by Hogarth

Below 'The Festival of the Golden Rump'. A satirical print (1737) which helped to provoke the Licensing Act

Fountain Court, Middle Temple. Fielding was a law student here in the late 1730s

A view of the Thames in the late 1740s, looking eastwards, by Canaletto

heart. In Dorset he had to support a wife and six children on a stipend of
£30, and according to a contemporary account he regularly found himself
taken away to jail at the suit of local tradesmen. But none of these circumstances would have lowered him in Fielding's estimation. It is universally
agreed that Young furnished the original for Parson Adams, and about the
warmth of their mutual regard there can be no dispute.

Another local figure about whom Fielding entertained quite different
feelings was the notorious Peter Walter, a grasping land-agent and money-
lender, who provided the basis for another character in *Joseph Andrews*, that
is the unlovely Peter Pounce. All the Augustan satirists had by this time
had a go at Walter, who had acquired a fortune of something like £200,000.
At his death in 1746, he was said to have augmented this by another £80,000.
Like Colonel Charteris, he founded his wealth on money-lending. Already
into his seventies, Walter was still busy adding to his estates and financial
interests. He had bought at the beginning of the century his seat of Stalbridge Park, four miles down the river from East Stour. Here he lived in a
remarkably parsimonious fashion, exercising a fierce surveillance over all
local affairs. In the late 1730s, for instance, he enclosed some common land
to which the people roundabout considered they held a traditional right of
pasturing. They accordingly broke in, uprooted trees, smashed fences and
so on. Walter dispassionately made a log of the damage done and brought an
action in court. When the case reached Dorchester assizes, a defendant named
Thomas Weston—with 'a good estate' in the parish of Stalbridge—complained about Walter's overbearing conduct: 'The plaintiff Mr Walter is a
great man in the west and particularly in and about Stalbridge and will do
what he pleases and will not bear contradiction as he is lord of the manor of
Stalbridge he will have absolute direction in the parish . . .' One interest of
this passage is that the case came on the assizes in the very first years of
Fielding's practice on the Western Circuit. But he would not need firsthand
experience in the court room to know about Walter's iniquities. To fill out
the allusions in Pope, Swift and Fielding, modern scholars have desperately
cast about to catch Peter Walter *in flagrante delicto*, but his stealthy depredations on the public are hard to pin down with clearcut evidence. That is
why he prospered so well in his own day.

At East Stour Fielding could lose himself in hearty physical activity and
quiet mental pursuits. But the world of Walpole and the theatrical battles
did not come to an end, any more than the need to eke out a better living.
One side of Henry's nature would have prompted him to remain in Dorset,
but there was also a combative strain in his make-up which would not allow
him to hide in the shadows when there were prizes to be won. There was
another consideration now: Charlotte was expecting a baby. She might
have preferred to bring the infant up in the tranquil Blackmore vale; but she

loyally accompanied her husband to London. The exact date of their return
is unknown but it is likely that they were back by the end of the year. For
Henry had a new role at the Little Theatre in the Haymarket; he was no
longer simply a resident dramatist, with a minor share to take in production
—he was himself the manager, artistic controller, director-in-chief. The
next two years were to see him achieve unparalleled influence and renown;
he made the theatre count in national life as it has rarely done, before or
since.

6

The new troupe were known as 'the Great Mogul's Company of Comedians'.
Fielding was probably responsible for organising the company and recruiting
players. The Little Theatre had not had permanent occupants since
Theophilus Cibber took his seceding actors back to Drury Lane in March
1734 (see page 70) but occasional performances had been mounted—for
example, Colley Cibber's amazing offspring Charlotte Charke had played
Macheath in Roman dress, presumably just for kicks, as well as those
contrasting male leads, Lillo's George Barnwell and Rowe's gay Lothario.
The company which Fielding assembled was made up for the most part of
unfamiliar names; they were based on a nucleus of the younger players from
Drury Lane. The new team took proper shape only in the middle of the
season, around February 1736. Altogether that season they acted only 95
times, most of these in the spring, with no fewer than eleven new plays in
their repertoire: far above the normal proportion. From the start Fielding
must have enjoyed the support of some eminent figures in the opposition;
certainly his schoolfellow Lyttelton and his new patron Chesterfield;
perhaps also William Pitt, now beginning to unleash his formidable talents
in parliament, and the young Duke of Bedford. For the company was from
its inception an exponent of the theatre of commitment; it pioneered new
forms and stretched the frontiers of drama, but it drew primarily on an
underlying vein of political fervour.
   The impact this company of unknown performers made is remarkable.
It is not as if they had no competition. At Drury Lane, under Fleetwood's
management, Macklin had now acquired James Quin to supplement the
talents of Kitty Clive and Theophilus Cibber. (In fact Macklin had been
lucky to survive unscathed the previous summer, when he had been accused
of murdering a fellow-actor. He had got away with the lesser crime of manslaughter, and had been sentenced to be branded on the hand with a cold
iron. His return to the stage occurred, to warm applause, just as Fielding
made *his* re-entry to Haymarket.) John Rich was doing his inimitable things

at Covent Garden; Handel intermittently presented oratorio there. The Nobility Opera, with Farinelli starring, was at the King's Theatre in the Haymarket, across the way; at Lincoln's Inn Fields, Henry Giffard had brought the company from Goodman's Fields for a short season. There was plenty of choice open to the theatregoer.

Within a matter of weeks, however, all London was talking about the Great Mogul and his company. (The nickname of grand mogul had first been applied to Colley Cibber, on account of his position as arbiter of all things theatrical during his Drury Lane days. It may have been acquired on the hereditary principle by his son, though there was less ground for it in the case of Theophilus.) The breakthrough came with a play by Fielding himself, which opened on 5 March. Its title was *Pasquin*, which in the cant of the day meant simply a satire or lampoon; and indeed the subtitle made this clear—'or a dramatic satire on the times'. A newspaper advertisement promised that although 'the clothes are old', the jokes would be entirely new. Reverting to the well-tried rehearsal formula, Fielding sets his scene in a playhouse; first Trapwit attempts a run-through of his comedy 'The Election', and then Fustian tries out his blank verse tragedy, 'The Life and Death of Common Sense'. The comedy has some affinities with *Don Quixote in England*, whilst the technique of the tragic burlesque recalls both *Tom Thumb* and *The Author's Farce*, especially in the portrayal of Queen Ignorance. There is however a new quality of engagement in the writing. Up till now Fielding had been a witty and detached observer of the human comedy. Now he infuses his play with a sharp critical attitude, which supplies the cutting edge his works had sometimes lacked. He uses his personal experience to good effect (Fustian's account of his difficulties in getting his drama staged makes obvious application to *The Universal Gallant*, just over twelve months earlier).

Both portions of the play excited great interest, and a fashionable mob traipsed regularly from Grosvenor Square and Pall Mall to the small playhouse, which became a sort of anti-establishment rallying-point. Even Farinelli was forgotten; the other theatres found their audiences dropping to a trickle. The vigour and boldness of Fielding's personal satire, which took in many conspicuous figures apart from the inevitable Walpole and Cibber, were chiefly responsible for this furore; but we must not forget the youthful élan of the company. Within the familiar vehicle of 'rehearsal' they managed to convey tremendous immediacy. Fielding at last was reaping the reward for his troubled apprenticeship: a contemporary print shows him presented by Queen Common Sense with a purse of gold, whilst a harlequin —representing John Rich—receives a halter instead of the fat profits to which he was accustomed. There are many indications of the popularity of the show: thirty-nine successive performances, more than sixty altogether that season. There was a pamphlet published offering a 'key to *Pasquin*'. Rich put on an afterpiece called *Marforio* by way of reply, but it was a total flop. Admittedly, the noise which *Pasquin* had made was in part fomented for political reasons; but we should remember what the theatrical historian Arthur Scouten tells us: 'People did not go to see Fielding's productions at the New Haymarket because they were consumed with indignation against Sir Robert Walpole; they went because they found pleasure in the lively entertainment provided by "the Grand Mogul's Company of Comedians".'

When the play reached its twelfth night, already an assured success, Fielding had a brilliant stroke of invention. For the part of Lord Place, a supercilious courtier in the comedy section, he enticed over from Drury Lane the extraordinary Charlotte Charke, youngest daughter of Colley Cibber. She was paid well above the going rate, four guineas per week, and on her benefit night, with favourable accountancy, was permitted to clear sixty guineas. When *Pasquin* finally began to lose favour, Fielding put her straight into the role of Agnes in a production of George Lillo's *Fatal Curiosity*, mounted on 27 May. He had overseen the rehearsals with great care, had written the prologue and generally worked to make this interesting but flawed tragedy into a success—which it proved to be. She then went into Fielding's own shows the following season, playing important male parts.

If it seems strange, even in our liberated times, that a girl of twenty-three should take these masculine roles, then further acquaintance with the lady will remove or confirm the oddity, depending on one's point of view. She had been married at the age of seventeen to an ex-dancing-master turned theatre musician called Richard Charke. Charke was a gambler and whore-monger, and their life was a misery until he ran off to the West Indies to escape his debts; he died within two years. Charlotte Cibber can only have married him in order to escape from the laureate's peculiar household; her father was in the situation of a music hall comedian who had been knighted and made director of the National Theatre. The strong probability is that her sexual tastes were exclusively lesbian. She was on a bad footing with her father and brother by this time; she had upset the Drury Lane management with a scurrilous play attacking Fleetwood. It was not surprising that she consented to join Fielding's troupe and even to ridicule her father's pre-tensions in a scene of 'The Election'.

When Fielding moved out of theatrical life she drops out of his story, but she continued to endure a tragi-comic existence. She had spells as a strolling actor (the gender is deliberate, since she specialised in roles such as Marplot and Macheath), as a puppet-show manager in the fairgrounds, and even as the director at the Little Theatre for a brief but disastrous term. She is thought to have married again but the details are blessedly obscure. Her autobio-graphy, published five years before she died in 1760, tells of strange escapades with the heroine passing much of the time as a man. Nobody believes everything she narrates but her nature was bizarre enough to make most of it possible. Her wildness may have touched a chord of sympathy in Fielding, and her undeniable courage would have appealed to him. Her life was a running protest against the limitations of a woman's role at this period and, the Great Mogul was open to any gesture against conventional mores—the more flamboyant the better.

Fielding again carried the fight to his enemies with a new afterpiece to *Paqsuin* which he first presented on 29 April. It was a travesty of a Drury Lane pantomime called *The Fall of Phaeton*, devised by that eccentric choreographer John Rich with music by Arne. Fielding's burlesque is called *Tumble-Down Dick: or Phaeton in the Suds.* Among the slightest of his pieces, it consists of close parody of the original, sometimes line-by-line. Priests in a temple become yokels in the fields; the divinities are turned into low-life London characters. Rich is the chief target of the satire, and he received an ironical dedication when the play was printed. But Cibber, Fleetwood and others come in for a share of attention. Mrs Charke's role was a direct answer to the part created by Kitty Clive at Drury Lane. This may seem a disloyal act on Fielding's part: we must be careful not to sentimentalise his character or underestimate the bitterness of these theatrical wars. As Arthur Scouten has observed:

Those who picture Henry Fielding as himself a Squire Allworthy, mild and benevolent, will not recognise the portrait of the manager of the New Haymarket that emerges in the Calendar of performance for the 1730's. Instead will be seen a bold and shrewd contriver intent on being a trouble maker, a promoter who did not scruple at persuading Charlotte Charke to play a role which ridiculed her father, Colley Cibber, who was ready to cry 'Foul Blow' upon any setback, and who was both sensitive towards criticism and ready to take extraordinary measures to secure publicity.

I am not sure that Mrs Charke needed all that much persuasion to guy her father, but it may be so.

Fielding continued to perform on 'forbidden' days during Lent, even during Passion Week. He specialised in new plays and would put on two novelties the same evening, quite against the ruling practice. His presentation was lively and original; during a Fielding show nobody slept in the audience. Among the other new plays, none, of course, could rival *Pasquin* in popularity, but some (like *Fatal Curiosity*) did extremely good business. There was a play by James Ralph, who may have helped to assemble the company, and more than one ballad opera. Mrs Charke was allowed to have a run-out as Captain Macheath, a role she always relished.

For most of 1736 the events at the Little Theatre overshadowed all other dramatic happenings. The pattern was disturbed only once, and *The Beggar's Opera* chanced to be at the centre of the episode. A revival was planned at Drury Lane in December, perhaps to show the upstarts in the Haymarket how such classics *should* be done. Unfortunately the casting of Polly Peachum raised difficulties. Should it be Mrs Clive, the actress-turned-singer, with a well-established reputation in the role? Or should the part go to Susanna Cibber, the sister of Thomas Arne and now the wife of dumpy Theophilus?* Perhaps Cibber junior had been deliberately stirring up trouble; he was capable of it, especially when the worse for drink. The problem would be to settle his motivation; his two-year-old marriage was already breaking up, and he was as likely to want to spite Susanna as to disoblige Kitty, who was generally a placid enough person. Fielding, who was ready enough to satirise any of the periodic Cibber mishaps, duly took Mrs Clive's side in his next Haymarket play. And Kitty, certainly the inferior singer, got the part.

7

Late in 1736 Fielding embarked on what was to be his last season in the theatre, though nobody knew it at the time. What happened is quite well known, in outline at least: Fielding's increasing boldness as a political dramatist provoked the ministry to bring in a Licensing Act, to regulate theatrical performance, which survived on the statute-book until 1968. In the eloquent phrasing of Colley Cibber's autobiography, 'Like another Erostratus [Fielding] set fire to his stage, by writing up an Act of Parliament to demolish it.' It was a cruel fate, after all those years of hack-work, to find his career blocked just when he had achieved the most brilliant success; and it is doubly to Fielding's credit that he was to go on and pluck two more successful careers out of the bonfire.

The Haymarket company continued to do well in the early part of the season; there was no new item by Fielding, however, and he may have been taking another vacation at East Stour. His daughter Charlotte was born on 27 April, and it is likely that his wife would have welcomed a chance to show off her first-born to friends and relatives down in the country. The couple may still have been living in Buckingham Street, assuming the accommodation was large enough, for the baby was christened at St Martin's in the Fields, which was the parish church. By the beginning of 1737, if not before, Fielding was back in London. Early in March a couple of new parishioners

---

*For the complexities of the Cibber-Arne relationships, see the family tree on page 41.

came to lodge at the house of a stay-maker in Exeter Street, a little further along the Strand from Buckingham Street: their names (Samuel Johnson and David Garrick) would have meant nothing to Fielding, of course—they were just two poor young men making their first sortie into the capital. But Johnson had with him the manuscript of a tragedy called *Irene*, and Garrick was already stage-struck. It is not straining our imagination to suppose that this bedraggled pair would scrape up the money to visit the Little Theatre, which continued to draw in the crowds. And they may have ventured into Drury Lane, right by their lodgings, where (for some reason) Fielding had offered his latest play.* With conscious magnanimity Charles Fleetwood agreed to put on the one-act farce *Eurydice*, and it was premièred on a Saturday night in the middle of February.

A worse choice could not have been made, as it turned out. The footmen, traditionally insolent in the playhouse to make up for their obsequiousness elsewhere, decided to show their mettle. First they made a noise during the performance of Addison's *Cato* which led off the evening. Ejected from the boxes where they were permitted to sit until their masters arrived, they broke down a door to gain entrance to the galleries. Theophilus Cibber, who invariably seemed to get into such an act, attempted Catonian oratory to quieten the mob, but to no avail. The Sheriff of Westminster was then called in to read the Riot Act and round up the ringleaders. *Cato* then struggled to a conclusion of sorts—after which it was time for *Eurydice* to receive its baptism. Not surprisingly the audience was in captious mood and the farce went under to a torrent of jeering. Two days later the cast tried again, but the reception was again hostile. Fielding was forced to accept the situation. He published his play, 'as it was damned at the Theatre-Royal in Drury-Lane', and made a short farce out of the disaster. Originally entitled *The Damnation of Eurydice*, it was intended for performance at the Little Theatre on 15 March; but circumstances prompted Fielding to defer production for some weeks. All in all, it was not a very terrible misadventure. *Eurydice* is a travesty of the well-known myth, adapted to topical ends, with a dig at the castrato Farinelli and leading roles for Macklin and Mrs Clive. I doubt if anyone will ever want to perform it again.

Back at the Little Theatre, Fielding had a more important work lined up for production. This was the momentous three-act comedy entitled *The Historical Register for the Year 1736*. It opened on 21 March, puffed by a newspaper advertisement which asked the audience 'to cry at the tragedy and laugh at the comedy, being quite contrary to the general practice'. The reception was almost as enthusiastic as that for *Pasquin* a year earlier. Until 13

*Not long afterwards Johnson was to offer *Irene* to Fleetwood, but in the event it took until 1749 (when Garrick had become manager at Drury Lane) to get the play on to the boards.

April it was played together with *Fatal Curiosity*, and after that date with the
new farce, retitled *Eurydice Hiss'd*. In all it enjoyed thirty-five performances
to packed houses, up to 23 May. By that time the company had new plays
ready, possibly by Fielding; but the days of the Great Mogul were numbered.
The Licensing Act was already beginning its progress through parliament.

The ingredients of *The Historical Register* are much as before. We have a
dramatist taking critics through a rehearsal of his new work. Once again the
Cibbers, Farinelli, and John Rich are the objects of ridicule. But the venom
against the Great Man, Robert Walpole himself, is even more intense than
before. The setting for the play-within-the-play is the island of Corsica, a
thinly veiled allegory of England. Walpole is presented later as the cynical
fiddler Quidam. Charlotte Charke appeared as the noted auctioneer Christopher Cock, rechristened Hen; and there is a reference to Mrs Cibber's
quarrel with Kitty Clive (originally the two Pollies were shown in contention,
but the scene was excised after the first night). Theophilus Cibber is
portrayed as Pistol, a role in which he specialised. The youthful cast put
over this daring material with insolent charm, especially when they had an
opportunity to guy the prime minster, who appears as charlatan, mountebank, and con-man. Audiences flocked to the Haymarket to enjoy this
mixture of abrasive satire and amusing cabaret turns. The text was soon in
print, with a pirate version probably issued by an Edinburgh printer
indicating the scale of national interest.

Colley Cibber appears this time as Ground-Ivy, a leading votary of the
God of Wit. His exchange with the bastard son of Apollo shows Fielding
capitalising on the notorious 'improvements' which Cibber had inflicted on
a helpless Shakespeare:

GROUND-IVY.   What are you doing here?
APOLLO.   I am casting the parts in the tragedy of *King John*.
GROUND-IVY.   Then you are casting the parts in a tragedy that won't do.
APOLLO.   How, sir! Was it written by Shakespeare, and was not Shakespeare one
of the greatest geniuses that ever lived?
GROUND-IVY.   No, sir. Shakespeare was a pretty fellow and said some things
which only want a little of my licking to do well enough. *King John* as now writ
will not do.—But a word in your ear. I will make him do.
APOLLO.   How?
GROUND-IVY.   By alteration, sir. It was a maxim of mine, when I was at the head
of theatrical affairs, that no play, though ever so good, would do without alteration. For instance, in the play before us the Bastard Faulconbridge is a most
effeminate character, for which reason I would cut him out and put all his
sentiments in the mouth of Constance, who is so much properer to speak them.—
Let me tell you, Mr Apollo, propriety of character, dignity of diction, and
emphasis of sentiment are things I chiefly consider on this occasion.

Apollo diffidently asks whether it will not be a change for the worse, in view of Shakespeare's popularity and Ground-Ivy's feeble hold on popular esteem; but of course the old actor-manager will not listen. The changes proposed are just such as he made to plays like *Richard III*; 'it will not do' was his stock manner of refusing plays offered to him.

One admiring spectator was the Earl of Egmont, who attended the first night and wrote of the play, 'It is a good satire on the times and has a good deal of wit.' A newspaper report stated that the *Historical Register* was greeted 'with the greatest applause ever shown at the theatre'. Three weeks later, when the new farce *Eurydice Hiss'd* joined the repertoire, Egmont was back at the Little Theatre. He described it in his diary as 'an allegory on the loss of the Excise Bill'. The whole play 'was a satire on Sir Robert Walpole, and I observed that when any strong passages fell, the Prince [of Wales] who was there, clapped, especially when in favour of liberty'. Frederick was by this time openly estranged from his father, and a symbol of opposition to Walpole. *Eurydice Hiss'd* is slighter than its companion-piece; it would last only a matter of half an hour in performance. It involves a mock-tragedy devoted to 'the rise, progress, greatness, and downfall of Mr Pillage', namely 'the author of a mighty farce at the very top and pinnacle of poetical or rather farcical greatness'. This figure represents Fielding, brought low by the failure of *Eurydice*, and at the same time Walpole, whose credibility had been destroyed (or so the play insists) by his abortive Excise scheme. This self-referential satire has some of the force we encounter in Swift, where the narrator likewise becomes implicated in the follies he aims to scourge. Taking us through a rehearsal of the tragedy is a playwright named Spatter, who was played by Charlotte Charke. It is notable, too, that in the role of the Muse we find Mrs Eliza Haywood, who had performed Mrs Screen in the *Historical Register*. Her talents in the sphere of serious acting were limited, but like other members of the Haymarket cast she was adept in broad burlesque cameo-parts. Whether or not Fielding, like Pillage in *Eurydice Hiss'd*, had been able to 'to write nine scenes with spirit in one day', his drama certainly bubbles with spontaneity and freshness. Murphy tells us that he would scribble his plays on odd scraps of tobacco-paper, after a good evening spent at a tavern, and this may not be stretching the truth very far.

All this now came abruptly to an end. For some time the ministry had been casting round for a pretext on which to introduce more control of theatrical matters. An independent MP had brought in a bill 'for restraining the number of houses for playing of interludes' in 1735—the archaic diction reflects the attitude towards the acting profession still current. This measure, which would have confined performing companies to those with a royal patent, was aimed at Goodman's Fields more than any other theatre, as a reputation for vice and debauchery still clung to the East End house. Walpole attempted to get the Lord Chamberlain a more central role in 'supervising' plays to be presented, and rather than accept this amendment the sponsor withdrew his bill. It was merely a temporary respite. Two years later the effrontery of 'Mr Fielding's Scandal Shop' at the Haymarket passed beyond the bounds of Walpole's patience. Not only were there two new plays by the manager making obvious fun of the prime minister: *Pasquin* had been briefly revived, and a lost play called *The Fall of Bob, alias Gin* (alluding no doubt to the Mother Gin riots against Walpole in 1736) also reached the stage early in 1737. On 7 May Fielding received clear warning with an article signed 'An Adventurer in Politics', prominently displayed in the ministerial organ, the *Daily Gazetteer*. Fielding replied as 'Pasquin' in the opposition journal *Common Sense* on 21 May, but he had cooked his own goose by this time. When the Adventurer, possibly a pseudonym for Lord Hervey, replied on 4 June, the bill to introduce stringent licensing regulations had already received its first reading.

The ostensible reason for tightening up was the imminent production of a farce called *The Golden Rump* by Giffard's company, now at Lincoln's Inn Fields. An extraordinary amount of mystery surrounds this play, whose text does not survive. It was based on a satirical print called 'The Festival of the Golden Rump', which showed the King as a satyr, exposing his naked posterior to the Queen, dressed as a priestess, who was injecting his anus with 'aurum potabile'. Walpole stood by, in the robes of chief magician. A long explication of the print appeared in *Common Sense* on 19 March, and indeed the cartoon had doubtless been published precisely to give an opportunity for this elaborate 'vision' of sordid politics. The satire, graphic and written, is as direct a challenge to the court as it ever received. A play on this theme would have been dynamite, and almost certainly obscene into the bargain.

But the projected farce may have been a put-up job. One early source—the burlesque autobiography of Theophilus Cibber, published in 1740—suggests that Giffard was suborned, and took the play to Walpole according to a prearranged plan. There is no proof, and since Fielding may be the author of this 'autobiography' we must treat its account with caution. On the other hand, the belief of Horace Walpole that there *was* a genuine *Golden Rump* farce, intended as serious criticism, and that this work came from Fielding's pen, is even more difficult to accept. Years later Horace Walpole said that he found an incomplete copy of the play in his father's papers, but if this is so it has never surfaced again. Most of those who have studied the problem are inclined to take a position nearer to that of the burlesque autobiography, without committing themselves to every detail of the account. It is safest to admit that we do not know the full circumstances.

What is unarguable is the rapid passage of the Licensing bill. By 21 June it had gone through all its stages in parliament and received the royal assent. There were two key provisions: all theatres had either to hold a royal patent or receive a special licence from the Lord Chamberlain; and all new plays (or additions to old plays) had to be submitted to the Chamberlain's office two weeks in advance of performance, so that the text could be censored as it was thought necessary. Nearly all the squawking concerned this second requirement, but at least one leading historian of the stage, Professor John Loftis, has argued that the first provision was the more cramping to drama. Biographers of Fielding generally quote at length from the onslaughts upon the bill mounted by Lord Chesterfield and Samuel Johnson, the first in a speech to the Lords, the second in an ironical 'Vindication of the Licensers of the Stage', published two years later. Their eloquence seems to me frigid, and it is unfair to underestimate the degree of provocation which Walpole had experienced. Fielding and his troupe had deliberately sailed as near the wind as possible, like a small child trying to see just how far a parent's tolerance will extend. He was a willing martyr, and to assume otherwise is to credit him with exceedingly low intelligence or knowledge of the world. Everything we know about the man resists that conclusion.

Anyway, he was out of a job. Within a matter of days, three unlicensed playhouses had to shut their doors: the Little Theatre, naturally enough, and also Lincoln's Inn Fields and Goodman's Fields. Giffard, who may have been owed some *douceur* in return for services rendered in the *Golden Rump* affair, managed to get round some of the provisions. Having once announced an auction of a 'large quantity of theatrical goods', he changed his mind and reopened the Goodman's Fields house in 1740; a year later David Garrick made his London debut there. What Giffard had done was to advertise 'a concert of vocal and instrumental music, divided into two parts'. In the interval a comedy was presented *gratis*. Since the Act only forbade theatrical performances for which admission charges were imposed, he could claim that the occasion did not qualify as a theatrical performance under the Act, and so the £50 fine was inapplicable. Other rebels made various attempts to defy the law. But most of the profession bowed to what they saw as the inevitable, leaving the field clear to Drury Lane, Covent Garden and the Opera House. Fielding was one of this number. By the time Giffard had worked out his 'concert' dodge, he had entered a totally different sphere of life.

Much has been written about this sudden break in his career. Most people have viewed it as a kind of fortunate fall, though admirers of his drama have been less inclined to view the resulting shift as wholly a good thing. It was certainly a decisive turning-point. Up to this time in his life Fielding had lived by his wits, and even the responsibilities of family life had not brought him within the pale of respectability. Now this was to change; his prolonged adolescence was over. The Licensing Act must have impressed on his mind just how marginal his condition had been up till then, from the point of view of society at large: technically, the Act was an amendment to an old *vagrancy* statute. He was exactly thirty, and he was going to have to start all over again.

FOUR

A Career and a Calling

1737-42

I

On the first day of November in 1737, Henry Fielding officially transferred his allegiance to the law. He was admitted to the Middle Temple on payment of the appointed fee of £4; in the admissions book he was registered as from East Stour in the county of Dorset, the son and heir apparent of Brigadier General Edmund Fielding. There is no mystery about his choice of this particular inn of court. The long family links with the law had been recently cemented by the calling of his cousin to the bar at the Middle Temple. Solid, dependable Henry Gould had taken his first meritocratic step to the judicial bench when he became a barrister in 1734. Using his utterly Gould-like talents to the full, he was already a rung ahead of Henry on the ladder of preferment, though three years younger than his cousin. Fielding, for his part, had decided it was safer to join the Goulds than to try and beat them. He now had a second daughter, Harriet, to provide for.

With their passion for the explicable, scholars have managed to make this step seem a forgone conclusion. They present Fielding's entry into the legal profession as an easy and predictable stage in his life. They point out that Henry's ancestors and living relatives were strongly represented in the legal profession. They search out allusions in the plays which betoken a latent interest in the subject. The older studies wrongly assert that Fielding had actually gone to Leyden to study law. They leave one with the impression that Fielding had half-intended to turn in this direction all along, and needed only the provocation of the Licensing Act to pluck up courage for the deed.

All this is highly misleading. In the first place, the legal background was on the Gould side, and Fielding had spent much of his first thirty years repudiating that inheritance. Secondly, most of the references to the law in Henry's plays are opprobrious; he shares the habital satirist's attitude towards 'vile attornies', and exhibits no respect for the dignity of judges or barristers. The truth is that Fielding had been doing all he could to keep out of this all-too-predictable way of life. It was an abrupt and jolting transition. If he had been able to get some form of subsidy to run an Opposition newspaper, he would probably have preferred that. Had he not been saddled with a wife and two young children, he might have continued to follow the reckless instincts, derived from his paternal ancestry, that welled up perpetually in his blood. Half of his nature would approve of the new course of living, but half of it would resist.

As it was, he found himself what we now call a mature student, but with no generous government grant to support him. He had to live off the remnants of his patrimony and also whatever was left of Charlotte's fortune. In the summer of 1737 he had apparently gone down to East Stour, to help wind up the estate. The trust established after his mother's death was now about to be dissolved, as the youngest child Edmund was on the point of reaching his twenty-first birthday. The estate was divided into six equal parts, one for each of the children—an equitable way of doing it, not always attempted when primogeniture still ruled most family arrangements. A Salisbury attorney called Robert Stillingfleet (sometimes thought to be the original of shifty lawyer Dowling in *Tom Jones*) oversaw the various transactions. In the summer of 1738 Henry and Charlotte sold their share for £260; the property involved ran to 'three gardens, three orchards, fifty acres of land, eighty acres of meadow, one hundred and forty acres of pasture, ten acres of wood' and a few buildings. The farm had been neglected and by current agricultural price rates (which were normally calculated as a given number of years' rent) the sum does not look a high one. Thus ended Fielding's association with his boyhood home—although he was to preserve strong connections with the West Country.

Back in London he applied himself with the utmost diligence to his studies. Everyone who knew him agreed that he had an astonishing capacity for sustained concentration. Arthur Murphy tells a story of occasional relapses into the bohemian ways of his youth, when Fielding would enter into 'the wild enjoyments of the town', followed by a burst of frenetic work:

He has been frequently known, by his intimates, to retire late at night from a tavern to his chambers, and there read, and make extracts from, the most abstruse authors, for several hours before he went to bed.

It is an enviable gift, and one that Fielding could enlist only while he was young and strong. Within a few years his constitution was undermined, and it became more difficult to harness the two sides of his character in this uncomplicated fashion. Meanwhile Charlotte appears to have stayed behind in Salisbury, for a year or so at least. Fielding must have taken a bachelor apartment in London, but we do not know in which quarter: almost certainly he would not stray far from his old haunts around the Strand, equally convenient for pursuing his studies or for enjoying a convivial night out.

By July 1739 he had decided to bring his family up to London. A letter to his bookseller conveyed apologies for not settling a debt (the kind of message in which he was well versed) and also enclosed a request:

Disappointments have hitherto prevented my paying your bill, which I shall certainly do on my coming to town which will be next month. I desire the favour of you to look for a house for me near the Temple. I must have one large eating parlour in it—for the rest shall not be very nice. Rent not upwards of £40 p. an: and as much cheaper as may be. I will take a lease for seven years. Your answer to this within a fortnight will much oblige

Your humble servant
Henry Ffielding.

It is worth adding that the 'Ff' at the start of his signature is no affectation along the lines of ffoulkes-ffotheringham. The doubled consonant was simply a way of writing a capital *F*. We see, too, that the first two vowels in his surname occur as we should expect them today. The family tradition had been to put the *e* before the *i*. A famous but unauthenticated anecdote has the fifth Earl of Denbigh, Henry's second cousin, asking him why he spelt the name differently. 'I cannot tell, my lord,' is the reputed answer, 'unless it be that my branch of the family was the first that learned to spell.'

With or without Charlotte, Fielding would have to plough through many of the prescribed tomes which made up a central part in legal education. Reports, abridgments, dictionaries and the like furnished a considerable share of the literature. There would be occasional moots or mock-trials for the trainee advocates; they might also visit the court in session at Westminster Hall, to hear eloquent pleading from men like William Murray, later the great Earl of Mansfield, or Dudley Ryder. But it was not a notable period for study at the Temple. 'Legal education in the eighteenth century,' remarks Sir William Holdsworth, 'is a very melancholy topic':

Neither at the Inns of Court nor in the Universities was there any effective teaching of law ... The law student was obliged to get his knowledge of law by means of undirected reading and discussion, and by attendance at chambers, in a law office, or in the courts ... At the Middle Temple the student's obligation to perform exercises, and his obligation of residence, could all be commuted for a money payment. All that survived were certain exercises called 'candle exercises', because they were performed after supper by candle light.

It says much for Fielding's strength of purpose that he survived these difficulties and managed to acquire a remarkable mastery of the law within a few years. Many of his fellow-students were not much more than pleasure-seekers, young men with money and a taste for urban living. They had no need to proceed to the bar, and indeed many had no intention whatsoever of doing so—the Temple was to them a kind of finishing school which provided a base for the real object of existence—the social round. Fielding on the other hand was forced to apply himself, as he needed the income which only a qualified barrister could aspire to. With commendable speed he realised his plans. On 20 June 1740 he was called to the bar. He had achieved in less than three years something that usually took six or seven.* From now on he was styled by his enemies 'Counsellor Fielding'; a poem had even been written expressing surprise when he first took up the study of law, and the scapegrace scribbler turned respectable legal gentleman was a still more obvious target.

His finances were on the mend, but very shaky for all that. In 1738 his uncle George, a Colonel in the Guards who had lived a typical Fielding life of activity, died and left Henry certain reversionary annuities. He expected to get fifty pounds a year from this source; but nothing the Fieldings did ever satisfied the close gaze of a lawyer, and the testator appears to have forgotten a number of financial engagements into which he had entered. Charlotte did not live long enough to receive her share, and if Henry did it was years later. Struggling for a foothold in his profession, he went down to the Dorchester assizes in 1740, a few weeks after qualifying, in the hope of sorting out the conveyance of the East Stour property. The attorney Stillingfleet had seemingly done him out of some of the money due. On 15 July he wrote to his uncle Davidge Gould, from Basingstoke, a regular stopping point on the journey westwards. Gould replied from Sharpham Park a week later, sending some of the necessary deeds but expressing little hope for the outcome of the suit. No record of the verdict has been traced (eighteenth-century legal archives often omit this inessential detail), but the omens were not good. According to a story which appeared many years later in a Salisbury newspaper, the estate passed into the grasp of Peter Walter, that insatiable predator. East Stour was right on his doorstep, and he was busy acquiring new properties up to his death in 1746. It sounds all too plausible, and all too symbolic.

Dorchester was to be a regular call for Fielding in the next few years, as he rode the Western Circuit. Assizes were held three times annually at Winchester, Salisbury (alternating with Devizes), Dorchester, Taunton (alternating with Wells), Exeter, Bodmin, and Bristol. The majority of

---

*Sir William Holdsworth indicates that the speed of Fielding's *ex gratia* call can be explained 'partly because he was of twelve years' standing in the University of Leyden, and partly because he was "a near relation to Mr. Gould, one of the Masters of the Bench, who from his own knowledge assured their Masterships of the said Mr. Fielding's great application and progress in the study of the law" '. The biographers have usually ignored the part nepotism played in such transactions.

cases were relatively small, and few advocates can have made their fortune on these petty squabbles about ownership or criminal actions over infringements of the game laws by sullen peasants and impoverished yeomen. In criminal cases the prosecuting counsel had much the freer hand, as the accused was obliged largely to conduct his own defence—his counsel was allowed to speak only on points of law, and could not examine witnesses. Excluding judges and serjeants at law, there were only about two hundred barristers at this date, virtually all of them based in London. Some of Fielding's friends from the Temple made themselves specialists in equity, and indeed two contemporaries (Charles Pratt and Robert Henley) rose to be Lord Chancellor successively in the 1760s. Fielding was joining an élite, but there was an élite within the élite; the lower rungs of the profession were neither dignified nor remunerative.

Meanwhile little was done for a long time to remedy the abuses concerning the other arm of the law, as represented by attorneys like Walter and Stillingfleet. Their training was wholly unregulated until 1729; even after that they were generally held in little respect, and many people would have responded to a jibe in *Tom Jones* (XVIII, vi), where Partridge speaks of a debt 'which an attorney brought up by law-charges from 15*s* to near 30 *l*'. Earlier in the same novel occurs a graphic account of a trial presided over by the brutal Judge Page. Though nearly eighty, Page was still riding the Western circuit in 1739; and the episode described in *Tom Jones* (relating to the Salisbury area) must have been part of barristers' folklore. All in all, it was a patchy sort of existence for Fielding. Whilst his health lasted, he could cope with the long horseback journeys, the hasty study of a brief, the fugitive contacts and the fearsome judges. But he did not make a huge amount of money, and was soon casting around for alternatives. A proposed legal textbook, perhaps on Crown Law, never materialised. In fact, two years after obtaining his call, Fielding did find a new source of income and a new focus for his energy: he turned to the novel. But even while still a student at the Temple, he had diversified his literary skills, with a periodical called *The Champion*.

2

It was in fact a newspaper, issued on three days a week. There were four pages, and it cost $1\frac{1}{2}d$ a copy. As well as ordinary news items and a selection of advertisements at the back, there was in each *Champion* some substantial editorial comment, usually in the form of a leading article. It was a standard recipe for journals at this date. So, too, was the adoption of a special *persona* for the conduct of the paper: in this case, Captain Hercules Vinegar (a name borrowed from a prize-fighter), presented as a national censor and scourge of current abuses. Together with an assortment of relatives, such as a worldly-wise father and a pair of gadabout sons, Captain Vinegar promised to cast a searching eye on the march of events. There are broad similarities with the circle of Sir Roger de Coverley, which had been described in *The Spectator*, thirty years earlier, by Addison and Steele. But Fielding brought freshness and vigour to these familiar modes, and certainly there is a more robust quality to *The Champion* than was apparent in the genteel *Spectator*.

The first number appeared on 15 November 1739, and the paper ran in its original form for something like three years (there were attempts later to revive it, under different management, but they did not amount to much). However, Fielding's active involvement was a good deal shorter. From the start he was assisted by James Ralph and possibly others. Since the time of their early association on *The Temple Beau*, Fielding and Ralph had been linked by satirists and journalists, but the man from the colonies had done relatively little to gain public attention. A few poems and plays, mostly adaptations from older writers, now and then draw him out of the pit of anonymous hack-writing; but until he gained some important patrons in the next decade he remained a figure of fun in most people's eyes. In desperation he abandoned his loyalty to Walpole. It was probably Fielding who recruited his services for the new venture, and on the whole he repaid this confidence. Both men were partners in the enterprise, with five others; Ralph was officially responsible for the directly political part of the journal, but in practice Fielding's articles overlapped with his. Fielding withdrew from the running of the paper some time in 1741; his own statement puts this at June, but the remaining partners set it a few months earlier.

In the first period of *The Champion*, however, it was Fielding's sharp and aggressive writing which set the tone. He wrote at least sixty-four leading articles by June 1740; we know this because a collected edition of these issues came out in 1741, and Fielding's contributions are identifiable by certain code letters used as a signature. There are reasons for believing that he wrote quite a lot more than these leaders. Moreover, he continued to take a leading share for a further period of up to a year; these numbers were not collected, and have up till now not figured in editions of Fielding's works. No complete run of the paper is known to exist, but enough issues survive to show that Fielding's vigour was unabated. He left off writing for *The Champion*, it emerges, on ideological grounds. The surprising fact seems to be that he tired of the paper's continual harassment of Walpole. It was one thing for the convert Ralph to keep up the onslaught; for Fielding, the campaign became increasingly stale and unproductive.

From the start a central feature of *The Champion* had been its stout opposition line: in other words, its perpetual buzz of criticism and innuendo directed against Walpole, usually designated by some transparent nickname. Popular variants were Brass (from his effrontery and perhaps his wealth), Forage (from an ancient accusation of graft, when he was secretary for war, back in Queen Anne's reign), Bob Booty (used by Gay in *The Beggar's Opera*), and many more. The anti-ministerial forces were now closing in for the kill. Ever since the Excise Crisis of 1733, Walpole's power had slowly begun to crumble at the edges. Though he successfully negotiated the elections of 1734, he had gradually to compromise more and more. In 1737 his close confidante Queen Caroline died a painful and lingering death; the Opposition so much resented her alliance with the ministry that they meanly tried to avoid even token expressions of mourning. Lord Chesterfield, writing to Fielding's friend Lyttelton, actually expressed the hope that peers not on the government payroll would refuse to comply with the official order for mourning. Meanwhile the international situation was growing tense. For years the mercantile community had been grumbling about the depredations of Spain upon British shipping. For its own purpose the opposition was ready to capitalise on this xenophobia and frustration. All this time Walpole had been resisting the pressure to go to war, once remarking to the Queen that although 50,000 men had been slain in Europe within a single year, not one was English.

But finally the pressures were too strong even for Walpole to resist. A master mariner named Robert Jenkins was induced to appear before the House of Commons in early 1738, to display with a flourish his ear, pickled in a bottle. It had, he explained, been cut off by the Spanish coastguards at Havana. This may have been true, but the event had taken place in 1731—since when Spain had been rather less indiscreet in her surveillance of British trading ships. Nevertheless, remote as the provocation might be, it was enough to turn the tide of public opinion. Walpole's masterful repertoire of delays and shuffles could prevail no longer. In October 1739 England began hostilities against Spain, and so began the War of Jenkins' Ear, the first stage in a long involvement with European contests which dragged on for a generation. It was understandable in a way, since the lucrative colonial trading posts were a key element in the national strategy; but it seems today a shabby end to the long period of peace over which Walpole had presided. 'It is your war,' he said to his importunate Secretary of State, the Duke of Newcastle, 'and I wish you well of it.'

Early signs were good. Admiral Edward Vernon managed to take the virtually defenceless Portobello, a minor success which prompted an access of unrealistic joy at home. However, Spanish resistance increased as the war went on, and Vernon's attempt to capture Cartagena, further to the east of the Panama isthmus, ended in abject failure. The idea was to mount a combined military and naval attack on this important trading port, in the hope of capturing some rich galleons and destroying fortifications. But the whole operation was mismanaged; the resources needed were not available (cheeseparing and corruption had kept naval spending below the necessary level), and the men were badly trained. Worst of all, the military side of the adventure was in the hands of the incompetent General Wentworth. Only about one in ten of the army personnel returned from this expedition, graphically described by an eye-witness, Tobias Smollett, in the novel he published seven years later, *Roderick Random*. Bitter irony suffuses his picture of top-level planning:

Here again certain malicious people took occasion to blame the conduct of their superiors, by saying that ... they not only wasted time unprofitably, which was very precious, considering the approach of the rainy season, but also allowed the Spaniards to recollect themselves from the terror occasioned by the approach of an English fleet, at least three times as numerous as ever appeared in that part of the world before. But, if I might be allowed to give my opinion of the matter, I would ascribe this delay to the generosity of our chiefs, who scorned to take any advantage that fortune might give them, even over an enemy.

Another attack, on Santiago in Cuba, proved equally unsuccessful. The war drifted inconsequentially on, with smugglers being the only people really to gain.

It was in this atmosphere that Walpole spent his last two years in office, with *The Champion* in full cry against him. Now and then the target shifted to Colley Cibber, but even then the minister was a veiled presence behind the laureate. In response the government's own organ, the *Daily Gazetteer*, mounted a campaign of equal ferocity against Fielding, portraying him as an ingrate who had accepted favours from Walpole and then turned to abusing him. He is depicted once as a bully in the streets, singing ballads on Tom Thumb to the mob until the magistrates have to be summoned—an idea close to one set out in Cibber's *Apology* (see page 106) and which might possibly have derived from the pen of the versatile Theophilus, who was now turning his hand to party journalism. The charge of ingratitude becomes ever more frequent, until in late 1740 one pamphlet retailed gossip to the effect that Walpole had been forced to send Fielding bail money when the latter had been arrested in a country town. (There is no evidence to support this tale, though it is not out of the question that it had some truth in it.) Fielding more or less admitted that he had some obligation to the prime minister, when he wrote in a *Champion* leader (4 October 1740) that he had once accepted a few 'pills' from a quack named Roberto, 'to stop the publication of a book, which I had written against his practice, and which he threaten'd to take the law against me, if I published'. Nobody is certain quite which book was involved. The likeliest candidate seems to be *Jonathan Wild*, first published in 1743 but—as many suppose—drafted some time earlier. It may be, of course, that the work was suppressed for good, in which case we are wasting our time guessing at its identity.

Not all *The Champion* was taken up with politics. There are some lively pieces of social satire; some effective Lucianic allegories in the mould of the later *Journey from this World to the Next*; and occasional snatches of literary criticism. Fielding anticipated some of the concerns found in his introductory chapters to the various books of *Tom Jones*, for example in considering the need for a balance or 'Golden Mean' in writing (15 March 1740), or the baneful effects of malicious criticism (27 November 1739). But most of the literary or dramatic material occurs in papers dealing with the Cibbers, especially Colley.

As I have said, the laureate often stands in the role of a surrogate for Walpole; but he comes in for his own share of attention, particularly after the publication of his famous *Apology* in April 1740. The act of committing autobiography seemed to most contemporaries unpardonably egocentric, to start with: there was no real tradition in this line of writing. Cibber's affected, prissy style attracted a good deal of unfavourable notice; and his occasional lapses of grammar were mercilessly exposed by the Popian party. All the same, no one could deny that Cibber had lived a long and interesting life (he still had seventeen years to go, but nobody would have thought that). In addition, he had always been at the centre of things, and his account of theatrical events makes him even today an indispensable source for the theatrical historian. Readable and candid, Cibber's book hardly deserves the labels which were attached to it on publication: terms like *pert* and *frothy* seem to belong to the writer's character, rather than to the *Apology* itself. For some time Fielding had been on bad terms with Cibber both *père* and *fils*, although the wild Charlotte Charke retained his affection. Even if the *Apology* had taken a neutral stance with regard to Fielding's stage career, he would have been looking in the text for some chance to satirise Cibber. As it was, Cibber went out of his way to rile Fielding; and this in what is, overall, a notably good-humoured book. Not surprisingly *The Champion* repaid the insult with interest.

In the middle of his book Cibber turns to the activities of the Haymarket company a few years earlier. It was assembled, he reports, by 'a broken wit', whose doings are rather cruelly summarised:

This enterprising Person, I say (whom I do not chuse to name, unless it could be to his Advantage, or that it were of Importance) had Sense enough to know that the best Plays with bad Actors would turn but to a very poor Account; and therefore found it necessary to give the Publick some Pieces of an extraordinary

Kind, the Poetry of which he conceiv'd ought to be so strong that the greatest
Dunce of an Actor could not spoil it: He knew, too, that as he was in haste to get
Money, it would take up less time to be intrepidly abusive than decently entertain-
ing; that to draw the Mob after him he must rake the Channel and pelt their
Superiors; that, to shew himself somebody, he must come up to *Juvenal's* Advice
and stand the Consequence:

> *Aude aliquid brevibus Gyaris, & carcere dignum*
> *Si vis esse aliquis——*

> Juv. Sat. I.

('If you want to be somebody important, dare to do something that merits exile or
prison.')
Such, then, was the mettlesome Modesty he set out with; upon this Principle he
produc'd several frank and free Farces that seem'd to knock all Distinctions of
Mankind on the Head: Religion, Laws, Government, Priests, Judges, and
Ministers, were all laid flat at the Feet of this *Herculean* Satyrist! This *Drawcansir*
in Wit, that spared neither Friend nor Foe! who to make his Poetical Fame
immortal, like another *Erostratus*, set Fire to his Stage by writing up to an Act of
Parliament to demolish it. I shall not give the particular Strokes of his Ingenuity
a Chance to be remembered by reciting them; it may be enough to say, in general
Terms, they were so openly flagrant, that the Wisdom of the Legislature thought
it high time to take a proper Notice of them.

Needless to say, this calculated refusal to name Fielding was intended to
annoy him; and it succeeded. Hercules Vinegar, having been thus indirectly
implicated, wasted no time in launching a counter-attack. On 22 April *The
Champion* carried a witty castigation of Cibber as 'One who hath played a
very comical part, which, tho' theatrical, hath been acted on a much larger
stage than Drury Lane.' The *Apology*, we are given to understand, treats
'of all manner of matters promiscuously; that is to say, of ministers and
actors, parliaments and play-houses, of liberty, opera, farces, C.C., R.W.
and many other good things'. (This nicely catches the inconsequentiality of
Cibber's mode of narrative.) Fielding then turns to the much-criticised style
of the *Apology*, ironically arguing that since the book 'is writ in no other
language, *ergo* it is writ in English'. A week later *The Champion* returned to
the fray, satirising the laureate as a 'Great Writer' fully worthy of the great
man at the head of national affairs.

Such repeated onslaughts could become tediously iterative, and indeed in
the columns of opposition newspapers it was usual for the hacks to fall into
that trap. But Fielding commands an unflagging invention and a superb
insouciance of tone which lifts his productions above the mass of polemical
writing directed against the court. On 6 May Captain Vinegar announced
that he had done 'with this excellent work, the *Apology* which is really a suet
pudding full of plums . . . As in a rapid stream, the waves of words pass by

so quick, that it is very difficult to separate or fix distinct ideas on any particular body of water; you cannot distinguish one wave from another, and you have from the whole, only an idea of a river.' Fortunately Fielding did not observe this self-denying rule: on 17 May he was back with the 'Proceedings of a Court of Censorial Enquiry', in which first Pope and then Cibber (as Colonel Apology) are arraigned—the first because he failed to castigate the roguery of 'one Forage, alias Brass, alias His Honour', and the second for making an assault upon the English language with 'a certain weapon called a goose-quill, value one farthing'. The lively court-room scene is one of the very best things Fielding had written in his entire career to date. A string of witnesses is brought in, but finally Cibber escapes with the verdict 'chance medley', i.e. a sort of manslaughter defined by jurists as 'not altogether without the killer's fault, though without an evil intent; homicide by misadventure'. The paper ends with a characteristic touch: '*Brass* was then brought to the bar, but it being late, and his indictment so very long, that it would have reached from Westminster to the Tower, his trial was deferred.' Fielding deftly enlists his legal knowledge to fill out the common opposition clichés regarding Walpole (such as the period he had spent in the Tower during 1712, accused of corruption). It is in *The Champion* rather than the plays that we get the first strong hints of Fielding's potential as a novelist, so soon to be realised.

But in 1740 the quarrel with Cibber still commanded his urgent attention. More strictly, with 'the Cibbers', for Theophilus figures almost as often as his father, portrayed as the blustering self-publicist 'T. Pistol' or as one of the 'Bob-tail Writers' employed by the government. In the middle of this year, the young Cibber had seen fit to publish proposals for a subscription volume—no less than an autobiography off his own bat. This was too much for the satirists. By now Theophilus was a universal figure of fun, principally because of a comically sordid escapade in 1738. His four-year-old marriage with the gifted mezzo-soprano Susanna (sister of Thomas Arne) was already on the rocks. He was plagued by debts, and on one occasion fled to France to get away from his more pressing creditors. When he came back his wife was living with a well-heeled MP named William Sloper, who had abandoned his 'independent' principles for a commodious court office. At first Cibber connived at the arrangement, and simply went on carousing as if nothing had happened. But when Susanna left with her protector for a house near Windsor, and deserted the stage, Theophilus thought it was time to take action. He assembled a body of three armed men and dragged her back to London. Sloper chased after them on horseback and attempted to reclaim Susanna at an inn in Slough; but at this stage he was rebuffed. Theophilus took a roundabout route into London, and then set up his wife at the home of a playhouse candle-snuffer named Stint. Eventually a party headed by

Thomas Arne came to the house and wrested Mrs Cibber back; she was taken away to Berkshire and indeed lived with Sloper until he died in 1743.

All this came out in the most public fashion imaginable, for the egregious Cibber promptly brought a suit against Sloper for criminal conversation. He asked for damages of five thousand pounds. The suit came on at the King's Bench on 5 December 1738, with the Lord Chief Justice himself presiding. The solicitor-general led for the plaintiff, while the strong defence team of lawyers included William Murray. It was not hard for the complainant to establish the facts that Susanna had lived with Sloper, or that he had regained her by force. An effective closing speech by Murray crowned a series of strong items of defence evidence, to show that the cohabitation of Sloper and Mrs Cibber had been 'concerted by' Theophilus. The jury awarded a token sum of ten pounds, after retiring for no more than half an hour. In the following year a second suit, relating to Susanna's forcible detention in Berkshire, yielded slightly more satisfactory results from the plaintiff's viewpoint: he was awarded five hundred pounds damages. But his character was irretrievably blackened.

The hapless Theophilus, never a favourite with theatrical audiences, now had to face increasing hostility and contempt. Several pamphlets were published about the affair; it would seem too good a chance for Fielding, with his inside knowledge of the principals, to omit all literary response, but we do not know for certain what his contribution was. A more or less factual account of the trials, published by 'T. Trott' in 1740, may conceivably derive from him: 'Thomas Trott' was the name used for Colley Cibber's servant during Vinegar's censorial court proceedings (*Champion*, 17 May 1740). There is a clear reference to the case in a poem included in Fielding's *Miscellanies* three years later; the work in question was an early one but much revised before publication.

> But verdicts of ten thousand pound
> Most sweetly to Ursidius sound.
> 'We'll all,' he cries, 'be cuckolds, *nem. con.*
> While the rich action lies of *crim. con.*'

It would be surprising if Fielding was content with so brief a word on the subject.

At all events, the threat of an apology for the life of Theophilus quickly brought a blocking measure. In July 1740 a bogus version of this work appeared, ridiculing poor Theophilus and naturally flinging dirt at both Cibber *père* and Walpole in the process. The object of this attack was forced to hand back the subscription money he had collected, and look elsewhere for funds. Many people have supposed that Fielding was the author of this mock autobiography, but there is no clear indication. The publisher is named as James Mechell in Fleet Street—a very minor figure in trade with no known links to Fielding. Much of the time the drift of the pamphlet is political: for example, Theophilus is accused of 'gazetteering' on the ministry's behalf, while Walpole is alleged to have masterminded the whole affair of *The Golden Rump* (see above, page 94). Nowadays scholars are disinclined to allot any share in the book to Fielding. In the same year, the notorious Edmund Curll (now drawing to the close of a career unmatched in audacity and commercial enterprise) published a typical gallifmaufry entitled *The Trial of Colley Cibber, Comedian*. This reproduced *inter alia* Fielding's *Champion* papers concerning the *Apology*, and ended with a true Curllian advertisement, recommending that the ingenious Henry Fielding Esq. (who 'married one of the pretty Miss Cradocks of Salisbury') should own himself the author of 'eighteen strange things called tragical comedies and comical tragedies'. He will then be in line for a place in 'the immortal *Poetical Register*', that is a hack compilation of literary biographies. It was lucky for Fielding that Curll was near the end of his time. A sustained campaign of harassment from that quarter was enough to break the strongest nerves.

3

Robert Walpole was in decline; but he was an unconscionable time in going. Throughout 1740 and 1741 the protracted twilight of his ministry suffused the political sky. Initially Fielding did all he could to speed the premier's departure, with repeated efforts to discredit his policies in *The Champion*. But such attempts had been never-ending for a decade and more. Would the Great Man prove able to withstand yet another crisis, as he had done so often in the past?

Fielding's admission to the bar in June 1740 made no obvious difference to his literary activity. In the following October an impressive team of booksellers, including John Nourse and Andrew Millar, brought out in three volumes, *The Military History of Charles XII King of Sweden*, a long narrative of the king's exploits by his chamberlain, Gustav Adlerfeld, now translated from the Swedish via a French version. Charles had been one of the greatest figures on the European stage in the early part of the century. Born in 1682 he had exercised absolute control over his country, a situation aided by his decision to abolish the national senate, and earned nicknames such as 'Alexander' and 'the Madman of the North'. After exile in Turkey, he was engaged in the latter part of his reign in a war against a ring of enemies—Russia, Denmark and (crucial for English diplomacy) Hanover. It was for the most part a losing struggle; and in December 1718 he was himself killed at the siege of Frederikshald in Norway, possibly by a stray bullet fired by one of his own soldiers. His extravagant life interested authors of every description; Defoe and Voltaire wrote biographies, whilst Samuel Johnson contemplated a play on the subject. (To judge by *Irene*, the world has not greatly lost by his failure to carry out this idea.) A receipt dated 10 March 1740 survives to show that Fielding was responsible for the translation published that year, either alone or with unknown assistants: he was remitted £45 as part-payment.

Four months later, in January 1741, Fielding published two much shorter items. One was a poem in heroic couplets entitled *Of True Greatness*. It was to stand two years later at the head of his *Miscellanies*, where items as notable as *Jonathan Wild* and *A Journey from This World to the Next* first appeared: so its author must have regarded the work with some favour. The poem is dedicated to George Bubb Dodington, of whom we shall hear more in due course. A familiar contrast is set up between the court favourite, surrounded by creeping sycophants (an unlovely image of the active life), and against this the self-satisfied hermit, railing at 'busy cities, splendid courts'. Be careful, Fielding adjures this embodiment of contemplative living, 'that no envy mixes with thy gall'. The poem thus dramatises a conflict within Fielding that he had never been able to handle satisfactorily. The tribute to Dodington reads in a somewhat fulsome manner today ('Maecenas you, in no Augustan age'), but some passages have the authentic Popian moral energy:

> Lives there a man, by nature formed to please,
> To think with dignity, express with ease;
> Upright in principle, in council strong,
> Prone not to change, nor obstinate too long . . .

(*Council* then would have the punning sense of 'counsel', since the spellings were interchangable.) When the poem was reprinted in the *Miscellanies*, Fielding omitted a self-justifying preface, which claimed that he had been reviled for writings which he had never seen until they were published. He also reveals that he had been offered money to suppress his publications—but again we are not told which. Perhaps he protests too much; in general Fielding chose to abide by the standards of his age, and his pose of virtue strains our credence at times.

The other poem to come out that January was called *The Vernoniad*; it was one of the last and fiercest of Fielding's assaults upon Walpole. It is presented as a fragment of ancient epic, using the well-established Scriblerian device of laborious pedantic notes by a well-meaning but imperceptive

ommentator. The subject is the taking of Portobello, or rather its aftermath
of delay and muddled purposes. Walpole is depicted as Mammon, possessor
of a sumptuous palace—this was Houghton Hall in Norfolk, which the
prime minister had been stocking with splendid furniture and a magnificent
collection of paintings. (Despite jibes that he was a philistine, Walpole
actually showed more advanced taste in the fine arts than most of the
opposition *littérateurs*.) Mammon succeeds in blocking Vernon's triumphant
progress, by raising contrary winds that condemn the admiral to a state of
becalmed inutility. The implication is that Walpole wished to frustrate the
war effort as it would benefit productive classes such as the merchants, and
thus weaken his own corrupt hold on society. It is a spirited rendition of the
theme, and gives no sign that the opposition believed their day was about
to dawn. Fielding writes as though belabouring a well-entrenched citadel of
power. Neither is there any hint in the poem that he was personally growing
weary of the struggle.

But the truth was that things were on the point of sudden reversal.
Fielding gave up his share in *The Champion*, and by June of 1741 was
voting—without support from his fellow-managers—not to reprint the
earlier essays in a collected form. The other partners carried the day, and
the reprinted *Champion* duly appeared. Meanwhile, in parliament the
opposition was making headway. In February they had even felt strong
enough to propose a motion that the premier should be removed from the
king's counsel for ever. They had miscalculated, and found that the remnant
of Tories in the House were little inclined to see Tweedledum Walpole
replaced by Tweedledee Pulteney. But it was a temporary setback only.
The septennial election was due that summer. Writs for it were issued at the
end of April, and the nation anxiously awaited results. Even when the polls
were declared, the exact colouring of an eighteenth-century parliament was
in doubt until it actually met; there were about 150 new men at Westminster,
as things turned out, and nobody could say quite which way they would
jump. Walpole himself hoped that he might command a majority of about
forty, whereas Bubb Dodington looked for the Opposition to acquire a lead
of fifteen members.

In the event Walpole managed to hold on to a majority of fourteen. But
he had lost influence in crucial areas, notably Scotland and Cornwall. He
had forfeited the support of the Duke of Argyll, a leading Scottish grandee,
and all but six of the boroughs north of the border returned opposition
candidates. Even more disastrous in some respects was the debacle in
Cornwall. Though not a populous county, this was vital for electoral
purposes because it contained no less than twenty-one parliamentary
boroughs. Most of these had less than a hundred electors, and were consequently easy and inexpensive for the government to manage. Up to the 1734

election Walpole had been able to count on a large block of support from this quarter. But the Prince of Wales had, since that time, broken openly with his father. As Duke of Cornwall he possessed a good deal of electoral influence, and in 1741 he proceeded to use this on behalf of the Opposition. The net result was that a safe government majority had been transferred into a marginal situation, with Walpole able to cling on only through desperate defiance. He lost significant divisions on procedural and business matters; by Christmas it was evident to all that he could not hold out much longer. To the end, he retained the confidence of the King, built up over so many years of close alliance—though not very much personal warmth was in evidence. But, for the first time in British history, royal favour was not enough. George had to accept Walpole's resignation, and early in February the old servant was removed 'upstairs' as Earl of Orford.

When the moment finally came, Fielding was not among those who joined in the celebrations. A few weeks earlier he had signalised his change in allegiance with a satire called *The Opposition: A Vision*, which depicted the self-styled 'patriots' as a wagon-load of aimless and mud-spattered travellers. Their cart is stuck in the mire, and it is only the arrival of fresh asses from Scotland and Cornwall (the new MPs) which propels them into clumsy motion. They are met by a cheerful, plump gentleman in a coach and six—Walpole, of course. After various adventures, the travellers decide to ditch their wagon and hitch themselves on to the coach, where they had formerly ridden at his invitation. At this point the vision disperses: it has all been a dream. Fielding's prediction of a further spell of power and prosperity for Walpole was to be negated by events within a very short period. But he had shown his new colours, and he who had long been a thorn in the minister's flesh became at the end an apologist for Walpole.

This was one of the boldest and most surprising steps in his entire career. Most of Fielding's admirers have attempted to find worthy or at least venial reasons for the apparent *volte face*. And it is not impossible to find aspects of opposition policy which could warrant a fundamental reconsideration of their programme and aims by a supporter, even one so long and fiercely committed as Fielding had been. But the truth is probably simpler. After years of starving to serve high principles, Henry took stock of his position: he had a growing family, with another child (his first son Henry, born in 1742) on the way. As things were then organised, his options were few, and perhaps he should not be blamed too much if he took the road of discretion. It needed a degree of valour, besides; his opponents would infallibly accuse him (as they duly did) of taking money 'to betray his paymasters and his paper, out of which he had for some time extracted a precarious subsistence'. Fielding may well have been disillusioned with factious and ineffectual opposition doings, but we must not whitewash his conduct; he changed ides, it appears, less on account of ideology than in order to pay his bills.

4

n the end it was not to matter very much. Partly this was because the fall
f Walpole ushered in a new political era, with former loyalties stretched and
resh alliances rapidly born. But more important was the fact that Fielding
ad found a completely new avenue for his talents, which was to determine
is future and to render his past in some manner irrelevant. In 1741 he
emained a struggling lawyer and a less than full-hearted political journalist,
vhose early promise as a writer had been baulked by the Licensing Act.
3ut during the course of that year a series of accidents gave him a renewed
iterary opportunity, and *Shamela* was the outcome. A year later *Joseph
Andrews* enlarged and enriched this mode of expression. The *Miscellanies*
ollowed after one more year, with *Jonathan Wild* a further extension of
ielding's fictional talent. It was a remarkable turnabout.

The datum line, as it were, for all these events is supplied by the publishing
st of 1740. Among the crop of books in that year, as we have seen, was
Colley Cibber's *Apology*. Rather later, on 6 November, came the first
nstalment of Samuel Richardson's hugely popular novel *Pamela*. This story
f a prim maidservant repelling the advances of her master, Mr B, had
aught the public's imagination as no other work of English fiction had
nanaged to do. There were soon three large editions; everyone was reading
he book; and grave moralists joined with fashionable ladies to laud its
nerits. A flood of tributes appeared, many of them bearing some loose
elation to poetry. The work was issued anonymously, but a trickle of
omplimentary letters grew steadily until the author had a fine collection of
nsolicited testimonials, which he carefully filed away. There were imitations,
ontinuations, adaptations, dramatisations, panegyrical essays, pirate
ersions. Pamela's adventures were not long afterwards represented in
aintings upon a fan and in a waxworks exhibition. The inhabitants of
lough were so gratified to learn of Pamela's marriage (the village black-
mith read the story aloud to them) that they went off and rang the church
ells. Modern television soap-opera has taken enough of a hold to elicit
oral tributes for deceased characters from the viewing public, but a
ommunal response on this scale is something different.

The author of this remarkable hit was a prosy, obese little printer of
fty-one, by the name of Samuel Richardson. His origins were obscure, but
is progress through life had been remarkably orthodox and unmysterious.
t seemed a case of virtue rewarded, indeed, as in the case of his creation
amela. He had worked his way up through the echelons of the printing

business; he had married the boss's daughter, and on finding himself a
widower had repeated the process with a different family firm. Now a master
tradesman in his own right, he had acquired some valuable official contracts;
by 1742 he was to take over the *Journals* of the House of Commons, and some
years before he was printing newspapers including the leading government
organ, the *Daily Gazetteer*, one of the most regular scourges of Fielding. A
political component therefore existed within the elaborate pattern of anti-
pathies which divided the two men. (It was Ralph Courtville, who regularly
drafted *Gazetteer* ripostes to *The Champion*, who passed on a characteristic
tribute to *Pamela*: 'If all the books in England were to be burnt, this book,
next the bible, ought to be preserved.') But most people, even Pope, seem
to have agreed on the transcendent value to be set on humdrum Samuel's
middle-aged fantasy; the heroine became a type of purity and prudence:

> Her birth, her beauty, crowds and courts confess,
> Chaste matrons praise her and grave bishops bless

(to misapply some contemporary verses). Few were able to resist the appeal
of this astonishing success, a sudden meteor that flashed across the imaginative horizon of the nation during Walpole's last winter in power.

Fielding was unimpressed. Or rather, though he disliked most of what
Pamela stood for, he sensed the source of its power—and rejected its implied
ethic. Alone among the imitators, he was able to give his parody a truly
Richardsonian heartbeat, however the tone is altered and the themes trans-
formed. Long before Richardson had his disappointing sequel ready—
Pamela's adventures in high life, lauded as before by ladies in Reading and
Oxford deans when published in December 1741—Fielding had got in his
blow. On 2 April of that year, just after the first part of *Pamela* reached a
third edition, there appeared in the bookshops *An Apology for the Life of
Mrs Shamela Andrews*, designed (or so the title page tells us) to expose 'the
many notorious falsehoods and misrepresentations of a book called *Pamela*'.
It, too, was anonymous; but rumours of Fielding's authorship soon got
about, and there is not the faintest reason to question this ascription. As the
title indicates, Colley Cibber's *Apology* was to come in for its share of
ridicule; in a sense, *Shamela* is the book called *Pamela* as the laureate might
have written it. There are other incidental targets: the dedicatee, 'Miss
Fanny', can be identified with epicene Lord Hervey, courtier and friend of
Lady Mary Wortley Montagu, who had been indelibly imprinted with this
nickname in a corrosive passage by Pope.

But most of the way Fielding contents himself with Richardson, and
especially with subverting the moral assumptions of *Pamela*. The original
heroine had been demure, coy, some might say affectedly innocent. Shamela

is sly, a pert minx who uses sex consciously to entrap men as Pamela had done—so Fielding suggests—by a more or less socially conditioned reflex. Mr B. becomes cloddish Squire Booby, Parson Williams is a vicious whore-master, and the boasted quality of 'virtue' becomes 'vartue', a vulgar pronunciation which symbolises the reduction of chastity into mere virginity as an asset on the marriage market. What Fielding produces is, in his own words, 'an antidote' to *Pamela*, that is a revelation of its inherent moral crudity. But this ethical programme is carried through with extraordinary comic *brio*; many of the events and motifs of the original novel are trans-formed into absurdity and farce, as in Shamela's breathless recital of her baggage:

Mrs Jewkes went in with me, and helped me to pack up my little all, which was soon done; being no more than two day-caps, two night-caps, five shifts, one sham [false sleeves with ruffles to put over plain ones], a hoop, a quilted petticoat, two flannel petticoats, two pair of stockings, one odd one, a pair of laced shoes, a short flowered apron, a laced neck-handketchief, one clog, and almost another, and some few books: as, *A full Answer to a Plain and True Account*, &c. *The Whole Duty of Man*, with only the duty to one's neighbour, torn out. The third volume of the *Atalantis*. *Venus in the Cloister: or, the Nun in her Smock*. *God's Dealings with Mr Whitefield*. *Orfus and Eurydice*. Some sermon-books; and two or three plays, with their titles, and part of the first act torn off.

This catches a number of features in the character of Pamela; her half-suppressed vanity, her inconsequentiality, her laborious ways of itemising finicky detail ('one clog, and almost another'), and her prosaic literalness of style. Shamela's luggage includes a mixed selection of books, ranging from devotional manuals to scandalous romances, obscene offerings from Curll's 'chaste press' and current pantomime libretti. The girl's inability to dis-criminate is imaged by her garrulous style, which is Pamela's tilted over only a little into outright silliness. In a way, *Shamela* reinstates Pamela as a chambermaid, where Richardson had shown her magically evading the limitations and attributes of her role in society.

Of course, Fielding was not really 'fair' to Richardson. He extrapolated from minor incidents and read attitudes into the characters which their creator would have disavowed. But, quite apart from the high comedy generated, Fielding had a literary justification. Disregarding all the moral, political and theological points on which he differed from Richardson, he disliked above all the expressive crudities of *Pamela*—its lapses into pompous explanation, its cruelly verbose style, its awkward construction and desper-ately unreal situations. Recently these flaws have been wiped off the slate by Richardson's admirers: symbolic power has been seen as more important than such banal qualities as truth to life, and the very clumsiness of execution has been thought somehow to contribute to the tale's 'authenticity'. It is true that in *Clarissa*, a few years later, Richardson did devise a compelling, almost mythic narrative which elicited Fielding's ungrudging admiration. But even the first part of *Pamela* has its *longueurs*; the second part has little else, and we may be grateful that the author's plans for a further instalment were stillborn. There is a good deal to admire in *Pamela*, and yet one feels that Fielding went to the genuine weak spots in its artistic composition; flaws that result from a certain amateurish, non-imaginative side of Richardson. The effect was to spur Fielding into showing what he could as a novelist, with his incomparably fuller literary training, his wider background, his subtler aesthetic perceptions and his suppler, more resourceful handling of language. *Shamela* was an amusing counter, but ultimately negative in its impact. The chance presented to Fielding was to create an alternative model of fiction, to outdo Richardson rather than to deliver a tit for tat. Within a further nine months the idea had become a reality.

Joseph Andrews was published on 22 February 1742, coinciding almost to a week with Walpole's final eclipse. It must have been written in the later months of 1741. Again the original title page carried no hint of the author's identity; the only person named was Andrew Millar, a Scot who had built up a successful bookselling house in London. (One of his authors had been James Thomson, famous as a leading opposition dramatist as well as for *The Seasons*; it is possible that it was he who brought Fielding and Millar together.) The two volumes of *Joseph Andrews* cost six shillings a set; 1,500 copies were printed. As it turned out, two editions amounting to 5,000 further copies were called for within a year; Millar must comfortably have recouped the sum of £183 11s which he paid for the copyright. The book did not enjoy quite the extreme degree of popularity that had belonged to *Pamela*; but it was a commercial and critical success, insofar as these things can be measured today. Among the numerous progeny of *Pamela*, it is immensely the most interesting work in its own right. Unlike its fellows, it could have survived in a world without Pamela.

Naturally it was not to be expected that everyone would approve. One of Richardson's friends, the influential physician and writer Dr George Cheyne, called the book a 'wretched performance', which would 'entertain none but porters or watermen'. But he was addressing none other than Richardson—they had begun to correspond in the mid 1730s—and knew what his insecure acquaintance wanted to hear. Cheyne had composed a number of treatises on diet, urging temperance in the consumption of both food and drink. He also berated plump little Richardson for his tendency 'to rotundity and liquor'. (The lesson would have carried more weight

Left Samuel Richardson, Fielding's great rival among novelists

Below Prior Park, outside Bath, where Fielding often visited the owner, Ralph Allen

Original illustrations to *Joseph Andrews* (1743)—actual size

J. Hulett inv. et sculp. Publish'd March 1. 1742/3 by A. Millar.

THE

HISTORY

OF THE

ADVENTURES

OF

JOSEPH ANDREWS,

And his FRIEND

Mr. *ABRAHAM ADAMS.*

Written in Imitation of
The *Manner* of CERVANTES,
Author of *Don Quixote.*

By HENRY FIELDING, Esquire.

Illustrated with CUTS.

The SEVENTH EDITION, revised and corrected.

VOL. II.

LONDON:
Printed for A. MILLAR, in the *Strand.*
M.DCC.LXIV.

Title-page of *Joseph Andrews,* Millar's seventh edition (1764)—actual size perhaps if Cheyne himself had carried less: he could be seen hulking his thirty-two stone frame up and down the inclines of Bath.) Fielding had satirised him in *The Champion*, and would do so again. Another rather stuffy response came from the fastidious young poet, Thomas Gray, who had been at Eton ten years after Fielding, and whose *Elegy* was as yet but a gleam in his poetic eye. Gray wrote to a friend in April 1742:

I have myself, upon your recommendation, been reading Joseph Andrews. The incidents are ill laid and without invention; but the characters have a great deal of nature, which always pleases even in her lowest shapes. Parson Adams is perfectly well; so is Mrs. Slipslop, and the story of Wilson; and throughout he shows himself well read in Stage-Coaches, Country Squires, Inns, and Inns of Court.

Luckily this thin-lipped patronage was not the rule. The popularity of *Joseph Andrews* spread to France, particularly after a translation by the Abbé Desfontaines in 1744; and in England a more representative opinion was that of the highly intelligent bluestocking, Elizabeth Carter. A blue-stocking, moreover, who 'could make a pudding, as well as translate Epictetus' (Dr Johnson). She found in the work 'a surprising variety of nature, wit, morality, and good sense,' pervaded too by 'a spirit of benevol-ence'. Miss Carter was later to become a friend of Richardson, when (it is to be hoped) she learnt to keep quiet about her opinion of *Joseph Andrews*.

The novel provides a more serious (though far from solemn) critique of *Pamela* than had the brisk and purely farcical *Shamela*. Its hero is 'brother to the illustrious Pamela', a footman in the service of Sir Thomas Booby, who is himself the uncle of Richardson's Mr B——. When the story begins Sir Thomas and his lady are on a visit to London, attended by Joseph. The squire dies suddenly and inconsequentially, in the midst one might say of a subordinate clause:

At this time, an accident happened which put a stop to these agreeable walks ..., and this was no other than the death of Sir Thomas Booby, who departing this life, left his disconsolate lady confined to her house as closely as if she herself had been attacked by some violent disease.

Lady Booby soon recovers from the shock, and within a week has started to make advances to her astonished footman. Joseph is presented as Pamela's rival in chastity—an application to the male sex not altogether risible in Fielding's day, but certainly a virtue not associated with servants below stairs. He wards off further trials of his virginity, with the result that his employer turns him away with the 'small remainder' of his wages (eight pounds a year) which is due. He accordingly sets out for the Booby's country seat, since there lives in the same village his beloved Fanny. Ten chapters have elapsed while the situation is thus outlined. The next thirty-eight are taken up with Joseph's adventures on the road to Booby Hall. The final book, containing sixteen chapters, relates the outcome with the principal characters all assembled in the country. The pace is rapid: neither the journey nor the subsequent doings can occupy more than about ten days. It may be added that the seat of the Boobys is commonly identified with East Stour, and the geography is tight enough to establish strong Dorset connections. (Peter Walter, for example, appears as the rascally steward Pounce, and that is a local as well as a moral piece of casting.)

The plot may appear not much more than a string of casual adventures on the open road; but as always Fielding introduces a degree of organisation and symmetry. There are four books, containing in all sixty-four chapters. Four was traditionally the number symbolic of concord and justice; square numbers were associated with virtue and reason, and so the 16 chapters of Book Four enact the process of everything coming to rights (as well as completing the pattern of 64 chapters *in toto*, expressing a larger congruence). Modern readers sometimes find it hard to take these arithmetic meanings at all seriously, but there is no doubt that Fielding was the kind of writer who enjoyed adjusting such patterns. The older numerological techniques were dying out in this period, and nobody in the eighteenth century composed such fantastically elaborate configurations as those which had delighted the Renaissance. But moral thinkers still insisted on the ultimate 'fitness' of things, that is the workings of the universe exhibited the regularity and harmony of God's design for mankind. Equally, aesthetic commentators emphasised the need for poetic justice, in other words the sharing out of fictional rewards and punishments according to a scale of worth. Fielding's tidy-minded construction, therefore, helps to fulfil his ethical scheme.

Nor can we overlook the fact that, for contemporary readers, there was a strong flavour of parable in the novel. Joseph and Abraham were Old Testament figures commonly used in Christian manuals to stand for chastity and charity respectively; the embodiment of these qualities in the book, of course, is found in Joseph Andrews and Abraham Adams. Modern scholarship has uncovered a good deal of buried allusion in Fielding's work, much of it suggesting his commitment to a broad Anglican theology known as 'Latitudinarianism'. We may reasonably doubt whether he absorbed quite so many of the devotional texts as some critics would require him to do: creative writers are not scholars, and even when we can prove them to have read a given volume of sermons (say), that is not the same thing as remembering it. I think it is fair to suppose that Fielding meant us to pick up the straightforward biblical overtones of his story—for instance, the reference to Potiphar's wife (Genesis 39) in the early episode of Lady Booby and Joseph (Book I, Chapter 5). It is certain, too, that Adams is presented as the good parson, almost in Chaucer's fashion, standing for good sense and benevolence. He displays a mixture of innocence and tough-minded, even combative energy which clearly attracted Fielding. Roughly speaking, we may define Fielding's theology as one of practical compassion. He was not much given to deep metaphysical enquiry, and he did not explore recondite existential states. He believed in the possibility of making the world a better place by sensible reform, and he opposed both the pessimists (Hobbes, Mandeville, etc.) and the ultra-spiritual (Wesley, Whitefield, etc.). It is, of course, an undramatic sort of religion, quite bereft of the cosmic intensities of Donne or the visionary stridency of Blake. But it formed a useful basis for his tolerant and humane comedy. Fielding can be severe but he is seldom malicious.

His own phrase for what he was doing is given in the preface: the 'comic epic-poem in prose'. There is in fact a neat little proportion sum: as the serious epic is to tragedy, so his new 'province', the novel, is to stage-comedy. Its main theme is to be the ridiculous, and that in turn derives from one broad category: affectation. Branching out from that concept are two predisposing qualities, vanity and hypocrisy. It will be seen that Fielding has marked out a niche for himself within the contemporary map of literature. He has also defined a subject-matter and justified a particular manner of approach: for a hectoring tone would clearly be inappropriate to the scale of offence he intends to expose.

The early novel was inherently a critical instrument: it deflated the high-flown expectations of 'romance', however we interpret that word of many meanings. Unlike the traditional story of marvellous happenings (like Robert Greene's *Pandosto* (1588) which provided the source for *The Winter's Tale*) the new fictional mode tended to avoid improbability. Unlike chivalric romances of the Arthurian type, the novel specialised in a strong feeling of the here and now. Unlike the immense slow-wheeling convoys of narrative launched upon an ocean of words by Madame de Scudéry, '*reine du tendre*', the innovative form aimed for a certain directness and uncluttered quality. (*Clarissa* and *Sir Charles Grandison* remain in the archaic vein, from this point of view: but *Tom Jones* and *Amelia* do not, long as they are, for they have a steady impetus and a definite sense of time passing.) Finally, unlike the widely published collections of love letters that appeared through-out Fielding's lifetime, the novel proper sought to place sexual passion in a wider context of human dealings. The epistolary genre, whether using letters from a nun to a cavalier, from a nobleman to his sister, or from a lady to a lady, placed its entire emphasis on things amatory or erotic. Some of the writers, notably Eliza Haywood, had a genuine talent which shows through the limitations of the form; but there is usually little social placing, little human complication, little of the *density* of coverage we expect in a novel. Perhaps the compilers of these works (very often translated) are not to be blamed. They seem to have got only a matter of four or five pounds per book on average, where playwrights and poets might easily achieve ten times as much. Prose fiction still had little respectability, and Fielding was the first considerable author able to demand a worthwhile sum for a novel.

On the title-page, *Joseph Andrews* is described as 'written in imitation of Cervantes, author of *Don Quixote*'. We shall be looking more closely at the impact of Cervantes on Fielding and other English writers in the next chapter. For the moment, the most obvious point of comparison is that between the don himself and Parson Adams, each of them innocents abroad in a corrupt or hostile world. (It is worth stressing that the title page promises the adventures of Adams as well as those of Joseph. A more accurate short-title might be *Joseph Andrews and Abraham Adams*.) Where Quixote was a man deluded by the false lights of romance, Adams is an unworldly country curate. Both are poor, well on in years, shabby. There is one important difference: Quixote is, for all his likeable qualities, alienated from reality to the point of outright madness. His chivalric dreams carry him right away from good sense, and our sympathy is generally tinged with pity. Adams—ridiculous too in his way—maintains more of our respect. Christianity and classical learning are never seen as inherently absurd: quite the reverse. The society that treats Adams' beliefs as safely outmoded (just as though they were the antiquated fictions of a Quixote) stands self-condemned. That Adams never travels without a sermon, 'for fear of what may happen' (III, vii) is comic, but it proceeds from a rooted Christian strength. At this particular juncture Adams reads his sermon, play-acting in the role of a Socratic teacher, but he also manages to give a good ducking to a foolish squire, whom we see as addicted to scoffing and childish irreverence. People often take Adams for a weak man; they soon learn to their cost that his remote ways can rapidly vanish when action is needed.

Of course, it is not true that Fielding *invented* the novel: twenty years earlier, Defoe had written a series of remarkable first-person narratives, including *Robinson Crusoe* (1719) and *Moll Flanders* (1722), and even before Richardson came along there were popular stories of love and adventure published in large numbers. In the 1730s perhaps a dozen books of this kind appeared each year on average. What *Joseph Andrews* did was to give the novel a more clearcut function, a more expressive literary form, and a wider range of resources. Fielding took a newly fashionable way of writing and made it serve the serious purposes of 'high' literature, when it could have drifted away into a short-lived fad.

Joseph Andrews uses a variety of satiric methods to point up what Fielding sees as the unreality of Richardson's vision. Irony, mock-heroic, burlesque, and parody are invoked to suggest that *Pamela* is no more than a moralistic fairy-tale; real life, Fielding indicates, involves a wider range of personal challenges. In the words of Ronald Paulson:

Richardson sees life as a single-minded conflict between two people, one good, the other evil. He is interested only in the sensibility of one woman, alone in a closet with her daydreams and wish fantasies ... To what he considered the narrow world of *Pamela* Fielding opposes the wide world of epic with all classes and all manners of locales. His settings are out-of-doors, on roads, in inns, in coaches, on horseback ... Life is not a private relationship between a man and a woman but a journey on which one passes through all kinds of experience and meets a great variety of people.

In other words, Fielding's basic model is epic rather than romance; and this permits him to deal with sexual morality in a more inclusive frame of human reference than was possible for Richardson or the popular epistolary authors.*

But none of this will properly account for the success of the book. It is true that Fielding had an exceptionally clear sense of what he was doing. We can readily grant that he brought to his task a great skill in construction (rather more, to tell the truth, than his plays would have suggested) and a broad-minded Christian outlook. These things might guarantee literary respectability or moral orthodoxy. What animates the novel is Fielding's buoyant narration, combined with his vivid human awareness. Above all, it is the character of Adams which elevates *Joseph Andrews* above everything else its author had yet produced.

The parson is briefly described in the third chapter of Book One. He then disappears until Joseph meets with him at the Dragon Inn—at which point the whole momentum of the fiction is immediately stepped up. He is a contradictory figure. Adams is both strong and weak, an example at times of fortitude and at times of vulnerability. He is desperately wrong about some things (such as the sales potential of his manuscript sermons) and crucially right about others, especially topics of morality. He is always liable to offer 'philosophical observations on the folly of growing warm in disputes', and then five minutes later to be engaged in a heated argument with the first person he encounters. Impulsive, generous and unpredictable, he looks forward to later comic characters such as Sterne's Uncle Toby and Scott's Jonathan Oldbuck. But he also prefigures in many ways the lineaments of

*Ronald Paulson, *Satire and the Novel in Eighteenth-Century England* (1967), p. 109. This book contains an excellent discussion of the satiric and critical aspects of Fielding's work as a novelist.

Samuel Johnson as they were indelibly to be etched by Boswell. Johnson was already living, of course; in fact he was only two years younger than Fielding. But it is the older man, described in Boswell's *Life*, whom Adams again and again recalls. I mean the Johnson who recited speeches from *Macbeth* when crossing Scottish heathland, or the one who exchanged ribaldry with a Thames bargee, or the one who was ready for 'a frisk' at three in the morning with his young friends up from Oxford. There is a quality of spontaneity in Adams which consorts oddly with his clerical dress and his profound absorption in classical texts. Like Johnson, he seems to live all the more vibrantly in the present because half of his mind is adrift in the ancient world. His shabby presence dignifies the novel, and his roughly good-hearted manners shame the civilised and polite Augustans who walk through its pages. With Adams, Fielding had made the quantum leap from very good to great writing.

Not, needless to say, that life came to a halt on that account. There was a sad reminder of the mutability of things just three weeks after the publication of *Joseph Andrews*. Henry and Charlotte lost their five-year-old daughter, named after her mother, who was buried in St Martin in the Fields on 9 March. The funeral expenses came to £5 18s, indicating that the ceremony was not skimped. Four men were employed to bear the tiny coffin. Charlotte (according to her husband's later account) comforted herself with the reflection that her child would not grow up to experience such a loss. But the death of 'one of the loveliest creatures ever seen' deeply affected both parents. The facts I have cited come from the sexton's register, which also shows that the body was brought from Spring Gardens, which lay on the west side of the parish, close to the corner of present-day Trafalgar Square where the Admiralty Arch is now situated. The Fielding family had presumably been lodging there since the previous autumn. However, the name of Henry Fielding is not to be found in the rate-books (only the householders were listed), and there is no way to be certain.

Three months after his novel appeared, Fielding made a brief return to the theatre. A one-act ballad opera, *Miss Lucy in Town*, was presented at Drury Lane; it was a sequel to the seven-year-old comedy *An Old Man Taught Wisdom*, and seems to have been a collaborative work. When it was written and why Fielding permitted its performance at this juncture, we can only guess. We can, however, be fairly sure that the collaborator was none other than David Garrick. Thomas Arne supplied music, where the chief responsibility lay with the great tenor John Beard and the durable Kitty Clive. Comedy was principally in the hands of Charles Macklin. Controversy still dogged Fielding: one character, Lord Bawble, was widely seen as a satire on a rakish peer, probably Lord Middlesex; either the Lord Chamberlain or the official licenser was called in, and on 22 May the production was stopped. It returned to the stage that autumn, with a few discreet alterations. Garrick, incidentally, had only reached Drury Lane a season before, after spectacular success out at Goodman's Fields in *Richard III*. He and Fielding soon took to one another, and it is a shame that the great actor should have entered the London theatre at the period of Fielding's departure. Their blended talents might have given us some major landmarks in drama. As it was, they tried once more. *The Wedding Day*, an early comedy in five acts, which Fielding had first sketched out when he was starting as a playwright, was revamped for Drury Lane. It was performed in February 1743. Despite a splendid cast, including Garrick himself, Macklin, and the charming Irish actress Peg Woffington, the piece proved a failure: it lasted only six evenings, and brought Fielding the inconsiderable sum of £50. On the last night, we are told, no more than five ladies attended. It was the last of Fieldings' plays to be performed in his lifetime.

Other miscellaneous writing kept him busy. He wrote a vindication of the octogenarian Duchess of Marlborough, relict of the great general, whose energies seemed to increase as she advanced in age. When she was not instigating pamphlet wars, she was endlessly litigating, sometimes against the more distant members of her own family. She won over the most unlikely people: in his declining years Pope embarked on a flirtatious correspondence with Sarah, though her temper survived better than her red-haired beauty of long ago. Colley Cibber nurtured a passion for her over half a century. Fielding's defence was probably sincere, though it is uncertain how intimately he knew the Duchess. Andrew Millar gave him five guineas (half the copyright fee paid for *Miss Lucy in Town*); it is to be expected that the Duchess supplied a more liberal reward, since her notorious meanness did not extend to persons who composed panegyrical accounts of her behaviour.

There was, finally, a projected translation of the comedies of Aristophanes. A single play was published in May 1742, to entice an audience for the venture as a whole. But *Plutus, the God of Riches* failed to do its allotted task: no more in the series ever appeared. Despite a preface and a judicious dedication to Lord Talbot (son of a recent Lord Chancellor, Etonian and budding politician), the volume attracted little notice. Fielding again had a collaborator—this time it was the Dorset curate, William Young. Now there is an old and probably reliable tradition that Young was the origin of Parson Adams, although I am not sure about the need for imaginative artists to have an 'origin' for whatever they create. At all events Young and Fielding somehow divided the responsibility for the translation. Most biographers assume that Young did the hard linguistic bits and then Fielding added a few masterly touches in the margin. That does not correspond to my own sense of his character; if he was involved in something, he liked to immerse himself completely. Nor was attention to detail foreign to his nature. But we have no evidence on the point, and it is perhaps better to resist the urge to guess.

Fielding was now thirty-five, and had come a long way to rehabilitate himself. He had made a start in the legal profession, even if he had not yet achieved any great prominence. More significant was the way in which he had picked up his literary career from its low point five years earlier. He was ready to make a direct bid for public recognition.

In June 1742 he issued proposals for a subscription edition of his miscellaneous works, in three volumes. A note was added that 'publication of these volumes hath been hitherto retarded by the author's indisposition last winter, and a train of melancholy accidents scarce to be paralleled.' The way was now clear for the set to appear. Could everything, at long last, be turning in the right direction?

FIVE

Risings and Reversals

1743-48

I

Fielding's *Miscellanies*, published in April 1743, mark a very important juncture in his life. They were planned both as a literary display and as a financial venture. In the first respect the three volumes made up what Norman Mailer calls 'advertisements for myself', a retrospective exhibition of earlier productions together with some brilliant new works. In the second respect they were designed to set Henry's insecure livelihood on a sounder footing.

His career as a barrister had not proved particularly remunerative—hence, no doubt, the frenzied efforts to cobble together a play for Garrick. Old General Fielding, his father, had died in 1741: I say 'old', since he had lived two or three lives in his epicurean, insatiable way, and though he was not much more than sixty, one gets the sense of a raddled countenance and a bloated corpse. Much more affecting had been the death of Henry's eldest child Charlotte; as we have seen, she was carried off just before her sixth birthday. The cause was almost certainly an influenza epidemic which raged that winter; resistance throughout the community was low (above all among children) after the extremes of weather which had prevailed for two years. The dreadful winter of 1740 left paupers dying in the streets of London; half the nation's sheep perished in the prolonged cold, and the price of food shot up to record levels. The frost fair on the Thames was a mere picturesque side-effect: for most people reality was far grimmer. Then in 1741 came a roasting summer, as though by way of compensation. In this period there were always more burials than baptisms in the capital: around 1740 the proportion was about 9 to 5, and the mortality rate among infants must have been even higher. Some of the waifs would at least fare better as a result of the new Foundling Hospital, which was granted a charter in 1739 and began to operate early in the next decade. Hogarth was an important supporter of the scheme, and Handel gave a great deal of help—he even bequeathed the score of the *Messiah* to the hospital. Ralph Allen was another considerable benefactor. Most relevant of all, the Duke of Bedford

(Fielding's main patron, along with Allen, in his latter years) was Head of the Corporation of the hospital. There is a commendatory reference in *The Champion*, but perhaps not quite as much active involvement on Fielding's part as one might have expected—he was after all to be author of 'The Foundling', as *Tom Jones* was first known.

He was himself beginning to suffer from gout, a harbinger of later ill health. The preface to his *Miscellanies* describes his situation at this time

I was last winter [1741/42] laid up with the gout, with a favourite child dying in one bed, and my wife in a condition very little better, on another, attended with other circumstances, which served as very proper decorations to such a scene . .

He means visits from the bailiffs and similar importunate gentlemen. The whole picture recalls Hogarth's *Distressed Poet*, first published seven years earlier and reissued with variations in 1740. As well as the two girls (the ill-fated Charlotte and her sister Harriet), there would soon be another mouth to feed—a boy, named Henry after his father. He lived to the age of eight, and it is only in the last decade that scholars have discovered that he ever existed.

Naturally the couple were finding it hard to make ends meet. In his desperation Henry had borrowed the considerable sum of £200, and now his creditor was suing him in the Court of Common Pleas for payment in full. On 7 July 1742 judgment was awarded against Fielding, with a small additional amount for damages. He did not himself appear in court, as he was away on the Western circuit. When the assizes ended Fielding seems to have gone to Bath to take the waters. There he was in easier contact with a new friend, the benevolent entrepreneur Ralph Allen, who was to play a significant part in his career from now on. An early story had it that Allen gave Fielding enough money to pay off the debt. We cannot be sure of the details, but there is no doubt that the two men came together about this time*—and Allen's mission in life was to do good, not always by stealth.

He is a fascinating figure. Nearly fifteen years older than Henry, he enjoyed no advantages of birth. He came originally from Cornwall, and as a boy entered the postal service. At seventeen he was already deputy postmaster for Bath. When he was twenty-six he produced a completely new scheme for the national carriage of mail, involving considerable economies, chiefly through the suppression of corruption. Allen took over in effect as manager of the postal services; in an age suspicious of state intervention, he naturally performed as a private contractor, undertaking to raise the revenue above

*The indications are that Allen may have entertained both Fielding and his own great friend Pope at his home, Prior Park, around October or November 1741: but absolute proof is lacking.

£6,000 per year. If he failed, he would have to reimburse the government; his assets could be seized and his guarantors stripped to the bone. But if he succeeded, the excess revenue would all go to the contractor, i.e. himself. In the event Allen made an annual profit of £500 for the first five years, and as time went on the proceeds expanded. He claimed to have increased revenues by a million and a half pounds in the forty years of his operations: by 1760 his own income from this source was £10,000 or more each year. It is a most characteristic eighteenth-century success story. It was a kind of government service, and it certainly made a large contribution to the speed and efficiency of commercial transactions. Allen's reward was not a C.B.E. but a contract on better and better terms.

Meanwhile he had bought the stone quarries on Combe Down, perched along the southern slopes above Bath. It was just at the moment of the city's great expansion into the leading pleasure ground of England. There was a huge demand for building-stone, and the warm-coloured, soft Bath stone from the Combe Down quarries filled the need. Along with the social arbiter Beau Nash and the architect John Wood, Allen was one of the creators of Bath. (All three were self-made men.) The grand occasions planned by Nash, the Roman splendours imagined by Wood, needed a fabric and a commercial intelligence to support them. Allen supplied both. Georgian Bath is built of oolitic limestone, and much of it was dug from the earth by Allen's workers. Streets, squares, parades went up; hospital, church, assembly room. Crowning all was Allen's own magnificently sited Palladian mansion, Prior Park, gazing down on the houses below like a benevolent aristocrat surveying his retainers.

And that was not far from the truth, as regards Allen himself. Almost as soon as John Wood had begun to plan the mansion, Alexander Pope offered his services as design consultant, and advised the owner on suitable decorations. An impressive tribute from the poet came in a work published in 1738:

> Let low-born Allen, with an awkward shame,
> Do good by stealth, and blush to find it fame.

Pope began to make regular visits to Prior Park and termed his friend 'the most noble man of England'. He also introduced Allen to leading figures in the Patriot opposition, among them Fielding's schoolfellow George Lyttelton. It is likely, too, that William Pitt—boy-wonder of the Patriots, and beginning to make a major impact on political affairs—got to know Allen by the same agency. Pitt, of course, had been another contemporary of Henry's at Eton. He was MP for that unreal constituency on the edge of Salisbury, Old Sarum, and must have seen Fielding from time to time. The connections were all welding together nicely: for the novelist to join the Allen circle at Prior Park was to cement literary and political links that were easily fractured in the less cohesive social world of London. As time went on, Fielding had more and more occasion to take the road to Bath—which happened to be the first complete stretch of turnpike highway (Allen no doubt had a finger in that pie, too). The waters may not have done his physical ailments much good, but his worldly prospects flowered as soon as he made the acquaintance of the 'benevolent man', the former postal clerk Ralph Allen.

2

The first thing to notice about the *Miscellanies* themselves is a feature of the contents we might rapidly pass over today: the list of subscribers at the head of Volume I. Proposals had been issued a year before, and in the end Fielding attracted 427 names. 214 orders were placed for the 'fine paper' (i.e. larger) sets, which cost two guineas instead of a single guinea for the 'coarse' paper sets. The amount grossed by this means would be rather more than £800. The bookseller Andrew Millar then deducted the expenses of printing and distribution, but these are unlikely to have cost more than £200 at the outside. Millar was to make his profit from a separate edition, that is sets without subscribers' names, aimed at the general public—these were published three weeks later. We may be confident that Fielding cleared a sizable sum, certainly not less than £500.

One or two exaggerated claims have been made for the distinction of this list of subscribers. It was large but not outstandingly so; and its social composition, though impressive, was less gilded than that some other books had drawn out. Aristocrats were present in reasonable abundance, headed by the Prince of Wales, who put himself down for fifteen sets. The Duke of Bedford, the Earl of Chesterfield and the Duke of Newcastle were also there. And so was the Earl of Orford, for ten sets—that is the recently deposed Robert Walpole, a fact which seems to confirm a measure of rapprochement between Fielding and his old adversary. Other politicians listed are Lyttelton, Pitt, Henry Fox, and Bubb Dodington (but portly old Bubb subscribed to almost everything, good and bad). Literary and theatrical personages include Garrick, Kitty Clive, Peg Woffington and Edward Young, author of *Night Thoughts*. Two names absent are those of Pope and Ralph Allen; but we know that the poet actually ordered sets for Allen and himself. Samuel Richardson, it may be added, is nowhere to be found on the list.

If any power-base is evident in the register of names, then this is assuredly the legal profession. Fielding expressed his gratitude in the preface, asserting that from this source he derived 'more than half' of the list. Actually about seventy of the subscribers are identified as members of one or other among the inns of court, or else designated 'attorney', 'serjeant at law', etc. A considerable number of others who bear no such identifying label had in fact legal training: it was still common for the sons of gentry or even peers to complete their education by spending some time at one of the inns. Local connections are represented by James Harris, Dr John Barker of Salisbury, and Peter Bathurst, until recently MP for the borough. It is interesting to note that nine per cent of the subscribers were women, just about the average for a literary venture of this kind. Overall the list has a somewhat meritocratic air: the Gould associations of professional industry are more in evidence than the Fielding swagger and sociability (a statement which would not apply to all subscriptions of this period, for high-toned nonentities enjoyed seeing their names at the head of a book which they had no intention of reading).

Turning to the contents proper, we must consider the three volumes separately. The first is the most genuinely miscellaneous. It is made up of a large number of items, mostly short, composed at various times over the previous fifteen years or so. First come the poems, running to no less than thirty-eight items. Of these the most substantial are five verse-essays. 'Of True Greatness', dedicated to Bubb Dodington, had been published separately in 1741 with a preface (now omitted). As we have seen, it dramatises Fielding's besetting dilemma by attacking both the court-follower and the misanthropic hermit:

> He flies society, to wilds resorts,
> And rails at busy cities, splendid courts.
> Great to himself, he in his cell, appears . . .

The author had still not properly come to terms with the split in his own personality; he attempts to steer a course between active and contemplative life, but produces no convincing middle way. 'Liberty', addressed to Lyttelton, employs some popular ideas of the day, much in vogue among Whig patriots, but again Fielding is unable to synthesise the materials with complete success. More effective is the lively satiric epistle addressed to his friend John Hayes, a lawyer from the Midlands. But today there is more enjoyment to be extracted from the light verse, mostly youthful gallantry and elegant fun. 'A Description of Upton Grey', written in 1728, is an amusing genre-piece with affinities to some of Swift's poetry. 'Advice to the Nymphs of New Sarum' (1730) is rather Popian in style, reflecting the strong influence of *The Dunciad*. A number of trifles to 'Celia' obviously go back to the days when Henry was courting Charlotte. Their titles reflect the kind of interest to be found: 'To Celia, Occasioned by her apprehending her house would be broke open, and having an old fellow to guard it, who sat up all night, with a gun without any ammunition', or 'To the Same, on her wishing to have a Lilliputian to play with', or 'To the Master of the Salisbury Assembly, occasioned by a dispute, whether the company should have fresh candles'. The poems have brittle charm enough to earn their keep as light relief in this collection; isolated, they would win few readers today.

The prose portion of this volume contains a number of extended essays on moral themes. The most important are 'An Essay on Conversation' and 'An Essay on the Knowledge of the Characters of Men'. Of these the former has to do with civility, social propriety and the idea of the gentleman. Fielding examines the basis of various 'rules for good breeding', and comes up with some typical Augustan answers: good breeding is 'the art of pleasing in conversation' (*conversation* here includes any sort of social situation), whilst 'In our behaviour to our superiors, two extremes are to be avoided, namely, an abject and base servility, and an impudent and encroaching freedom'. The fundamental imperative is expressed as the talent for 'contributing as much as possible to the ease and happiness of those with whom you converse'. The discussion is enlivened by anecdotes and examples:

Dyskolus has the same aversion to cards; and though competently skilled in all games, is by no importunities to be prevailed on to make a third at ombre, or a fourth at whisk and quadrille. He will suffer any company to be disappointed of their amusement, rather than submit to pass an hour or two disagreeably to himself.

Jane Austen would have approved of that touch. As for the 'Essay on the Knowledge of the Characters of Men', it is just what the title promises. The theme is the practice of simulation and dissimulation: Fielding enquires into the different forms hypocrisy may take, and sets out a view of human psychology to enable us to achieve some sort of insight into the layers of personality. It is a tougher-minded account of the games people play than some would expect when they have read Fielding's novels. Among the remaining items, the most striking is an essay 'Of the Remedy of Affliction for the Loss of our Friends', a classic piece of consolatory writing prompted by the deaths in quick succession of his father and his eldest child.

So much for the first volume. The second contains two plays, *Eurydice* and *The Wedding Day*, together with the fragmentary story entitled *A Journey from this World to the Next*. Only the last had been heralded in the subscription proposals. Apparently the plan had originally been to fill the volume with a completed *Journey*; but the work never attained a final state. We have already encountered the two plays, *Eurydice* at the time of its performance in 1737 and more recently the ill-fated *Wedding Day*, which Garrick had produced only two months before publication of the *Miscel-*

lanies. By far the most considerable item here is the *Journey*, an imitation of the manner of the Greek satirist Lucian, with touches here and there from the old Scriblerian fun-book. Fielding was later to describe Lucian as 'the father of true humour' and to link him with Cervantes and Swift. The present work can be divided into three sections; nine chapters describing the journey to Elysium; sixteen chapters describing the adventures (in various guises) of Julian the Apostate, whom the narrator meets on arrival in Elysium; and a single extended chapter concerning Anne Boleyn. Everyone has always agreed that the first portion is the best, and indeed Fielding seldom surpassed its finest moments—the city of Diseases, in Chapter 3, anatomising medical quackery, or the 'proceedings of Judge Minos at the gate of Elysium' in Chapter 7. This is a rapid account of the judgments meted out to various candidates for admission to paradise. Fielding characteristically comes down on the side of shabby humanity as against pompous hypocrites, like the self-styled patriot, 'who began a very florid harangue on public virtue and the liberties of his country'. Among those to gain admission is an author, proud of his dramatic works, who succeeds instead because he once 'lent the whole profits of a benefit-night to a friend, and by that means had saved him and his family from destruction'. Could this possibly be Fielding repaying a generous act by someone like Colley Cibber?

At the start of the next chapter we learn that the narrator, on entering Elysium, has been reunited with 'a little daughter whom I had lost several years before'. Unmistakably this is another reference to the death of Charlotte, and so the work must have been at some stage of composition as late as 1742. Dickens had a great admiration for this reunion, and indeed is one of several distinguished admirers of the *Journey*: he wrote to his old love Maria Winter in 1855 of its consolatory power. Gibbon, rather surprisingly perhaps, was equally drawn to the book. But it has never achieved a wide measure of popularity. I think it is the most under-rated among all Fielding's books; its wit, fancy, and invention provide a sparkling surface, while the deeper implications of the allegory recall Langland and Bunyan. No one who has avoided contact with the *Journey* can be said to have made the full acquaintance of Fielding. Its jumbled layout is partly a satiric convention (the bundle of papers, found in a garret lodging by a Fleet Street bookseller —very much the Scriblerian milieu); but these dubious origins nicely reflect the ambiguous feelings of contemporaries about 'visionary' works of the imagination. The suggestion is offered that the book was produced by an inhabitant of Bedlam; we are left to wonder if such outcasts do not possess a truer hold on reality than all the respectable and rational members of straight society.

The third volume is entirely taken up by the best known item in this collection, that is *The History of the Life of the late Mr. Jonathan Wild the*

Great. Wild had never been much lamented and of course he was not even lately deceased in 1743: it was eighteen years since he had gone to his end at Tyburn, when Fielding was only just leaving school. No one knows quite when the book came to be written. Some commentators have detected a germ of *Jonathan Wild* in a *Champion* essay of March 1740, and have regarded this as a possible starting date: but the hint is only a vague one. We can say that the *Miscellanies* proposals in June 1742 promise a history of 'that truly renowned person Jonathan Wyld, esq; in which not only his character, but that of divers other great personages of his time, will be set in a just and true light'. It is not clear whether this indicates a full realisation of the scope of the book, or merely a general outline of the theme. One theory is that Fielding composed the work in stages: first the life story of Wild himself, then the Heartfree episodes, and finally the wanderings of Mrs Heartfree. Others would reject this fragmentation theory, but would suggest that Fielding revised previously composed material during 1742, that is after the fall of Walpole. No certainty has yet been achieved on these points. For most readers it may not be a very important issue, but there are puzzling questions for anyone interested in Fielding's development as a writer. For instance, how was the composition of *Jonathan Wild* related to the creation of that very different comic masterpiece, *Joseph Andrews*? The most natural supposition would be that *Wild* is in substance the earlier of the two items; but some of the evidence seems to point in the other direction.

The equation of Wild and Robert Walpole had a long history. It is implicit in the satiric portrayal of Peachum in *The Beggar's Opera*, a play which was still performed but which achieved its greatest impact in the late 1720s, when Fielding himself was setting out as an author. Newspapers and pamphlets had made the same easy identification between the Great Man of politics and his opposite number in the world of crime. Both were seen as unscrupulous, merciless, subsisting by graft and intimidation. Each was thought to have methodised his craft; just as Wild had brought professional regularity to the thieves' kitchen, so (it was felt) Walpole had made political management into a kind of debased art. Unlike the prime minister, Wild had faded from the scene; but his memory had been kept alive in the numerous collections of criminal biographies, such as *The Lives of the most Remarkable Criminals* or *A Complete History of the most Notorious Highwaymen*.

Fielding makes no pretence of sticking closely to the true facts of Wild's career. He immediately fits the criminal out with a spurious genealogy, and his assertion that 'our hero ... made his first appearance on this great theatre the very day when the first plague broke out in 1665' has no basis in reality. Wild was baptised on 6 May 1683; we do not know the exact date of his birth, but it is most unlikely to have corresponded with the anniversary of the Great Plague. Fielding brings into the story a number of real-life characters such as his Newgate companion Roger Johnson (Book IV, Chapter 3) and the thief Joseph 'Blueskin' Blake (Book III, Chapter 14). There is a brief veiled reference to our old friend Mr Peter Pounce in Book I, Chapter 7. But these individuals are equally abstracted and typified; they consort easily enough with imaginary personages such as the good merchant Heartfree, or the vulgar Laetitia Snap. Often Fielding draws on a stock of Jonsonian 'humour' characters, almost allegoric in cast. The false Count la Ruse represents a standard eighteenth-century confidence trickster—it is a fact that many adventurers and charlatans adopted the title of count. (Some, like Lady Mary's friend, the bisexual Algarotti, or Cagliostro, who claimed to be a thousand years old, may have been real counts. But more often, as with Casanova, they looked forward to President Amin by awarding themselves all the dignities they required.)

In some respects *Jonathan Wild* is a bleak work. Its topsyturvy moral outlook is created first of all by the inversion of accepted language patterns, so that 'great' always indicates 'mean', and here Fielding's ironic play with cliché and thieves' argot is splendidly effective. But the unremitting exposure of Wild's evil makes the comedy rather black for some tastes. None of the good characters lives with anything like the intensity of Jonathan himself, brutal, self-absorbed and hideously clear about his purposes. At least *The Beggar's Opera* is diversified by music and laughter; there is a vestige of pretty pastoral in the low-life scenes. But *Jonathan Wild* never allows the pressure to drop below the savagely ironic note it strikes from the beginning: it is a fierce, single-minded work, aesthetically closer to Swift's *Modest Proposal* than to Gay's half-joyous *Opera*. Its laughter is not far from a grimace.

Later on Fielding was to turn towards serious criminology, insofar as the concept then existed, with his social pamphlets on highwaymen and kidnapping. There is not much evidence that he was, at this stage, particularly interested in the criminal mind. We are not invited to explore Wild's personality: he remains a monster out of pantomime or melodrama, more kin to Fagin than to Bill Sikes. His role in the book is to be flamboyantly wicked, with the aim of showing how strong-minded villainy prospers. The language used is that of disinterested and gentlemanly intercourse, but the reality is quite different. We see this at the opening of I, vi, when Count la Ruse finds his cash has gone:

The count missed his money the next morning, and very well knew who had it; but, as he knew likewise how fruitless would be any complaint, he chose to pass it by without mentioning it. Indeed it may appear strange to some readers that these gentlemen, who knew each other to be thieves, should never once give the least hint of this knowledge in all their discourse together, but, on the contrary, should

have the words honesty, honour, and friendship as often in their mouths as othe
men. This, I say, may appear strange to some; but those who have lived long i
cities, courts, gaols, or such places, will perhaps be able to solve the seemin
absurdity.

The beautifully casual *or such places* reinforces the suggestion that th
highest places in the kingdom (particularly Walpole's corrupt court) wi
display the same contradiction. And the effect is capped by a characteristi
touch of subtlety on the part of Fielding: he himself speaks of Wild and th
Count as 'gentlemen', obeying the same perverse decorum which he is in th
process of satirising.

There are flashes of pure comedy, as for instance in the illiterate lette
Wild sends to his intended bride Laetitia, 'which we challenge all the beau
of our time to excel either in matter or spelling' (III, vi):

Most deivine and adwhorable creture,—I doubt not but those IIs, briter than th
son, which have kindled such a flam in my hart, have likewise the faculty of seein
it. It would be the hiest preassumption to imagin you eggnorant of my loav . . .

But such comparatively innocent fooling soon gets dispersed in the genera
bitterness. There is no time to linger on absurdity; whilst the reader i
chuckling, the next great rogue (Wild or Walpole or Walter or Charteris
will have slipped off with his cash.

3

All now seemed set fair. *Joseph Andrews* and the *Miscellanies* had finall
established his reputation (Fielding's authorship of the former was acknow
ledged in the preface to the latter). He had made at least £750 from the tw
ventures. And on a personal front, the sad loss of his little daughter had bee
partially atoned for in the birth of his first son Henry. In May 1744 cam
another pleasant event, the publication of a novel by his favourite siste
Sarah, under the title of *The Adventures of David Simple*. A second editio
was soon called for; Fielding himself added a preface, denying the curren
rumours that he was the true author. He goes on to explain the need t
correct a few 'small errors, which want of habit in writing chiefly occasioned
and which no man of learning would think worth his censure in a romanc
[i.e. novel]; nor any gentleman, in the writings of a young woman'. At thi
time Sarah was thirty-three. She had lived with Lady Gould in Salisbur
until the old woman died in 1733, and kept up the house for a few mor
years. She was to write several more books, but none achieved as muc
popularity as this first venture. Later on she would settle in Bath and enjo

Ralph Allen's benign, if paternalistic, company; she may already have been introduced to the great magnate by her brother. Her own health was not good and Henry felt some solicitude on this account.

But the blow which he had to suffer shortly afterwards came from a different quarter. 1744 had been a relatively quiet year, with the false attribution of a silly pamphlet (duly denied in the preface to *David Simple*) the only event to disturb the placid course of life. Sadly, everything changed in the autumn. His beloved wife Charlotte, described in the *Miscellanies* as 'one from whom I draw all the solid comfort of my life', was now deteriorating in health. Perhaps, as the biographers suggest, she had not made a full recovery from her severe illness two years before. Late in the year her husband took her to Bath, but to no avail. The likeliest cause of her death was consumption, that ever-present scourge in all centuries before our own.

If we have no authentic narrative of Charlotte's last days, there is certainly one picturesque account of her life and death in the anecdotes left by Lady Louisa Stuart. It should be stressed that Lady Louisa was not born until after Henry Fielding's death and that her memoirs appeared as late as 1837, postdating by nearly a century the events here described. Though her grandmother Lady Mary Wortley Montagu was a reliable informant, Fielding's gifted relative had by this time fled from English respectability and was living in Avignon. It would be rash, then, to take all the details on trust; but the story may well give us the essential truth.

Sometimes they [Henry and Charlotte] were living in decent lodgings with tolerable comfort; sometimes in a wretched garret without necessaries; not to speak of the spunging-houses and hiding places where he was occasionally to be found. His elastic gaiety of spirit carried him through it all; but, meanwhile, care and anxiety were preying upon her more delicate mind, and undermining her constitution. She gradually declined, caught a fever, and died in his arms.

We should also take into account the effect on Charlotte of the loss of her eldest child. It is a total fallacy to suppose that people in the past were inured to such tragedies, simply because they occurred so remorselessly often. Moving letters of condolence are studded through almost any eighteenth-century correspondence. Queen Anne grieved over her repeated losses as she had the very first, and not just because she desired a protestant heir. When the tough, experienced Lord Treasurer, Robert Harley, lost an adult daughter in child-birth, Swift wrote him a long and moving commiseration. Another of the high-spirited Scriblerians, Dr Arbuthnot, wrote about Harley on the same occasion: 'I pity his case with all my heart, for what ever other affliction he has been used to he is much a stranger to domestic calamaties. I have a true sense of his present condition for which I know philosophy & religion are both too weak, & I believe it is the will of God that it should be so. I have lost six children.' The Augustans seldom burst out in *Kindertotenlieder*, but they felt these things as acutely as later generations. Who would doubt that Charlotte had been deeply affected?

She was carried back to London from Bath, and buried in St Martin in the Fields on 14 November, alongside her daughter. Where exactly the couple had been living is uncertain, but it was probably within the parish of St Martin's—Henry had never been tempted to move to the new residential areas over towards Oxford Street, or perhaps he simply could not afford it. The sexton's records indicate that £11 17s 2d was expended on tolling the great bell, lighted candles, black drapery and other accompaniments of the obsequies. It was probably at night, like most eighteenth-century funerals; if the widower attended, he was braver than Swift, who could not bear to witness the last rites when Stella was buried. Instead the Dean cowered in his lodging, unwilling to venture as far as his bedroom in case he should catch a glimpse of the candles aglow in the cathedral.

According to Lady Louisa Stuart, Fielding 'in the first agonies of his own grief, which approached to frenzy' could find relief only in weeping along with Charlotte's maid, whose name was Mary Daniel. People thought that he was in serious danger of losing his mind. For almost a year he remained prostrate, and it is not surprising that there is a gap in his literary output. Nor is there anything necessarily shameful in the fact that Mary, who shared his grief, should three years later become his second wife. All observers confirm Charlotte's angelic character; we should be very cynical to assume that her maid must have been hypocritical in mourning her in this heartfelt way.

It was a time of dissolution. Sickly Alexander Pope had somehow contrived to stretch out his life for fifty-six years, though beset by asthma, dropsy, urethral strictures and migraine; but in 1744 his feeble constitution finally gave in. Swift survived for another year, bereft of most of his senses. Robert Walpole, having outlived his inept successor as prime minister, underwent a painful few months with the stone. His doctors were headed by John Ranby, Serjeant Surgeon to the King, and a subscriber to Fielding's *Miscellanies* They prescribed a fiercely active drug called *lixivium*, which caused the dying man to beg for opium. He ultimately expired on 18 March 1745. As with Pope, it would have been kinder to let him depart in peace, untroubled by the ill-concocted remedies thrust upon him.* At least Fielding's moderate

---

*The physicians promptly launched into a pamphlet battle, urging the merits of their own particular remedy and blaming their rivals for all medical failures. Fielding entered the lists with a satire called *A Charge to the Jury*, drawing on his legal knowledge as well as the traditional suspicion of doctors. Appended to this item was a Scriblerian type *jeu d'esprit* called *A Project for the Advancement of Physic*—an easy remedy is proposed, that is the abolition of the whole College of Physicians. It is distinctly probable that Fielding wrote this, too.

eans prevented him from imposing such expensive agonies on Charlotte. The power vacuum caused by the fall of Walpole, three years earlier, had ill not been properly filled. Henry Pelham, brother of the Duke of New- stle, was the natural successor. But it took time for the Pelhams to establish omplete dominance over the confused political arena. Meanwhile the ation had drifted into the War of the Austrian Succession, a complicated uropean struggle where the interests of Hanover were rather more at risk an those of Britain herself. There were a few insignificant victories, a few qually inconsequential defeats. It is doubtful if Fielding paid much tention at this stage. He was slowly coming out of his torpor; and events ould ensure that the outside world would break in on him, whether he ked it or not.

4

nyone who thinks that Hanoverian Britain was a humdrum, sleepy sort of lace cannot have given much thought to the events of 1745 and 1746. As st mentioned, the country was already involved in a war—a muddled and pparently distant affair, but a war all the same. Then in the middle of 1745 ere began a series of adventures which have furnished matter for legend nd romance ever since. A life of Fielding is not the place to retell the story f the Jacobite rebellion at any length. Nevertheless, it is important to nderstand what a dramatic and constitutionally serious juncture this was.

The Young Pretender, Charles Edward, set out from the island of Belle le, off St Nazaire, on 4 July 1745. His own vessel was a privateer named the *u Teillay*; with it sailed a 68-gun frigate belonging to the French fleet, arrying 700 men, called the *Elisabeth*. This small convoy was sighted by a ritish man-of-war off the Cornish coast, and the ensuing skirmish permitted e *Du Teillay* to slip away alone and head for Scottish waters. On 23 July e Prince landed on Eriskay, one of the smaller islands among the chain at make up the Outer Hebrides. This was his first contact with Scottish oil. A couple of days later he reached the mainland on the coast of Arisaig, st to the south of Skye. The Rising had begun in earnest, even if recruits o the cause proved fewer than hoped for at the outset. Charles Edward sent ord back to Louis XV in France, asking for further support. Nothing much eemed likely to materialise in the short term, so the Prince and his followers oved inland a few miles to Glenfinnan, a narrow defile at the head of Loch hiel. Here on 19 August the standard of King James was unfurled, and his on proclaimed regent amid loud huzzas. The *Du Teillay* had been dispatched o France again, and there could be no turning back.

It took just over a year for the full drama to play itself out. The rebels had

their brief season of triumph, particularly their victory over General Co[
at Prestonpans on 21 September. The Prince now held Edinburgh, and
month later began his march into England. Carlisle fell to him on ₁
November, and the procession southwards continued, with the Stuart ki₁
proclaimed in every town on the route. By the end of the month the Jacob₁
army had reached Manchester, whilst General Wade's pursuing forc₁
(which had been sent to seal off the eastern route) were still ploughir
laboriously through Catterick, at the very least three days march behin₁
But things had gone awry. There had been hundreds of desertions fro₁
Charles's army; meanwhile, the Duke of Cumberland, the third son of Ki₁
George, had reached Staffordshire in a bid to halt the Jacobite progress ₀
London. At Derby a council of war was held, and rightly or wrongly t₁
Prince accepted the need to retreat. On 6 December his army turned abo₁
and began to retrace its steps. Although morale naturally fell at this wit₁
drawal, it was not quite the end of the Jacobite hopes. The army reach₁
Stirling in the New Year, and on 17 January 1746 they achieved a clearc₁
victory over the Hanoverian forces under Henry Hawley. General Hawl₁
was one of the most experienced soldiers taking part in the campaign—₁
had seen service at Sheriffmuir, back in the first great rising of 1715, as w₁
as more recently at Dettingen and Fontenoy. But his sixty-seven years stoo₁
him in little stead at Falkirk, when his troops suffered heavy losses.

At the same time, however, the Duke of Cumberland was making relen₁
less progress northwards. He pursued the Prince through Stirling and Pert
into the Highlands. The Jacobite tactics were mismanaged to an ev₁
increasing degree, so that the outcome became more and more inevitabl₁
As everyone knows, it was on the bleak moor of Culloden, a few miles ea₁
of Inverness, that the climax came, one wintry day in April. The Highlan
army were routed; Charles Edward himself escaped but many of his follower
perished during the battle. Some of the survivors were mown down in col
blood. Looting and terrorising of the local population went on for sever₁
days. Afterwards came the judicial slaughter: over a hundred peop₁
executed, a thousand transported. As David Daiches has written, 'Th
Battle of Culloden marked the beginning of the end of Highland societ₁
When tartan and the kilt and the romance of the clans revived again ₁
British esteem, it was to be in a mood of literary nostalgia and romance
There remained only for the Prince to perform his protracted act of escap₁
complete with a lone boat over the sea to Skye and all the paraphernalia ₀
mythic heroism. He finally got away from the coast of Arisaig, very near h₁
original landing place, on the morning of 20 September 1746. He made h₁
way to Paris, where he settled in some style on the Faubourg Saint-Antoin₁
It took little over two years for Louis XV to expel him as an impossibl₁
embarrassment, diplomatically and personally. Charles survived anothe₁

forty years, and after the death of his father in 1766 was officially recognised by Stuart supporters as the rightful king. But he declined into drunken debauchery, and lost all serious credibility. He died where he had been born, in Rome—a fitly circular life history.

The events briefly chronicled here were, of course, the subject of intense interest on the part of all men and women in Britain. Henry Fielding had no special personal stake in the matter, but he soon became deeply involved in the propaganda battles. The Rising, if it had done nothing else, would have given him something to write about—a commitment which could supply him with fresh creative energy. I do not mean that the yawning emotional gap caused by the death of his wife could simply be 'filled' by a political cause. It is rather that he needed the stress of urgent, swiftly changing events to rouse his full capacities. What was important was not so much the Hanoverian ideology as the biological excitement of warding off the Stuart threat.

Complex issues were involved. On one level the Rising had been intended to settle a constitutional problem: a question that had rumbled away in the background ever since the Glorious Revolution of 1688. There were broader political overtones, with Whiggish principles under challenge from what might be termed radical Tory ideas. A religious dimension existed, no one denies, but on the whole the Jacobite pretenders were not as devoutly Catholic as some of the Stuart monarchs had been—the Rising can scarcely be seen as a crusade on behalf of Holy Mother Church. More significant was the national conflict; the Jacobites were able to recruit many Scottish supporters among solid protestant folk whose dislike of England hinged on the terms of the Union forged in the year of Fielding's birth. Highland culture had long been under siege, and the roads and forts built by General Wade after the Fifteen had done something to abridge the isolation of the clans. But this process was now greatly accelerated. When Dr Johnson was taken round the Highlands by Boswell in 1773, the old ways were dissolving. A relatively primitive mode of life, predominantly oral in its culture, could scarcely have survived in the expanding and increasingly homogeneous world that hovered on the edge of industrialism. Yet it would certainly have held out much longer, but for the events that came to a head on Culloden moor.

Fielding had shown no prescience in this area. He makes very few references to the entire Stuart dynasty in the first period of his career as a writer. Even though his masters Swift and Pope had been close to much of the action (it could not have been otherwise, with the involvement of their close friends Bolingbroke and Atterbury), he had confined himself to an occasional sly joke at the expense of the Jacobite party. As late as 1744 he was satirising the expense involved in maintaining several thousand Hanoverian mercenaries. Now, in 1745, it had all suddenly become something everyone had to take seriously. Fielding's first recorded response came in his journal *The True Patriot*, beginning on 5 November, more or less as the Pretender began to storm the hastily-patched garrison of Carlisle. But it is possible that the Rising had an earlier effect on the progress of his work. The leading Fielding scholar now active, Martin Battestin, has suggested in a recent edition of *Tom Jones* that the great novel was already under way when the Prince landed in Scotland, and perhaps the first third of the text already written. According to this theory, the book was laid aside whilst more pressing business was transacted; then Fielding returned to his task in the spring of 1747. The evidence is inconclusive, but Battestin's argument certainly makes a good deal of sense. Ultimately the Forty-Five was to occupy a central place in the structure of *Tom Jones*, but it is far from clear that Fielding intended such a thing when he wrote the opening sections.

It will be best to defer full discussion of *Tom Jones* until we reach the time of its publication. Before that comes *The True Patriot*, a weekly journal which ran to thirty-three issues between November 1745 and June 1746. It was basically a four-page newspaper, with a heavy editorial slant in favour of the ministry and the Hanoverian regime. Fielding had a certain amount of help with the routine tasks of producing the copy, but the leading articles have always been regarded as his own work. The paper was distributed by Mrs Mary Cooper, but she is unlikely to have exercised any proprietorial functions. Just possibly there was some form of government subsidy; but if so no record can now be traced. At the same time Fielding entered the parallel field of pamphleteering with three short essays intended to arouse the public against the Jacobite threat. These items range from earnest exhortation to sharp satire of the Roman Catholic church; one incorporates an alleged eye-witness account of events north of the border. Vigorous journalism is all they amount to, but at least the pamphlets show the old combative Fielding reasserting himself.

As a more sustained effort, *The True Patriot* merits fuller attention. Along with the leading article, normally a trenchant statement of Hanoverian sentiments, there was a section of foreign news, but a more significant part was played by intelligence concerning the progress of the Rising. With some success Fielding attempted to distinguish in his coverage between the rebels and the rest of the Scottish people: 'Except outlaws, and one or two profligate younger brothers,' he wrote, 'there is not a single man of any name in the kingdom [Scotland], who hath given sanction to the Pretender's cause.' It might be worth adding here that Fielding always preferred the obsolescent form *hath*, and this can be used in helping to confirm or rebut attributions. Another more striking feature of the paper was an item it regularly carried under the heading of *Apocrypha*. This consisted of news items pillaged from other journals, to which Fielding added a brief sardonic comment. He enjoyed himself particularly at the expense of newspapers and obituary notices. It was a device foreshadowed in the 1730s by his old adversary, the *Grub-street Journal*; now Fielding brought his own verve and, so to speak, genial malice to the technique.

Tuesday. [Died] Mr. Tillock an eminent stocking-presser in Grub-street. *Wednesday*, Mr. Tillock is not dead but in perfect health. *It is unpardonable in these historians* to mistake in matters of such consequence, especially in their own neighbourhood.

There were straight obituaries, too: a dry and brief one for Peter Walter, who finally died in January 1746, 'worth upwards of £200,000'—modern estimates would suggest a figure half as big again. And a solemn, resonant tribute to Swift, who had expired three months before Walter.

He possessed the talents of a Lucian, a Rabelais, and a Cervantes, and in his works exceeded them all. He employed his wit to the noblest purposes, in ridiculing as well superstition in religion as infidelity, and the several errors and immoralities which sprung up from time to time in his age; and lastly, in the defence of his country, against several pernicious schemes of wicked politicians. Not only was he a genius and a patriot; he was in private life a good and charitable man . . .

Understandably Fielding wants to make Swift's career count in the present crucial juncture: the phrases about 'superstition in religion' and 'defence of his country' could have only one implication as the Pretender's army marched south into the heart of England.

The most striking individual paper appeared early in the series, that is on 19 November, when news of the Jacobite progress poured into the capital almost every day. It is a nightmare fantasy, with some affinities to the *Journey from this World to the Next*—although the mood is far more grim. Fielding describes how he dreamt of sitting in his study, surrounded by his children, when suddenly a knock at the door disturbs the tranquil scene. It is, in effect, the secret police, here decked out in Highland dress and carrying broadswords. Their mission is to drag Fielding off to Newgate on account of his treasonable pro-Hanoverian publication *The True Patriot*. He is carted off through streets full of bodies and rubble, and eventually reaches an internment camp at Smithfield—where his fellow-prisoners include such doughty loyalists as the Archbishop of York and the Bishop of Winchester. He goes on trial before a court owing its allegiance to the Stuart sovereign, and finds the judge speaking broken English. Sentenced to death, he passes

crowds of protestant martyrs on his way to the scaffold. Just as the executioner is tightening the rope around his neck, he is wakened by his
daughter, who tells him the tailor has brought the traditional 'birthday suit'
of new clothes worn on a royal anniversary.

It is a compelling vision of an occupied city, and one which it is hard to
read today without twentieth-century associations crowding into our minds.
Fielding plays on some old protestant fears with his hints of the Smithfield
martyrs in Queen Mary's reign; and he makes superb use of his familiarity
with the machinery of law. State trials were still a possible recourse for
British governments, and indeed the 1715 Rising had been followed by
highly publicised arraignments of the rebel lords. Fielding could not have
known that the 1745 rebellion would have a much less conspicuous judicial
aftermath. A few of the leaders were beheaded, but the only one to catch
the public imagination was slippery old Lord Lovat, a lifelong opportunist,
whose bulky figure and unrepentant gaze were memorably caught in one of
Hogarth's most popular prints. At Lovat's execution on Tower Hill the
grandstand collapsed, and the old man watched the carnage that ensued with
good-humoured lack of concern.

What would have happened if the Pretender had succeeded, we shall
never know. Fielding inserted in *The True Patriot* later on another 'dream'
prediction, with heretics burnt, bishoprics given to Jesuits, and the naval
hero Admiral Vernon dispatched at Tyburn. It seems a little farfetched today,
and the virulence of Fielding's anti-papist sentiment jars on modern nerves.
But we may be less confident than the Victorian biographers were that it
can't happen here.

Throughout the early months of 1746, as the tide turned against Charles
Edward, Fielding kept up the attack in his newspaper columns. He whipped
up support for a Hanoverian defence fund, defended the ministry against
opposition allegations of insufficient response to the Jacobite danger, and
generally beat the drum for King George. He reanimated Parson Adams
briefly in the loyalist cause. He attacked the expensive Italian opera company
when it reopened in January 1746; the singers were a natural target for public
resentment, as Catholics, and sturdy Hanoverians began to insist on concerts
ending with 'God Save the King' (the first time there had been a generally
accepted national anthem). Even Handel offered a chorus song for the
gentleman volunteers of the City of London to the words, 'Stand Round,
My Brave boys!' In February he produced a more considerable work, the
so-called Occasional Oratorio, which made use at one point of Thomas
Arne's six-year-old 'Rule, Britannia'. It was a great success and revived the
flagging fortunes both of composer and of nation. There used to be a suspicion that Fielding himself had become a 'gentleman volunteer', but his
gout makes that utterly improbable. He supported the young lawyers of the

Temple in a mild form of home guard training they took up;* perhaps he witnessed the confused scenes when the royal troops set out to cut off the enemy, a moment so vividly portrayed by Hogarth in his superb *March to Finchley*. In this rendition patriotic fervour is heavily qualified by carousing, drinking, and petty pilfering. But Fielding was generous enough in that sphere of morality, however implacable he might be in his larger political and religious attachments. Provided the soldiers were brave and loyal, he did not require their daily lives to be models of absolute purity.

After Culloden there was less and less for *The True Patriot* to do. Crowing over a fallen enemy was not really in Fielding's style. Accordingly he composed an eloquent final number on 17 June—prevaricating just a little on the issue of how severely the captured rebels should be treated—and laid down the paper. The circulation had evidently been declining as there was less imminent national danger. In addition, Fielding was finding it increasingly difficult to combine supervision of the weekly paper with his own activity on the Western circuit. And, yet again, his own financial affairs were in a state of embarrassment. This time it was not really his fault: or at least, his impulsive generosity was to blame. He agreed to serve as guarantor for a debt contracted by an old Salisbury friend, a civil lawyer named Collier who had subscribed to the *Miscellanies*. James Harris, still living down in Salisbury, was to stand bail for an equal sum. The case came to trial in the Court of the Exchequer during 1745, and Collier lost. He refused to pay the debt all the same, and so the creditor naturally tried to recover his money from the guarantors. Fielding fought on in the courts, but to no avail.

In June 1746, just as he laid down *The True Patriot*, an execution for £400, plus damages, was taken out against him. It was the last thing he wanted. He had spent enough time struggling against the debts incurred by his sociable way of life and his own extravagant nature. The 'Feilding' side of his character had almost ruined him; and now here was a crushing blow inflicted on him as a result of his courtroom activity—which he had thought to reflect a prudent Gould mentality.

5

Since the death of Charlotte he had been living with his sister Sarah and his two children in Old Boswell Court, off the Strand to the north of St Clement Dane church. He paid an annual rate of about seven pounds a year from

*Characteristically Ralph Allen had raised a company at his own expense in Bath. They were dressed in blue and red uniforms, and accountred with halberds, pikes, swords and drums. They paraded in the Market Place to the satisfaction of the local population. Allen spent £2,000 on this occasion: it encapsulates his entire role as a public-spirited Hanoverian activist.

1744 to 1747, which indicates that it was a fairly substantial property—tall and narrow, in what must have been a dark and winding court running through a not particularly fragrant area. (The meat trade, otherwise confined to the provision markets, made an exception and clustered thickly about Butcher Row; the shops had no glazing or protection, so that the meat hung in full exposure to soot and rain.) Still it was convenient for the theatres, and particularly handy for members of the legal profession. Two of the smaller inns of court were situated here, and in due course the half-timbered houses were pulled down to make way for the nineteenth-century law courts. Other lawyers chose the alley and its environs for the same reason. The presence of an abundance of coffee-houses and chopshops would also entice the gregarious Fielding.

Sarah must have been a great comfort to him; she could supply literary conversation as well as sisterly affection. She was working on a sequel to *David Simple*, which was ultimately published by Millar in 1747. This time she adopted the subscription method, and was rewarded with a list larger and more resplendent than that of her brother with his own *Miscellanies*. Ralph Allen, Lady Mary Wortley Montagu and even Samuel Richardson figure, as they had not on the previous occasion. Henry again supplied a preface, and this time he contributed a few letters of his own to the text. With Sarah seems to have come Margaret Collier, a family friend from Salisbury, whose elder brother Arthur was just now saddling Fielding with his unwanted £400 debt. Peggy Collier was to accompany Fielding on his final voyage to Lisbon and to witness his will. Female devotion cannot have been lacking in the household, especially when we remember that Mary Daniel had remained in service as housekeeper.

Fielding's own literary activities were sparse for a time. The poet and critic Joseph Warton visited him in Boswell Court during October 1746 and found him civil and agreeable. According to Warton, it was *Joseph Andrews* which Fielding valued above all his other works to date. This may now look an obvious preference, but it was a less automatic choice in the 1740s, when the novel was still a new and lowly regarded form of writing. October 1745 had seen a collected edition of his dramatic productions, in two volumes; but this was a made-up set, consisting of the unsold sheets from earlier printings. It illustrated Fielding's range and testified to his industry; the public doubtless wanted something new and vibrant from his pen, rather than these warmed-up effusions from the Haymarket days. What people did not know was that Fielding had his masterpiece already under way. Every theory of composition admits that *Tom Jones* must have been in progress by this time.

Two minor works call for brief mention. The more interesting is the earlier, a lively piece of Defoe-like opportunism called *The Female Husband*, which appeared in November 1746. It was a semi-fictional account of a woman by the name of Mary Hamilton, who had passed herself off as a man and married a girl in Wells. She had been tried at Taunton, and Fielding's cousin Henry Gould had personally interrogated her. Apart from this local interest, a second reason which may have led Fielding to the story was the similarity between Mary, or 'George', Hamilton and that other sad transvestite adventurer, Charlotte Charke. The sixpenny pamphlet rapidly ran through an edition of 1,000 copies, and more had to be printed. Fielding's admirers tend to dismiss *The Female Husband* as a sensational pot-boiler, but it has some vigour in execution. The other item, *Ovid's Art of Love Paraphrased*, was published in February 1747. It is a fairly uncomplicated prose version of the opening segment in the *Ars Amatoria*. Fielding evidently planned to do more in the same vein, assuming proper encouragement—something that cannot have been forthcoming. Again that stout uncomplaining scholar, William Young, may have given some assistance.

A small hiatus in the following months would indicate that Fielding was turning more of his attention to *Tom Jones*, which had now reached an advanced stage of composition. He was still forcing his gout-ridden constitution to undergo the pains and penalties imposed by the circuit of assizes. This meant long days spent on horseback or in draughty coaches along bumpy roads. His lodgings would not always be comfortable, and his days in court would be spent in cramped conditions, where judges, jury and advocates alike stood a perceptible risk of catching the dread 'gaol fever' (a kind of typhus) from prisoners in the dock. In 1730 this had happened at Taunton, one of the assize-towns Fielding knew best: Sir Thomas Pengelly, MP and Chief Baron of the Exchequer, was one of those to succumb to the epidemic. It could happen even in the capital. The 'Black Sessions' at the Old Bailey in 1750 carried off two judges, the Lord Mayor, an alderman, and several other persons involved. Fielding was lucky to be officiating elsewhere. Had the legal technicalities fallen out slightly differently, he might have found the infected prisoners appearing before him at Bow Street or the Westminster court-house—and that would have been that.

It was a relief to go down to Bath after the tiring circuit was over. The town was large enough to provide all the civilised amenities, small enough to avoid the urban blight which was starting to affect London. It had grown steadily since Queen Anne helped to make it fashionable at the start of the century. The long reign of Beau Nash had given it smartness without vulgarity. The buildings of the elder John Wood, many built from the stone out of Ralph Allen's quarries, fanned out across the sides of the Avon valley. Monumental designs perched elegantly on the irregular terrain. Long terraces and colonnades were made to clamber nimbly about the jagged landscape. There is something especially Georgian about this blend of

nature and art, formal and informal. Fielding must have felt intensely at
home there, with the town's dual constituents of culture and enjoyment. It
is thought that the summers of 1746, 1747 and 1748 were spent by Henry
and Sarah at a house subsequently known as 'Fielding's Lodge' at Twerton
—what is now the ugliest suburb of Bath. This story goes back to a former
Rector of Claverton, by name Richard Graves, best known for his
amusing satire *The Spiritual Quixote*, and most scholars believe it to be
reliable. Graves also tells us that Fielding dined almost every day with
Ralph Allen, up at Prior Park, and again this is in accord with the facts we
have.

This does not mean, of course, that all of *Tom Jones* was written in this
precise locality. Parts were no doubt composed in London; and Fielding
may still have stayed with friends like Harris in Salisbury. And another, less
authenticated, narrative tells of an incident when Fielding joined a distinguished house-party at Radway, Warwickshire, in the summer of 1748.
This was the estate on Edge Hill belonging to a thirty-year-old virtuoso
named Sanderson Miller, who was a pioneer in the taste for things gothic
and who erected some of the most likeable follies and mock-ruins ever
created. Miller had a wide circle of friends, and his guests on this occasion
were said to include William Pitt, George Lyttelton, and 'George Fielding',
an unidentified relative. Fielding, we are assured, read a portion of the
manuscript of his work in progress to the assembled company. An embellish-
ment upon this story, which appeared as far back as 1756, states that Radway
Grange is itself the original of Mr Allworthy's seat. It is at least true that the
'Gothick' style of the Allworthy mansion is unlike Prior Park; but more
likely Fielding was paying a compliment to his dedicatee Lyttelton, who had
followed Miller's designs in erecting a sham castle at Hagley. Pitt did visit
Lyttelton at Hagley during August 1748, so even if the three men were
together at Radway that year they could very well have travelled across from
Lyttelton's house. In any case *Tom Jones* must have been nearing completion by this date.

Back in London, Fielding had a number of distractions, both personal and
professional, from work on his novel. In the first place he had married again.
On 27 November 1747, which fell on a Friday, the wedding took place of
Henry Fielding, widower, and Mary Daniel, spinster. The setting was a
small church on the north side of Thames Street named St Benet's, Paul's
Wharf, which had been rebuilt by Wren after the Great Fire. It was a tiny
parish, with fewer than eighty houses, as against the five thousand or more
in St Martin in the Fields. Fielding did not possess any known connection
with this district, and he must have chosen the church on grounds of
privacy. Mary Daniel was already six months pregnant. There may have
been no father to enforce a shotgun ceremony, but that inveterate gossip

Left The bailiffs arrive. From a pamphlet of 1723

Below A satirical invitation to the execution of Jonathan Wild in 1725

A REPRESENTATION of the Execution of Lord LOVAT.

A. The Scaffold.   C. Cloth to receive the Head.   E. The Coffin.   came on the Saffold.
B. Lord Lovat's head on ye Block. D. The Executioner with ye Axe. F. The House from which he

Opposite above The execution of Lord Lovat on Tower Hill in 1747

Opposite below *The March to Finchley* by Hogarth (1746). The soldiers are heading north to meet the Pretender's forces

Left Ralph Allen, Fielding's patron

Below Ralph Allen's mausoleum at Claverton, near Bath

Left John Russell, Duke of Bedford, another important patron of Fielding

Below Bedford House, the Duke's residence, which stood at the north end of Bloomsbury Square

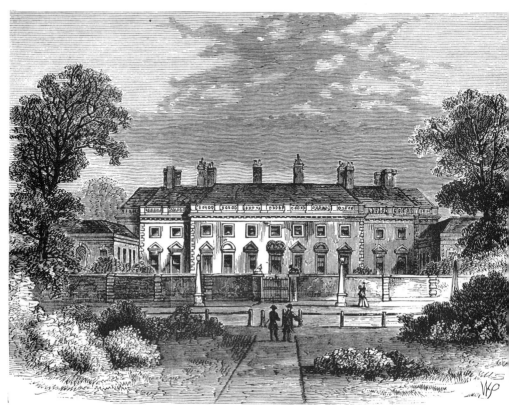

Horace Walpole came up with the story that George Lyttelton had applied suitable pressure:

Some gentlemen commending Mr L for having though a Lord of the Treasury voted against the ministry in the Bedwin election, Fielding started up, & striking his breast, cried, 'if you talk of virtue, here's virtue! I married my whore yesterday.' He had; Lyttelton made him.

The circumstance of Fielding, descendant of an aristocratic line, marrying his housekeeper naturally set scandalous tongues wagging. Fielding considerately found a place of retirement for his wife as the time of delivery drew near.

Mary was about twenty-six; not particularly pretty (Lady Louisa Stuart says she had 'few personal charms') but a tender and faithful woman. She lived to see the dawn of the nineteenth century, but it is only through her marriage that we can come at all close to her. Ever afterwards Henry was plagued with sneers for this unworthy alliance: Smollett accused him of marrying 'his own cook-wench', and even Lady Mary Wortley Montagu abated some of her normal charity towards him: 'His natural spirits gave him rapture with his cookmaid, and cheerfulness when he was fluxing in a garret.' ('Fluxing' means undergoing a medical course of purging.) When Fielding's political opponents had nothing better to throw at him, they could always be relied on to toss in a jibe at the expense of Mary.

For the moment she was protected. Henry leased two rooms in remote Twickenham, and here his son William was born in February 1748. There was not room for Sarah; probably a maidservant completed the household. The lodging lay tucked away down a narrow alley called Back Lane; it is said to have been a 'quaint, old-fashioned wooden structure'. Like many of Fielding's places of residence it is long gone, but it can be located in present-day Holly Road, near a sweeping bend in the Thames marked by Eel Pie Island. A quarter of a mile to the south stood Pope's old house, bereft of its master for nearly four years now, the grotto all hollow echoes and faintly absurd in its prolonged existence. A few minutes walk along the river bank, further upstream, past the residence of the painter Thomas Hudson, would bring one to Strawberry Hill, where Horace Walpole had settled in the previous spring, and where he was laying the plans in his mind for a new and eccentrically original house. It was a district famous for beautiful riverside villas; a few months before Henry installed Mary in the little wood-built retreat up the side lane, Horace Walpole was describing his surroundings in this way:

Two delightful roads, that you would call dusty, supply me continually with coaches and chaises: barges as solemn as Barons of the Exchequer move under my window; Richmond Hill and Ham Walks bound my prospect; but, thank God! the Thames is between me and the Duchess of Queensberry. Dowagers as plenty as flounders inhabit all around, and Pope's ghost is just now skimming under my window by a most poetical moonlight.

The prospect from Back Lane was doubtless more restricted, and the moonlight vistas less poetical. But it was a safe and quiet place where this difficult second marriage could make a start.

A second distraction was supplied by a surprising return to the theatrical world. It was in an area we should describe these days as 'fringe theatre'. Between March and June 1748 Fielding was engaged in a satirical puppet show in Panton Street, off the Haymarket right next door to his old stamping ground. He posed as 'Madame de la Nash,' said to be the proprietess of a breakfasting-room. The inception of this venture was noted in the press on 7 March, with a hint that 'the true humour of that most diverting entertainment [Punch and Judy] will be restored'; Fielding's own new *Jacobite's Journal* picked up the story for its 'Comical Occurrences' a week later. Nobody is quite sure what the content of these performances was; but it is safe to assert that the message would be political, that is to say pro-ministerial and anti-Catholic. Fielding may also have slipped in matter concerned with theatrical quarrels, for he remained a strong supporter of David Garrick, now the manager, and busy innovating at Drury Lane. Incidentally, seven of Fielding's own plays were performed that season at the two 'legitimate' houses, Drury Lane and Covent Garden.

All that, and *Tom Jones*, might seem enough to be going on with. There was also the little matter of Fielding's professional career at the bar. There are indications that he did not attend the spring assizes in 1748, and in view of the programme he had marked out for himself this would be a reasonable course of action. Later that year a story appeared in the press, with the dateline of Bridgwater in Somerset, reporting the death of Fielding's cousin Henry Gould 'as he was going the circuit'. *The Jacobite's Journal* repeated the item, with an encomium on Gould's merits. It was quite untrue— Gould survived for another forty-six years, as a matter of fact. Either Fielding was down in the West Country, or else he was singularly ill informed in London concerning events round about his old home.

The new *Journal*, which I have just mentioned, was yet another preoccupation of Fielding at this juncture. Again it was a weekly paper, very much along the lines of *The True Patriot*. A run of forty-nine issues extended from 5 December 1747 (no more than a week after his marriage to Mary) until 5 November 1748. The price was twopence. A woodcut illustration at the head is traditionally attributed to Hogarth, though the evidence is not

lefinite. Fielding had praised Hogarth as far back as *The Champion* and
Joseph Andrews, and they were old friends by this time; but that is all we
can say. In the *Journal* Fielding adopts the persona of John Trott-Plaid,
Esq., an unashamed Jacobite; 'A title which men assume in the most public
manner in taverns, in coffee-houses, and in the streets, may surely, without
any impropriety, be assumed in print.' It is a mere feint. Few of the opposition leaders had anything to do with the Jacobite cause, in 1745 and 1746
or at any other date. But Fielding enjoys bestowing on them what an
historian once called 'the perpetual reproach'. In his last paper Fielding sets
out as his justification 'a strange spirit of Jacobitism, indeed of infatuation'
rampant in the country when he began the *Journal*.

Yet the Stuart cause was virtually dead, and the true centre of the debate
is increasingly a different aspect of government policy—that is, the efforts
of the Pelham administration to achieve a satisfactory peace treaty to end
the War of the Austrian Succession. This was acutely necessary because of
the huge drain on national resources which this long-drawn struggle imposed.
The Secretary of State, the Duke of Newcastle, had been holding out for
better terms than many believed Britain could achieve. Eventually, an
agreement was signed by Britain, France, and the Dutch at Aix-la-Chapelle
in October 1748. One of the conditions accepted by the French was the
expulsion of the Young Pretender from Paris, which meant the effective end
of his hopes. Now, Fielding writes in his last *Journal*, the funds have gone
up and dejection has overtaken all factious opponents of His Majesty's
government. It is time to lay down John Trott-Plaid's pen.

The prime concern, then, is political, and this is reflected by two fairly
dull pamphlets which Fielding composed at the same time. But there is also
a good deal about the theatre in the columns of the *Journal*, and a revival of
the old *Tatler* idea of a national censor with a 'Court of Criticism'. More
enticing for the modern reader are the satirical tags applied to news items;
instead of 'Apocrypha' these are now given headings such as 'Credenda' or
'Comical Occurrences'. Some of Fielding's liveliest comedy is to be found
tucked away in these forgotten newspapers. The 'Gallimatia' attributed to
one Morgan Scrub, 'Grubstreet Solicitor', afford some splendid barbed
comments:

[Thursday. George Mackenzie, Esq. late Earl of Cromarty, and his lady and family,
set out from their lodgings in Pall-Mall for Devonshire, to the place he is banished
to for life, near Exeter. *Whitehall Evening Post*.] *If Ovid had been obliged to have
exchanged Scotland for Devonshire, he had never written his Tristia.*

which is at least as witty as anything Johnson wrote about the Scots.

(Cromarty was a supporter of the Pretender, captured and sentenced to death, but later reprieved.)*

Fielding was well accustomed to abuse, but at few stages of his career did he draw more flak than now. Opposition papers like *Old England* were savage in their attacks, dragging from the past every minor peccadillo and misjudgment. It was natural that the unacceptable marriage he had made should be hauled into the argument every time. But he had even to endure reminders of his rakish father, and the suggestion that both the general and his son had 'coupled' with a kitchen-maid:

> This difference only 'twixt the sire and son,
> The first had money but the other none.

He was no doubt glad enough to lay down the *Journal* in early November. It was his last sustained piece of party political·writing. Besides, there was a much greater event in the offing.

6

Progress on *Tom Jones* had necessarily been slowed down by all the other pressures of a crowded life. However, by 1748 the work was coming to completion. The novel had been composed in bursts, and a concerted effort enabled Fielding to dispose of the last third of the text towards the end of the year. Scholars have tracked down a variety of contemporary references which seem to date particular portions of the book; but since these details could have been supplied during the act of revision, it does not seem very fruitful to analyse them at length. One important intermediary happening was the publication of Samuel Richardson's greatest novel *Clarissa*, which took place in stages between December 1747 and December 1748. This was too late to influence the overall character of *Tom Jones*, though as we shall see the situation is different with *Amelia*.

Fielding immediately came to admire *Clarissa*, and inserted two or three indirect allusions to the work in *Tom Jones*. He was sent an advance copy of the fifth volume by its author, and wrote to Richardson a letter full of glowing praise: 'Let the overflowings of a heart which you have filled brimfull speak for me. . . . Here my terror ends and my grief begins which

---

*Serious news items naturally received less facetious coverage—thus when old General Wade finally expired at Bath in March 1748, Fielding reprinted a newspaper account of his public career, with the addition: 'He was besides, in private life, a gentleman of the highest honour, humanity and generosity, and hath done more good and benevolent actions than this whole paper can contain.'

the cause of all my tumultuous passions soon changes into raptures of admiration and astonishment by a behaviour the most elevated I can possibly conceive.' He ends by a hearty wish for Richardson's success. There is an equally warm tribute in *The Jacobite's Journal* on 2 January 1748, this time relating to the opening instalment of *Clarissa*: 'Such simplicity, such manners, such deep penetrations into nature; such power to raise and alarm the passions, few writers, either ancient or modern, have been possessed of.' It is astoundingly generous in view of the previous coldness between these great rivals. Sadly Richardson was not able to respond in kind, even when Sarah Fielding brought out her approbatory *Remarks on Clarissa* soon after the publication of the last instalment.

The literary world was keenly interested in the progress of *Tom Jones*, a curiosity which the great impact of *Clarissa* must have intensified. On 19 January 1748 a well-known scholar named Birch, later to be Secretary of the Royal Society and to edit folio compendia of stupefying bulk, wrote to his patron of the expected novel: 'Mr Fielding is printing three volumes of adventures under the title of *The Foundling*. Mr Lyttelton, who has read the manuscript, commends the performance to me as an excellent one, and abounding with strong and lively painting of characters, and a very copious and happy invention in the conduct of the story'—just praise, of course. Later that year Birch got hold of a story that Fielding had been paid £600 for the manuscript, and he again cites the high regard for it which Lyttelton was expressing. Hostile critics were later to allege that Lyttelton had run around town organising the promotion of *Tom Jones*, and had prevailed on a herd of 'placemen and pensionaries' to puff it in the coffee-houses. This is obviously an exaggeration, but it is known that Lyttelton and Pitt did everything they could to advance the fortunes of the book—as why should they not? By December Birch was reporting that some of his friends had gained a sight of *Tom Jones*, and spoke well of its humorous and pathetic qualities. Meanwhile Lady Hertford, an ardent devotee of literature and something of a salon-frequenter, had read the first two volumes and declared a preference for the new book over *Joseph Andrews*. It was a verdict that posterity (having access to the entire novel) has amply confirmed.

Birch kept his ear close to the ground, especially in the company of members of the book trade. It is no surprise then to learn that his information about Fielding's financial returns prove to have been correct. An agreement was signed on 11 June 1748 between the author and his usual bookseller, Andrew Millar. Fielding made over the copyright of *Tom Jones* for a flat sum of £600. Later on, when the book proved so successful, Millar is said by Horace Walpole to have paid Fielding a further £100; but there is no documentary evidence of this. The original plan had been to issue the work by subscription, perhaps in the three volumes mentioned by

Birch. But when it appeared in the bookshops on or about 10 February 1749, it was a normal commercial edition, made up of six neat little duodecimo volumes. The demand was so great that the first edition was immediately snapped up, and by the end of the month Millar was advertising a second. At least 2,000 copies were printed of the former and 1,500 of the latter. A third edition, reset in a different type-face, amounted to 3,000 copies, and appeared on 12 April. The fourth followed in September, this time running to 3,500 sets. Within nine months the total printing had reached 10,000. Millar had made a huge profit; the original price had been 18s bound (cheaper in unbound sheets), and though the third edition was priced at 12s for a bound set, his gross income must have been of the order of £6,000 in the course of the year. Printing costs cannot have eaten up more than a third of this. The rumour got around that Millar was able to set himself up with a handsome equipage on the proceeds of the edition. It is easy to believe.

The fame of the book soon spread. By 1750 there were translations into French, German and Dutch; and of course the usual Dublin piracy crept out. The reception at home was overwhelmingly positive; even Fielding's opponents had to allow some merit to the novel. It took extreme nerve as well as perversity, in this climate, for *Old England* (a resolutely anti-ministerial organ) to describe the performance as 'beneath the dignity of regular criticism' and a 'motley history of bastardism, fornication and adultery'. Another stubborn resister was Samuel Richardson, who was deaf to the entreaties of his friends that he should at least *read* the book. He grew alarmed as a number of the ladies whom he had in tow admitted to have perused, and even enjoyed, this 'truly coarse-titled' novel, with its 'very bad tendency'. Nevertheless all the ladies continued to 'talk of their Tom Joneses and the men of their Sophias'. Elizabeth Carter, the talented blue-stocking of Deal, was impelled to desert her former favourite Richardson; whilst an old admirer, Lady Mary Wortley Montagu, sat up all night to devour a parcel of Fielding's works. She liked *Joseph Andrews* better than its successor (surprisingly she does not seem to have read the former until now); and indeed others considered that there was no character in the new book as strongly drawn as Parson Adams. But not everyone was as fastidious as Richardson or as cut off as Lady Mary, pottering about Lombardy and awaiting the mail from England. Just how powerfully the novel had caught people's imagination is shown by an event recorded in the press at the start of May. At Epsom races a match was run between a chestnut called Joseph Andrews and a bay called Tom Jones. Joseph was the winner this time.

Tom Jones survives as one of the best-known English novels, and it would be tedious to describe its plot or characters in any detail. The qualities for which Fielding is renowned—ebullient humour, gusto, magnanimity.

shrewd observation—are all fully in evidence. The story is full of incident, and teeming with comic adventures. At the same time there is an unfolding moral drama, in which the young hero is contrasted in his spontaneous and affectionate nature with the canny Blifil, Squire Allworthy's 'legitimate' heir. Both of Tom's evil tutors, Thwackum and Square, prefer Master Blifil—the only matter on which they can ever agree. Fielding superbly evokes the physical clamminess of Blifil; as with Uriah Heep, the threat he presents is in part one of sexual rivalry, and as with Heep there is a repellent and perverted quality in Blifil's advances to Sophia. The heroine is another triumphant creation: it was exceedingly difficult for girls to come across as living, breathing human beings in early fiction, if only because they had so few opportunities to express themselves in real life. The love story is tender without being mawkish, and Tom's noted virility is matched by Sophia's ardent and unflinching recognition of her feelings. It has generally been thought that Sophia was a portrait of Fielding's first wife, and while the character is no direct transcript from life there is every reason to suppose that some aspects of Charlotte do show through. Allworthy is thought to be an amalgam of Lyttelton and Ralph Allen, probably more of the latter; but if so the type-cast role has tended to suffocate the individual.

Another question might be asked: that is, whether Fielding is dramatising elements in his own psychic history. He was not exactly an orphan, but from the age of eleven he had no mother, whilst his father was an absentee most of the time. It is by no means fanciful to observe that Fielding was in a sense disinherited, a scion of the aristocracy brought up without any real expectations and split down the middle by a disintegrating family situation. Of course, Tom is far more than a transfigured Fielding, but he may serve that imaginative purpose among others. Recently, Ronald Paulson has pointed out that Tom's character and wanderings reflect aspects of Bonnie Prince Charlie, as these were seen by his admirers at least. Similarly Blifil is depicted in terms of those qualities which Jacobite sentiment attributed to the Hanoverians. This does not mean, of course, that Fielding emotionally identified with the Stuart cause; but it does provide a complicating factor to the feeling of the novel. The 'history' of Tom Jones is fascinatingly interfused with the history of the nation.

Tom Jones is deeply original in many ways. For example, Fielding's use of an introductory chapter to each book where the narrator can lay down the law and assert critical positions, gave the work an intellectual range and a dense literary texture which had been lacking up till then in the English novel. By comparison Daniel Defoe's stories appear thin-bodied and deficient in amplitude. There is no evidence that Fielding had read Defoe's fiction, by the way, and it is likely that he had managed to steer clear also of Eliza Haywood *et hoc genus omne*. Nothing in earlier fictional tradition accounts for what Fielding does with the form. The most important mode, as with *Joseph Andrews*, is the ancient epic—that is to say, the classical variety of Homer and Virgil rather than the Renaissance kind of Tasso and Spenser. To understand the workings of *Tom Jones* it is much more help to read *The Odyssey* than to look for 'sources' and hints in the writers of Fielding's own day. And quite apart from the epic poets there was his beloved Lucian, the master of wry disillusioned accents. A satirist of the second century, born in Syria, Lucian used the Greek language with a witty and clear-headed precision. As Gilbert Highet puts it in his survey *The Classical Tradition* (a good background book for Fielding):

'Lord!' he says, 'what fools these mortals be!'—but there is more gentleness in his voice and kindness in his heart than we feel in his Roman predecessors. His work ... forms a bridge between the dialogues of creative philsophers like Plato, the fantasy of Aristophanes, and the negative criticism of the satirists. He was Rabelais's favourite Greek author. Swift may have recalled his fabulous travel tales when he wrote about Gulliver; and Cyrano de Bergerac certainly did when he went to the moon.

Such men as this inspired Fielding much more than the hacks who had dominated prose fiction in English hitherto. So he invoked the spirit of Genius in *Tom Jones* (XIII, i):

Come thou, that hast inspired thy *Aristophanes*, thy *Lucian*, thy *Cervantes*, thy *Rabelais*, thy *Moliere*, thy *Shakespeare*, thy *Swift*, thy *Marivaux*, fill my pages with humour; till mankind learn the good nature to laugh only at the follies of others, and the humility to grieve at their own.

It was in such company that Fielding discovered the fount of true creative invention.

He once named the 'great triumvirate' of wit and humour as consisting of Lucian, Cervantes and Swift. Cervantes stood at the head of modern authors, and *Don Quixote* (1605–15) was pre-eminent among modern books. It was for Fielding 'the history of the world in general', an unrivalled picture of human destiny in its mingled comic and pathetic colours. Certainly Fielding's 'new species of writing' would have been impossible without the example of *Don Quixote*. At the end of his life his rival Tobias Smollett was embarking on the fifth translation into English of *Quixote*; this was to be the only version seriously to compete in popular favour with Motteux's early eighteenth-century translation, the one Fielding probably knew best. (It is, I think, safe to assume that he did not read Spanish at all fluently.) There were abridgments and copies, innumerable novels developing the 'quixotic' character (*The Female Quixote: The Spiritual Quixote*).

plays and poems building upon the original, continuing the story of the deluded knight of La Mancha. As for *Tom Jones* itself, the direct relation is less than in *Joseph Andrews*, despite the vague similarity of Partridge to Sancho Panza; but the informing spirit of Cervantes' book—realism without cynicism, compassion without mawkishness, wit without malice—is abiding throughout his disciple's work.

It is possible for scholars who look hard enough to pick up the odd allusion to other modern writers—for instance to someone like Paul Scarron, a popular French comic novelist of the mid-seventeenth century. But these do not emerge as significant 'sources' in any pervasive sense. Nor is *Tom Jones* to be described, except in the loosest possible way, as a picaresque work. Comparison with the genuine picaresque—say, *Lazarillo de Tormes* (1554) or *La Vida del Buscón* (1626)—will soon show the differences. In these latter cases the *pícaro* hero is just what the word means, that is a rascally but cunning good-for-nothing—the very opposite of Joseph and Tom, innocents abroad in a world of corrupt or sophisticated exploiters. A much nearer equivalent in English is provided by the early novels of Smollett: even Defoe's Moll Flanders, her sex notwithstanding, has a bit of the *pícaro* about her. But Fielding's interests lay in another direction.

What Fielding did was to adapt the high forms of classical literature to modern experience. He attempted in prose what the Augustan satirists had done in mock-heroic poetry: that is, he stretched ancient modes rather than taking the fashionable ones to hand. The old term 'neoclassical', little used now and often disparaged, is really quite applicable in his case. He writes about the 1740s with two thousand years of authorial practice to guide him.

One of his great innovations was to make the introductory chapter to each book (a device pioneered in *Joseph Andrews*) into a kind of chat with the reader on literary and moral topics. Of course, the narrator in these chapters is not in a strict sense the 'real' Fielding; it is a specially contrived mouthpiece for the author, emphasising some of his own qualities and suppressing others. We know that Fielding's own moods and personal circumstances were sometimes at variance with the tone of his disquisitions in the novel. Like Mozart, he was capable of producing sublime comedy whilst his own life took a grim or tragic course. And the naïvely optimistic, perpetually cheerful Fielding is a delusion, as anyone would expect in the light of the events we have witnessed.

It remains true that generations of readers have come to feel as though a warm personality were in the room with them as they savoured the genial narrative and ironic asides:

Examine your heart, my good reader, and resolve whether you do believe these matters with me. If you do, you may now proceed to their exemplification in the following pages; if you do not, you have, I assure you, already read more than you have understood, and it would be wiser to pursue your business or your pleasures (such as they are) than to throw away any more of your time in reading what you can neither taste nor comprehend. To treat of the effects of love to you must be as absurd as to discourse on colours to a man born blind, since possibly your idea of love may be as absurd as that which we are told such a blind man once entertained of the colour red: that colour seemed to him to be very much like the sound of a trumpet, and love probably may, in your opinion, very greatly resemble a dish of soup or a sirloin of roast beef.

Fielding is clearly enjoying himself here. He is exercising his rights as a benevolent despot, which were set out at the start of the second book. But he does not bully us and needle us like Swift, or even pester us with enforced intimacy quite as Sterne does. He puts us in our place, with good-humoured concern for our welfare. He has the air at times of a long-suffering Dutch uncle, ready to share a joke but never scrupling to advise and guide us. His natural form of expression was not so much the moral essay as the discursive chat practised in the heyday of radio by J. B. Priestley or C. S. Lewis—he would have made a superb broadcaster, with his fund of anecdote and his eloquent use of plain words.

The film of *Tom Jones* made by Tony Richardson in the 1960s caught many of its most attractive features—not just the physical fun, but the ironies and satiric insights, too. Other aspects of the book naturally resisted translation into the terms of a movie. There were few means at Richardson's disposal to bring out the elaborate symmetries of construction which are built into Fielding's narrative. And he could not do very much with the Jacobite rising, which is so carefully woven into the middle third of the novel. Fielding could rely on a total familiarity with these events on the part of his readers: a biographer can provide a rapid outline of the Forty-Five, as I have done, but a film-maker can scarcely interrupt his narrative to follow the Pretender's fortunes ('Meanwhile, back at the glen . . .'). Nevertheless, the cinema version introduced a wide diversity of people to *Tom Jones* for the first time, and many must have gone on to read the book of the film. It is significant that Fielding himself was ready enough to use the popular media of his day.

Tom Jones confirmed Fielding's position as one of the greatest living writers. But even before the book appeared, a fresh turn occurred in his jagged life history. At the end of 1748, now aged forty-one, he began a new career.

SIX

The Seat of Judgment

1748-52

I

During the course of 1748 two vacancies occurred in the magistracy of the city of Westminster. On 30 July the official 'fiat' was issued naming Henry Fielding as a Justice of the Peace to fill one of these positions. The commission took effect on 25 October, and next day Fielding took the oaths. A full year before, he had been named for the Middlesex commission; but since there was a property qualification for all county magistrates, not applicable in the case of Westminster, he was at first unable to take the oaths for Middlesex. In the meantime it seems, from recently published evidence, that he had obtained the post of High Steward to the Warden of the New Forest, thanks to the patronage of the Warden, John Russell, Duke of Bedford. It was not a particularly well-paid sinecure, and it had to be relinquished when in due course Fielding qualified for the Middlesex magistracy; but it was something to be going on with. Fielding had more than once defended the Duke's actions in *The Jacobite's Journal*, and now he was busy cultivating this important magnate through his agent Robert Butcher.

Fielding was entering the last, and in some ways the most distinguished, phase of his varied career. How improbable it would have seemed, only a decade earlier, that the roistering garret-writer should have arrived at the judicial bench! Some scornful comments were to be expected, and they were duly made. Opposition papers like *Old England* satirised his lack of legal knowledge (unfairly, on the whole), and pictured him as a poetaster who had occasionally flicked through a textbook on law: 'I have only read a few plays, and wrote some pamphlets during my state of probation,' he is made to admit, 'which qualified me very essentially for the gown.' With more reason, his critics drew attention to his dependence on the ministry, particularly the new Secretary of State, the Duke of Bedford. One mock-autobiography published in the columns of *Old England* shows the kind of hostile image it was possible to create:

Hunted after fortunes, and lived on kept mistresses for a while; scored deep at
the taverns, borrowed money of my landlords and their drawers; burrowed in
privileged places among the flatcaps of the town, stood bully for them, and p*xed
them all round; abused my benefactors in the administration of public affairs, of
religious dispensations, of justice, and of the stage; hackneyed for booksellers and
newspapers; lampooned the virtuous, wrote the adventures of footmen, and the
lives of thief-catchers; cramped the stage, debased the press, and brought it into
jeopardy; bilked every lodging for ten years together, and every alehouse and
chandler's shop in every neighbourhood; defrauded and reviled all my acquaintance, and being quite out of cash, credit and character, as well as out of charity
with all mankind, haunted by duns and bumbailiffs, hallo'd, hooted at and chased
from every side and by every voice, I escaped with whole bones indeed, but
damnably mangled into these purlieus of safety, where no venomous creatures
dare enter.

And so on. Some of the charges are old ones, though Fielding's tendency to
drink is now given more prominence. One phrase seems hard to reconcile
with everything we know about the character of Fielding—'out of charity
with all mankind'—but sadly it is probable that most of the other accusations
had some remote basis in fact, however unsympathetic the treatment here.*
   At the centre of these attacks stands one fact: Fielding's increasing
reliance on the patronage of the Duke of Bedford. Undoubtedly it was
through the intervention of Bedford, urged by George Lyttelton, that
Fielding obtained his appointment to the bench. The Duke was the heir
of a rich and illustrious line; he had succeeded his brother in the title at the
age of twenty-two, and joined the opposition to Walpole. After the great
man's fall he began to collect around him a group of followers known as the
'Bloomsbury gang', and gradually wormed his way into the Pelham administration. He also enjoys a minor niche in history as an early supporter of
cricket. Gray and Horace Walpole, who had been exposed to the game at
Eton, liked to sneer at 'dirty cricket-players'; one wonders if the tall,
muscular Fielding had more pleasant recollections from his schooldays. The
Duke lived in some style in Bedford House, at the upper end of Bloomsbury
Square. There were open fields behind the mansion even as late as 1800,
until the large-scale development of the Bedford estate towards what is now
Russell Square.
   As for his client, dependent, favourite—call him what you will—Fielding,
he was temporarily on the move. When he got back from the West Country

---

*Some of the contemporary slang needs explanation. *Drawer* is the old word for a waiter; the
privileged places are sanctuaries for debtors and criminals, such as Whitefriars (there may also be
a sneer at Fielding's new position of trust), a *bully* was a pimp, whilst *flatcaps* are evidently prostitutes. There is perhaps some irony in applying this jargon against Fielding, since he had made such
effective use of thieves' argot in *Jonathan Wild*—the thief-catcher named here.

Left Fielding's house in Bow Street, in the early nineteenth century

Below The interior of the court-house in Bow Street in 1777. Sir John Fielding is the figure on the bench (*centre, rear*)

Overleaf Central London in 1745. Westminster Bridge (*lower left*) was still under construction: it was opened in 1750

The Bench by Hogarth (1758)

A drunken brawl in Covent Garden

in the autumn of 1748, ready to take up his magisterial duties, he briefly took a house in Brownlow Street, running off the top end of Drury Lane. Within a few weeks he had shifted his abode to Meard's Court, Wardour Street, in the heart of modern Soho. It is a little odd to think of Fielding dispensing justice in a district now celebrated for shows not calculated to please the Christian moralist. But by early December he was settled in a more lasting home, that is a large house on the west side of Bow Street, a few yards from where Covent Garden opera house now stands. This was to be his private residence but also his official place of business as a JP— important functionaries often lived more or less on the job, as with Pepys at the Navy Office a couple of generations back. The court-room occupied the ground floor, and there were living quarters above. The freehold, it will be no surprise to reveal, belonged to the Duke of Bedford, who had leased it for twenty-one years to the notable former magistrate, Sir Thomas de Veil. Curiously, although de Veil had died in 1746, it was his executors who were responsible for the lease throughout Fielding's residence. It was not until 1766 that John Fielding took formal possession of the house, for which he paid Bedford a flat sum of £300 and a rent of £10. After de Veil a justice named Green had occupied the property, but he was removed from the roll of magistrates on 14 November 1748. By 9 December Fielding had taken up residence in this, the most celebrated home he ever had.

Three days later he wrote to the Duke, asking to be granted the lease of a house or houses with an annual value of £100. Unless he obtained such a qualification he was debarred from joining the Middlesex bench. It was normal to act in both capacities, and since the jurisdiction of the county extended into what was practically central London (including such hotbeds of crime as St Giles in the Fields and St George in the East), any sensible strategy for enforcing the law required close cooperative effort between city and county. Within a few days Fielding learnt that his request had been granted. On 19 December he wrote to thank the Duke: 'There is really no language which can express my full sense of your Grace's unparalleled goodness to me . . .' It meant giving up the post of High Steward, but that was a small sacrifice. Bedford's original plan was to lease Fielding a number of properties around Bow Street and Bedford Street. He changed his mind, and made over instead a number of properties chiefly in Drury Lane, worth £135 per annum. Bedford had recently bought these up, and two of his tenants in this theatrical area were David Garrick and the experienced manager James Lacy, who had put on Fielding's plays back in the Haymarket days. A nominal rent of £30 was charged to Fielding, but in the event he never paid 'one shilling ground rent', as his brother found after his death. A debt of £712 was wiped out by the Duke when the lease was surrendered. But this all lay ahead. On 13 January 1749 Fielding took the oaths for the

Middlesex commission, a ceremony repeated six months later when the qualifying properties had been reassigned. Understandably the dedication to *Tom Jones*, published in February of that year, refers to the 'princely benefactions of the Duke of Bedford': an honest acknowledgment, but at the same time further ammunition for Fielding's critics.*

The house in Bow Street had been taken over in 1739 by Sir Thomas de Veil, and it remained the centre of criminal investigation for well over a century. (Scotland Yard dates only from 1891.) De Veil had been a colonel in the Marlborough wars, and was already a man of forty-five when he became a magistrate in the same year that Fielding returned to England from Leyden. During the 1730s he had done a great deal to clean up the capital, and had smashed some of the gangs which were attempting to follow in the footsteps of Jonathan Wild. At the time of the 'Gin riots' in 1736 he had taken a strong line against the leaders, an example which Fielding was to copy during his own tenure. He was also a vehement Hanoverian and kept a vigilant eye on all suspected of Jacobite leanings— which meant, *inter alia*, all Catholics. During the Rising one of de Veil's duties had been to lead a party of men to arrest a harmless peer called Lord Dillon at his home in Barnet—the Dillons were Irish catholics, Stuart supporters almost by reflex, and his lordship needed to do nothing in 1745 to become guilty by historical association. De Veil was also ready to lead the Westminster militia, but the Pretender's retreat from Derby denied him that chance. He had picked up a knighthood the year before, when he had suppressed one of the intermittent footmen's riots in Panton Street (a haunt of Fielding's). He was still in office when he died from a stroke in 1746.

There was a brief interregnum before Fielding took over in Bow Street. But he was the natural successor to de Veil, and comparably energetic in seeking to root out crime. It would perhaps be more appropriate to say crime as then defined. Fielding's role was closer to that of a continental superintending magistrate than that of a modern English stipendiary. He was involved in detection, for the primitive force of constables was directly under his authority; he also had the prime responsibility for maintaining public order, and when the Riot Act was called into action it was he who,

---

*For this transaction, and other matters concerning Fielding and the Duke, see the important article by M. C. Battestin, with R. R. Battestin, 'Fielding, Bedford, and the Westminster Election of 1749', in *Eighteenth-Century Studies*, 11 (1977–78), 143–85. This prints for the first time eighteen letters by Henry, his second wife, his son and his half-brother. An incidental fact revealed by the newly published correspondence is the sad condition into which Fielding had already fallen by reason of his gout. One letter to the Duke's agent, dated 21 November 1748, begins, 'I am not yet, and God knows whether ever shall be, able to stand upon my legs . . .' Gout was then a less specific term than it has subsequently become; it was used of a wide range of rheumatic and arthritic conditions.

n the normal course of events, would be required solemnly to intone its
sweeping provisions. They included such clauses as these:

Be it further enacted . . . that if any persons unlawfully, riotously, tumultuously
assembled together, to the disturbance of the public peace, shall unlawfully, and
with force demolish or pull down, or begin to demolish or pull down any church
or chapel, or any building for religious worship certified or registered . . . or any
dwelling-house, barn, stable, or other out-house, that then every such demolishing,
or pulling down, or beginning to demolish, or pull down, shall be adjudged
felony without benefit of clergy, and the offenders therein shall be adjudged felons,
and shall suffer death as in the case of felony . . .

It was, we can safely assert, a tough job.

The new magistrate soon came face to face with the realities of his post.
On 2 November he committed a woman as a 'loose, idle and disorderly
person, not giving any good account of herself'. For the rest of that month
he was kept busy by a variety of crimes: stealing predominated, with shirts
and bundles of linen the most frequent items involved. But there was also a
case concerned with the theft of an iron fire shovel and a hearth brush. More
evocative in a way is the girl charged with failing to provide for a bastard
child—she could be glad that she came before Fielding and not someone
like Mr Thrasher, the corrupt justice in *Amelia*. Another of Fielding's early
hearings took place on 9 December 1748, when he sent a man to the Gate-
house gaol for stealing money from a clergyman's bureau. A week later 'one
Jones', ironically, was brought before Fielding at Bow Street, charged with
barbarously wounding a young woman on the head with a cutlass the night
before, without any provocation'. A succession of such cases came up for
trial, many of them by way of committal proceedings—the more serious
offenders were remanded to Newgate or other maximum security prisons,
insofar as a corrupt system could provide these. (Keepers made their living
principally from garnish, bribes paid by the more affluent inmates which
bought them better conditions—and even occasionally freedom.)

It is not likely that Fielding came to his post with any exalted ideas of the
mission he was called to serve. From his own days of poverty and wildness,
he would have known what the seamy side of London life was like. From his
years as a barrister he would have come to recognise the inadequacies,
deprivations and miseries which underlay a high proportion of crime.
Coiners, prostitutes, sneak-thieves and extortioners mingled in the dock
with murderers, muggers, and sodomites. Some of these men and women
were, no doubt, truly vicious and irreclaimable. But the state of the law did
not make it easy to distinguish these from genuine unfortunates or from
hapless victims of desperate social circumstances. From the start Fielding

showed himself a tough magistrate, although we can reasonably infer from the evidence that he was a just one—some might add, within the limits of the system. His enemies, as we have seen, were prepared to throw every kind of dirt at him. But they never make a single charge of any substance concerning the propriety of his conduct on the bench.

It has to be admitted that Horace Walpole does give us a distinctly unpleasant 'picture of nature' in describing life at Bow Street. He tells us how two men about town named Rigby and Bathurst

t'other night carried a servant of the latter's, who had attempted to shoot him, before Fielding; who, to all his other vocations, has, by the grace of Mr Lyttelton, added that of the Middlesex justice. He sent them word he was at supper, that they must come next morning. They did not understand that freedom, and ran up where they found him banqueting with a blind man, three Irishmen, and a whore on some cold mutton and a bone of ham, both in one dish, and the cursedest dirtiest cloth! He never stirred nor asked them to sit. Rigby, who had seen him so often come to beg a guinea of Sir C[harles Hanbury] Williams, and Bathurst, at whose father's he had lived for victuals, understood that dignity as little, and pulled themselves chairs, on which he civilised.

Now all Fielding's biographers have been inclined to treat with the utmost scepticism the details of this story, which dates from the May following his appointment. I think it rings pretty true. Horace Walpole showed himself less than fair to Fielding on other occasions, and the persons present may have been respectable enough—the blind man was certainly Henry's half-brother John (of whom more in a moment), and the whore *may* have been his wife Mary, though I would not be so positive as the rest of the biographers on this point. Nevertheless, it may well be that Fielding continued to live in a rough-and-ready fashion after his translation. Habits of forty years do not drop off in a matter of weeks. He worked hard, in cramped and apparently 'fetid' surroundings, and it is more than likely that he wanted to relax in the evening. I should be very surprised if the three Irishmen were there to discuss finer points of jurisprudence. Fielding could be ill-tempered and unmannerly, and it is a distortion to portray him as uniformly sweet or ingratiating.

He was, after all, engaged in a bitter struggle against dreadful odds. He had to be available at all hours of the day and night, and could no longer recruit his health with essential rest—as even the harsh circuit existence had permitted. The slums of London lay all about him; the notorious district of St Giles was within five minutes' walk, and next to it sprawled the 'hundred of Drury', where the theatre involved fewer people than did organised sexual activity. The resources at his disposal were slender. For the parish of St Giles, with a population of 30,000 people, the list of ward officers ran: five constables, ten headboroughs, ten surveyors of the high-way, ten scavengers. St Mary le Strand had just one constable and two scavengers for something like 2,500 inhabitants; St Paul's, Covent Garden, a burgess with one assistant plus four constables to police a district with 5,000 residents. (I shall explain the role of these officers presently. For the moment it is enough to emphasise that there was as yet no corps of trained Bow Street runners, a force whose innovation we owe to the Fielding brothers.)

It was the kind of work which could only be done properly in the eighteenth century if the incumbent possessed a large private income, and this of course was anything but the case with Fielding. Ralph Allen could have made faster inroads into some of the problems, simply because he had the money to command men and materials when they were needed. But Fielding soldiered manfully on. It was not the degree of legal eminence he would have wished for: at the back of his mind he may still have harboured the old dream of rising to position of Justice of the King's Bench, like his maternal grandfather. Later on his cousin, still an obscure member of the bar, was to become a judge in the Exchequer and the Common Pleas. But the Gould illusions confronted the Fielding realities: a muddled life, a mixed reputation, and a notorious marriage. Worst of all, his health was steadily declining.

2

During this period of hectic activity Henry could give less attention than he wished to family matters. Another daughter was added to the household in Bow Street, she was christened at St Paul's, Covent Garden, on 6 January 1749, under the names Mary Amelia. Unhappily she was to survive only eleven months more. A week before Christmas she was buried in the same church. Although he lived technically in the parish of St Paul's, Fielding was still very close to his old haunts. The gentlest of saunters would have carried him back to his former parish of St Martin's. Few people can have changed their residence so often without altering their general locale. Fielding operated within something like one quarter of a square mile, the whole of his time in London. As playwright, law student, barrister and magistrate he was surrounded by the same familiar landmarks, between Temple Bar and Charing Cross. Then as now, careerists tended to drop their former associates as they moved up in the world, deserting the scene of their imprudent youth. Fielding stuck to the same quarter of town. If he frequented the Rose Tavern in Russell Street during his dramatic days, he is unlikely to have kept away from this enticingly adjacent hostelry now he was the Bow Street magistrate. If he had spent convivial evenings at Old Slaughter's coffee-house as a bachelor and a newly married man, it is hard to see him imposing any self-denying ordinance in middle age.

By now his half-brother John was sharing his home. John was a child of General Fielding's second marriage, and had reached the age of twenty-eight. He had been totally blind for about ten years: the cause is not known. He was to follow Henry into the Commission of Peace and make an even greater contribution to penal matters. But it was as manager of a joint venture called the Universal Register Office, opened on 19 February 1749, that John was to engage in his only active collaboration with his elder brother. The office served as a kind of Universal Aunts, indeed the latter title may have been partly borrowed from this source (there was, too, an old phrase 'universal maid', meaning a general servant). The firm was in business as an employment agency and as an estate-management service; it engaged in money-lending, insurance, and all kinds of brokerage. Its advice function extended to travel, which anticipates Thomas Cook in the field of tourism by almost a century. Since it was a hard time to get servants —it always has been—Londoners were particularly glad to use the office for this purpose. It was lucky that nobody had yet invented the newspaper personal column.

As it was, the office prospered, with John in day-to-day control of its routine. After a short spell in Cecil Street the office moved across the Strand to the corner of Castle Court, opposite the recently built block of shops known as New Exchange Buildings—admired, as an historian of London puts it, 'as the latest idea in shop planning'. The office probably occupied the upper floor of one of the retail premises clustered round about —print shops, wallpaper-makers, ironmongers, druggists. A few half-timbered houses survived in this part of the Strand, although they were outnumbered by chaste Georgian frontages which made a striking contrast to the angular seventeenth-century façades alongside them. Within three years the brothers found it profitable to open a branch office in Bishopsgate, and the office in time attracted rivalry in the shape of the Public Register Office— equally a private enterprise, despite the official-looking title. Henry had twenty shares in the business, which he divided between his wife and surviving children in his will.

The multifarious character of the tasks undertaken by the Universal Register Office may be illustrated by one piquant example. It was the London outlet for the sale of a quack preparation called Glastonbury water. The brew had become famous after an old man named Matthew Chancellor had received a miraculous cure of 'asthma and phthisic'—the second word means consumption, but was loosely applied to any chronic lung condition. Chancellor was supposed to have dreamt that he should take a glassful of water regularly from the spring at the foot of Tor Hill, Glastonbury. Legend had it that the spring issued from the Holy Grail, brought to Glastonbury by Joseph of Arimathea—whose journey to Avalon with the Grail had been recounted by Malory and others.

In April 1751 Chancellor swore an affidavit concerning his cure, and immediately a stampede began. Invalids deserted Bath and the Bristol Hotwell in order to drink the waters at Glastonbury. Meanwhile the bottled variety was shipped up to London and made available through the Universal. A puff for the product appeared in a newspaper on 31 August, under the signature of 'Z.Z'. This item was later reprinted in the *Gentleman's Magazine* as the work of 'J[ustice]e F[ieldin]g'. It is not certain whether either brother wrote the article, and if so which. I am much more inclined to think Henry the author. We know that he went down to Glastonbury in August, with his wife and daughter, and returned to London next month greatly improved in health (as the papers reported). He was more experienced in journalism than John, and I suspect more unscrupulous in promoting any activity of his own. For example, he inserted some glowing references to the Universal into the first edition of *Amelia*, published three months later. Finally, he had a lifelong connection with Glastonbury, and a strong reason for celebrating the wonders of the mysterious hill he had gazed on as an infant. John had no links with the area whatsoever.

We are told that the fame of these healing waters was of short duration. A pump room was opened, on the Bath model, and Chancellor himself appointed pumper. But the venture never really threatened to rival larger spas: as Dudden wrote, 'the quiet old town bored fashionable people'. Meanwhile the office continued to sell Glastonbury water at a shilling a bottle (dose, half a pint every morning, *fasting!*). Without the inspiration of Henry's energy and acumen, the medicine fell into obscurity. If he had lived long enough to write another novel, he would assuredly have lauded the virtues of Glastonbury water in its pages.

In the event, *Amelia* contains tributes to Dr Ward's drop, a preparation of antimony and arsenic not very reliable in its curative properties (see page 213). There is appreciative mention of Dr Ranby, who had been involved in the battle of physicians after Robert Walpole's death. A kind word is even allotted to Dr James's powder, destined—as Cross memorably observes—'to shorten the life of Laurence Sterne and to kill Oliver Goldsmith'. James, bibulous schoolfellow of Samuel Johnson, had compiled a medical dictionary with Johnson's aid; his powders were tried out on George III during the king's first bout of madness. Most remarkable of all is the eulogy of Thomas Thompson, whose primitive physic occasions an extended sight—perhaps (Cross suggests) in lieu of a fee. Thompson had attended Pope just before the poet's death, and many believed that his ministrations had done nothing to defer that event. He also treated the Prince of Wales before poor Fred made *his* exit from the world, but it is not clear in this instance whether Thompson was allowed by the royal physicians to try out his remedies, lethal or otherwise. Another aspect of the quack is his alleged membership of the so-called Medmenham Monks, otherwise known as the Hell Fire Club, who practised satanic rites in a ruined abbey on the Thames near Marlow. The owner of this strange place was Sir Francis Dashwood who had subscribed to Fielding's *Miscellanies*. So had others alleged to be among the leading spirits, notably George Bubb Dodington and John Tucker. But we have no hard documentary evidence as to what went on at these revels, and indeed some historians have doubted if the Monks ever really existed.*

Thompson, at all events, started to treat Fielding around 1749. A newspaper report for 28 December describes what had happened:

Justice Fielding has no mortification in his foot as has been reported: that gentleman has indeed been dangerously ill with a fever, and a fit of the gout, in which he was attended by Dr. Thompson, an eminent physician, and is now so well recovered as to be able to execute his office as usual.

His old enemy, gout, was reasserting itself, and Thompson's 'cure' was apparently no more than temporary. Still, he remained loyal to the quack, as did the Medmenham brotherhood: Dashwood, Dodington and others gave evidence of his medical skill in a libel suit in 1752. Gout and smallpox were his specialities: enough patients survived his attentions, no doubt by mere chance, to allow him to go on practising and even flourishing.

Luckily Thompson made no pretence to obstetrics, and so the birth of a

*The myth that has accreted around the Hell Fire Club is exemplified in a popular book on the subject of the monks, published not so long ago. Its author draws a vivid picture of one of the 'parties' at the abbey. Dashwood is reclining at the head of the table, and near him 'Lady Mary [Wortley Montagu] was lying on another couch . . . She would leave the next day for Constantinople, where she was to write the series of letters on art, literature, gossip and politics which have made her famous. Later, she was to introduce from Turkey the technique of inoculation against smallpox.' William Hogarth is also there, sitting 'quietly in a corner sketching his fellow members' The 'half-witted Earl of Oxford' has a girl in his lap; he has been admitted to the club to spite his brother Horace Walpole. Bubb-Dodington (*sic*) is giggling as he chokes on vintage claret, with a naked nun perched on his huge belly.' It is a pity to have to remark that Lady Mary went to Constantinople in 1716, when Dashwood was eight years old, and brought back the method of inoculation in 1718, thirty-odd years before he acquired Medmenham. There is not a shred of evidence to connect Hogarth with the Monks; the statement that his sketches 'would later appear in the "Rake's Progress" and the "Harlot's Progress" ' again puts the scene back into the first third of the century. In any case there are no orgies in the *Harlot*, and nothing in the *Rake* that London night-spots could not afford to the artist's imagination. Lastly, the brother of Horace Walpole was Earl of *Orford*. Though always eccentric, he did not become insane until the 1770s—by which time most of those alleged to be present were dead.

daughter to Mary Fielding at the start of 1750 took place without alarms. She was named Sophia, commemorating Henry's finest literary portrait of a woman. Sophia was still alive when her father made his will in 1754, but she cannot have survived very many years longer. Sadly, Henry junior, the elder son of the family, died at the age of eight during this same year, 1750. So did two of the novelist's sisters; a third followed in 1751, which left only Sarah alive of the four girls born to Edmund and Sarah Fielding. It is the kind of horrific necrology with which people in earlier centuries were numbingly familiar.

3

Fielding did not take long to make his mark as a justice of the peace. On 12 May 1749 he was elected chairman of the Quarter Sessions at Hick's Hall, that is the courthouse in John Street behind Smithfield market. The next month, on 29 June, he delivered his first charge to the jury (a formal oration on the opening of sessions) at the Westminster Court House; it was published three weeks later 'by order of the court and the unanimous request of the grand jury'. Fielding sent a copy to the Lord Chancellor on 21 July, enclosing too his 'draught of a bill for the better preventing street robberies'. Curiously, another early novelist, Daniel Defoe, had produced towards the end of his career a scheme directed towards the same goal. Fielding's own charge calls on the citizens of Westminster to act as the natural censors of public behaviour. He inveighs against masquerades and dancing-parties, brothels and gaming-houses, blasphemy and libel. Even Samuel Foote's popular shows at Covent Garden theatre, involving mime and mimicry, come into the line of fire. This may suggest a puritanical Fielding very different from our general picture of his character. But moral reformation had always been an aspect of his practical Christian creed, and now that he had reached a position of some authority he intended to apply the existing law without fear or favour. There was widespread admiration for the stand Fielding had taken. People had been looking for a strong lead: even de Veil, energetic as he had been, had not been above suspicion of 'trading' and had achieved only limited success in cleaning up the city.

The problems were immense. London was a dirty, ill-lit place which in some quarters became lost in a tangle of impenetrable alleys and festering courts. This made the actual commission of crime easier; and of course it was not an environment conducive to high-minded civic virtue. Poverty, malnutrition, and squalor made life for a high proportion of London residents a short and unpleasant experience: the torpor depicted in Hogarth's *Gin Lane* (1751) was occasionally broken by a burst of destructive energy.

Many of these factors were to be analysed in Fielding's masterly *Enquiry into the Causes of the Late Increase in Robbers*, published just one month earlier than *Gin Lane*. More important than any other aspect of the situation was the total inadequacy of the machinery of justice and of policing arrangements.

Whatever one may think of the magisterial system, there is no doubt that the majority of JPs up and down the country attempted to dispense justice fairly according to their lights. But London had its own peculiar breed of 'trading justices', such as Fielding portrayed in plays and novels—corrupt and brutal to an astonishing degree. Moreover, the inquisitorial powers of the magistrate were such that an inactive or venal man could effectively paralyse criminal detection. At the start of *Amelia* Fielding drily observes, 'I own I have sometimes been inclined to think that this office of a Justice of the Peace requires some knowledge of the law . . . and yet certain it is, Mr Thrasher [the magistrate] never read one syllable of the matter.' In a tradition of genteel amateurism, corrupt individuals could make their jobs remunerative enough.

There was no proper police force. The so-called constables were just unpaid local citizens, obliged to serve for a year at a time in this unpopular capacity. Obliged, that is, unless they chose to pay a deputy to act on their behalf—and that inevitably meant introducing a further level of corruption. Fielding inherited eighty constables and found he could trust only six of these. There were other 'offices of burden', as the significant phrase ran. The archaic title of headborough belonged to a primitive kind of law-and-order functionary, going back to manorial times, whose utility in the eighteenth century was distinctly doubtful, and who sometimes confined his activity to feasting at the expense of the parish. In Westminster the burgesses were also unpaid conscripts, as were highway surveyors and scavengers allegedly charged with matters of health and safety in the streets. At least in 1750 there were probably fewer 'wandering hogs' than the capital had known in Elizabethan times, but dung-heaps remained and public nuisances went on unchallenged by municipal action. Worse, if anything, were the 'offices of profit', bought and then held for life (unless re-sold). Gaolkeepers and the officers of sheriffs and bailiffs generally fell into this category. Men in such positions recouped the purchase price by charging fees and fines to all with whom they came into contact. As we have seen, prison warders were notorious for extracting garnish from the unfortunate people who came into their custody.

As pathetic as any group were the watchmen, 'poor old decrepit people' as Fielding called them, paid a shilling a night to patrol the streets, armed with a lamp and a pole 'which some of them are scarce able to lift'. Notoriously they passed their evenings in the gin cellars, prudently avoiding the hreatening activity out on the streets. The last group theoretically on the ide of law and order were the thief-takers. Rewards had been paid to nformers for many years, and the profession of thief-taker institutionalised his unlovely and unreliable means of catching offenders. Not every such person developed into a Jonathan Wild, but they generally took care to mpeach the unsuccessful criminals rather than the real enemies of society.

Steadily Fielding set about reform. He had the assistance of a remarkable officer of the law in the person of Saunders Welch, the High Constable of Holborn. He was four years younger than Fielding, similarly robust in build, a self-confident extrovert who gained the admiration and friendship of Dr Johnson. The Great Cham even attended Welch's court for a whole winter, when the constable had been promoted to the bench: but all that he witnessed was 'an almost uniform tenor of misfortune, wretchedness and prolifigacy'. Also leagued in the fight to improve the state of criminal detection was Fielding's clerk Joshua Brogden, whom he had inherited from de Veil. When he wrote to Lord Chancellor Hardwicke he actually proposed hat Brogden should be appointed a J.P., but nothing came of this idea. It should in fairness be added that Fielding himself was not above looking for a tidy sinecure—no one could survive long in the eighteenth century unless he was alive to such possibilities. On 3 July 1749, when hotly engaged 'in endeavouring to suppress a dangerous riot', he still had a moment to write to the Duke of Bedford, asking for the post of solicitor to the excise 'now vacant by the death of Mr. Selwyn'. The Duke in due course made a different appointment, but he did arrange for Fielding to receive an annual pension out of secret service funds. This was an ordinary means of rewarding loyal public servants, and implied nothing truly clandestine or embarrassing. The amount was probably quite small—perhaps £100 per year.

'The 'dangerous riot' mentioned in Fielding's letter constituted his first major challenge as a magistrate. It involved a number of sailors, and it is significant that the ending of a war (in this case that of the Austrian Succession) always created a social problem with a large influx of discharged soldiers and seamen—the ending of the Marlborough wars had seen the same pattern, and the growth of piracy in the Caribbean owed much to this circumstance. More than forty thousand men had been demobilised after the Peace of Aix-la-Chapelle, and now in 1749 unemployment was at a high level. Modern research has shown that of forty-four persons who were hanged in London during the year (male and female), more than half had been at sea. Fielding's laudable desire was to clamp down on social predators who had been taking advantage of the lax enforcement of law; his campaign happened to coincide with a difficult economic situation and a tense feeling among ordinary Londoners.

On Friday 30 June, the day following Fielding's emphatic charge to the jury, a fracas developed at a bawdy-house called the Crown. Two sailors claimed to have been robbed but could get no satisfaction from the brothel's keeper. On the following night they returned with a party of shipmates, and proceeded to wreck the Crown. Considerately, they 'suffered no injury to be done to the poor damsels' who made their living in the house. Troops were summoned, but it took until three in the morning to disperse the rioters.

The next evening, a Sunday, some four hundred sailors arrived in force. They threatened to pull down all bawdy-houses, which would have been a lengthy undertaking. They duly set about one brothel belonging to Lord Stanhope, and then turned their attentions to the Star at the east end of the Strand. It was in a part of London long familiar to Fielding—his house at Old Boswell Court lay just around the corner. As it happened, he had gone away for the weekend; but Saunders Welch, returning from a visit to a friend, saw the glare from some distance off. He made his way to the Star, where the keeper, Peter Wood, told him the mob of sailors were threatening to take his house apart. Welch summoned troops from the Tilt Yard, in White-hall. The detachment of soldiers arrived to find the Star largely in ruins. However, they were able to contain the situation and made some arrests.

On Monday Fielding arrived back in town to take charge of operations. Separate bodies of rioters were now making attacks on scattered properties; they also went along to Bow Street and rescued one of their number who had been arrested the night before. Fielding thereupon sent Welch to the Secretary of War to get additional troops for the protection of his court. Armed guards were posted in the Strand and at other strategic points. A rumour had spread that many hundreds, if not thousands, of sailors had assembled on Tower Hill and were about to seize the royal armoury. It was an inflated estimate of the scale of trouble Fielding could expect, but he was probably right to believe that the riots would intensify unless strong measures were taken. It happened that the Star lay next door to a banker's establish-ment, and there was understandable concern lest the rioters should choose that for their next target. Fielding's concern is evident in a letter he wrote that Monday to the Duke of Bedford, which has come to light only very recently:

My Lord,
   I think it my duty to acquaint your grace that I have received repeated inform-ations of upwards of 3000 sailors now in arms about Wapping and that they threaten to march to this end of the town this night, under pretence of demolishing all bawdy houses. I have an officer and fifty men and submit to your Grace what more assistance may be necessary. I sent a messenger five hours ago to the Secretary at War but have yet no answer. I am, my Lord,
                                   Your Grace's most obliged
                                         obedient humble servant H ffielding

In the event, though the day brought further tension and sporadic violence, peace was restored and the riots ceased.

One of the prisoners who came before Fielding for examination and whom he committed to Newgate was a young barber and manservant called Bosavern Penlez. Despite his exotic name, he was thoroughly English—the son indeed of a clergyman from Exeter. On the Monday morning he had been found by two members of the watch, lying in a drunken stupor in Bell Yard, about a hundred and fifty yards from the demolished Star. Stuffed under his clothes the watchmen found a large quantity of women's linen, which he could not account for. Peter Wood subsequently deposed that the linen belonged to his wife, and had been stolen by Penlez during the riot. The keeper of a disorderly house is never likely to be regarded as a trustworthy witness and many people have doubted if Penlez had anything to do with the destruction of the Star. Whether he was engaged in looting, later on, is a different question.

Seven rioters had been arrested during the disturbances, but some escaped, died in custody or otherwise cheated the law. Only two were found guilty of offences under the Riot Act, and one of these was reprieved the night before his execution was due to take place. Only Penlez actually went to the gallows. There had been an aggressive campaign to get him a reprieve also, and when this ultimately failed there were ominous predictions that his execution on 18 October would inspire further disorders of an even more serious kind. The risk was heightened by the fact that fourteen other men were to be hanged on the same day, and all of them were sailors. It was quite common for friends and relatives of the condemned man to attempt to retrieve the body after it was taken down from the gallows—otherwise it went to the surgeons for their anatomical researches. On this occasion the Sheriff of London decided on a policy of maintaining what is now called a low profile. He kept the military presence in the background, and when the hangings were completed he handed the corpses over to the assembled sailors. Thus the frequent Tyburn riot was averted. Indeed, from this time onward it became less usual to allow the surgeons to carry away the body.

The whole affair had become a *cause célèbre*. It was not only the most dramatic episode in which Fielding was actively involved as a magistrate. It also marked the moment of his highest public visibility. The Penlez business was mixed up with wider political issues, and Fielding had to face criticism from a wide range of sources. On the narrow legal front, there were several aspects of the case which his opponents took up. Had Wood perjured himself in his charges against Penlez? Had the Riot Act been read in the due form? Was Penlez involved in rioting, looting or was he simply a sneak-thief who had taken advantage of the confusion? We still cannot answer these questions, although there are finite truths here if only we had the evidence. Then there are matters of judgment: was it necessary or appropriate to call out the troops? And was it reasonable for Fielding (who had attacked brothels in his charge) to devote so much zeal to prevent the mob from pulling them down?

In November Fielding produced his own version of events, in the shape of a pamphlet entitled *A True State of the Case of Bosavern Penlez*. It could not settle the issues I have mentioned, to the satisfaction of everyone that is; and critics exist right up to the present. In the narrative I have given, I have chosen largely to follow the fullest modern account, which was written by Peter Linebaugh in 1975.* His detailed information seems to me more reliable than that used by previous students of Fielding—who have generally seen the magistrate as acting in a firm and admirable manner. Linebaugh terms the *True State* 'frankly polemical and self-interested', which is apt enough. However, his own treatment is polemical in a different way—he sets out to explain the attitude of the London crowd to the surgeons' activities, and assumes (rather than demonstrates) the righteousness of their cause. Although he can find no evidence to support the accusation that Fielding was paid an annual sum by the pimps to leave them unmolested, he thinks it requires mention that the *Enquiry into the Causes of the Late Increase in Robbers* does not emphasise the role of prostitution in the structure of London crime. Moreover, Linebaugh considers it is worthy of comment that 'when he came to write of the riots in November . . . it appeared that the magistrate's duty lay less in bringing down bawdy-houses than in keeping them standing.' The strange logic here must be that, since Fielding attacked the houses of immorality in his charge, he ought to have condoned their destruction by the rioters, regardless of arson, looting, fighting and other disorders. We can argue about the effectiveness of Fielding's methods of suppressing the riot, although it must be remembered that he arrived on the scene when indecisive officials had allowed a considerable head of steam to build up. And we can wonder if the evidence really was sufficient to send poor Penlez to his death—although, again, the Old Bailey trial was not conducted by the Bow Street magistrate. What is surely hard seriously to maintain is that Fielding ought to have left the rioters to raze to the ground any house they considered to be one of ill fame.

*See Peter Linebaugh, 'The Tyburn Riot against the Surgeons', *Albion's Fatal Tree : Crime and Society in Eighteenth-Century England* (1975 and reprinted 1977). This is an interesting and well documented survey, but its political assumptions make it less than objective in its attitude towards Fielding. Nevertheless, he emerges with surprisingly clean hands: Linebaugh is compelled to admit that Fielding's conduct as a magistrate was not influenced by 'the dirtiest money on earth'— a very large concession at such a juncture. At the time, it is true, *Old England* suggested that Fielding had reasons of his own for protecting the bawdy-houses: from being a customer of the 'mothers of iniquity', it is alleged, he had become a patron. But it would not do to take everything in *Old England* for gospel.

4

After this controversial episode, Fielding must have hoped that life would settle down to more routine affairs—though he was anything but idle. From time to time he had to deal with cases involving organised vice, and there is no sign that he adopted a soft posture on these occasions. More run-of-the-mill offences were larceny and pickpocketing, though a case of house-breaking heard in July 1749 stood out because the property was that of a merchant just across the street from Fielding's courtroom. The Universal continued to operate, even if John rather than Henry took the leading share in that undertaking. Other relationships continued to flourish. In August 1749, while the Penlez story was still the chief topic of conversation, Fielding wrote to George Lyttelton the only letter to have survived between the two old friends, in which he congratulates Lyttelton upon his second marriage— the bride's dowry of £20,000 must have compensated for the absence of the bloom of youth. Fielding also took the chance to promote the interests of a more recent friend, Edward Moore, an unsuccessful linen-draper who had turned to the composition of sentimental comedy; but again his intercession failed. Men of power in the eighteenth century received a steady stream of such requests; and not even a close associate of long standing, as Fielding was, could always gain his point.

Things began to boil up again with the Westminster by-election, held between 22 November and 8 December. It was one of the noisiest contests of the era. The constituency had on its rolls some six thousand voters, more independent and politically aware than most electors in other parts of the country. Naturally Fielding gave his support to the ministerial candidate, who happened to be none other than Bedford's brother-in-law, Viscount Trentham. The opposition was represented by Sir George Vandeput, a baronet who belonged to a well-known city family: he had subscribed to the *Miscellanies* six years earlier. The struggle was bitter and prolonged. On 14 November trouble was heralded by a fracas at Fielding's old stamping-ground, the Little Theatre in the Haymarket. A visiting troupe of French actors were performing, much to the dislike of a claque organised by the opposition, who could rely on a solid core of chauvinism after the less than glorious outcome of the War of the Austrian Succession. According to the opposition, Trentham had hired fifteen bullies to defend the French players and to assault the patriots among the theatre audience.

During the contest the Penlez affair was dragged in at every opportunity, and Fielding found himself once more under attack for the part he had played. On 27 November he cast his own vote for Lord Trentham, and it is probable that he intervened in the pamphlet war. All the techniques of publicity then available were utilised by the rival factions: the Duke of

Bedford was said to have distributed a quarter of a million leaflets in support of his brother-in-law. This seems excessive, even though Westminster was notoriously the most volatile constituency in the land. We can be sure from extant ledgers that printing runs of 10,000 and more were involved, and small handbills may have been produced in even greater quantities. On the other side, the opposition had recourse to a form of *agitprop* almost resembling street theatre. A number of demonstrations were carefully stage-managed, including a procession through the streets headed by the ghost of Penlez. According to one story, Penlez came back from the grave to vote for Vandeput. There were many tradesmen around the Strand, who would not have held the franchise in most constituencies, and were willing to support the 'independent' candidate for a variety of reasons. But Trentham had behind him the Bedford money and influence (the Duke was by far the biggest landowner in the city), and he finally prevailed. The magistrates balloted 76 to 7 in favour of the ministerial candidate. Some accused them of bending the law to suit Trentham's interest, even to the extent of trumping up charges against opposition activists.

Fielding's own involvement became most visible after an affray on 24 November. Violence broke out at the hustings in Covent Garden, and some ministerial sympathisers were arrested by the high constable of the parish. They included Benjamin Boswell, said by many to be the ringleader of the pro-Trentham mob. Boswell was quickly bailed out by Fielding, which earned him the familiar taunts in the press: 'If any person happens to be taken into custody for riotous behaviour, Mr. Justice *Trotplaid* attends to prevent commitment.' Evidence discovered by Martin Battestin shows that Fielding was indeed responsible for procuring Boswell's release from the parish roundhouse. What we cannot say for certain is whether or not this was an improper act. Two years later the poet Paul Whitehead was still raking over the electoral coals, and accusing Fielding of perverting the course of justice. The charge stung Fielding, who committed a street-hawker to Bridewell for selling Whitehead's 'scandalous and libellous' pamphlet, and ordered the work to be publicly burnt in Bow Street. Fielding may genuinely have believed that Boswell was innocent, and it would be nice to think that this was so: but we are bound to regard the episode with some suspicion.

For his own part, Fielding seems likely to have had a hand in a ministerial manifesto called *Ten Queries Submitted to Every Sober, Honest, and Disinterested Elector*. Ten thousand copies were printed and distributed on 24 November. At about this juncture Fielding published his *True State* of the Penlez affair, which had been printed in September but not issued to the public. The occasion no doubt was an opposition pamphlet called *The Case of the Unfortunate Bosavern Penlez*, which treated the executed man as 'a harmless unthinking lad' who had been out on a pleasant frolic. A fortnight after the queries came a pamphlet entitled *The Covent-Garden Journal*, which anticipates the name of a periodical Fielding was to run in 1752. Opinion is divided on whether Fielding wrote this broadsheet, but on balance I am inclined to agree with Battestin that he probably did. No fewer than 13,000 copies were printed, at the expense of the Duke of Bedford. The putative author is 'Paul Wronghead, of the Fleet, Esq.,' an obvious thrust at Paul Whitehead, a hack writer who had spent years in the Fleet Prison and who was allegedly to become secretary of the Medmenham monks—a post his contact with Dodington, amongst others, may have brought him. By this time Dodington was in the opposition led by the Prince of Wales; he voted for Vandeput in 1749, and on his way to the poll 'met with a great crowd, but great civility.'

As I have said, Fielding supported what was ultimately the winning side. Trentham sat in the Commons until 1754, when he succeeded as the second Earl Gower: ahead of him lay a marquisate, and terms as a Lord of the Admiralty, as Lord Privy Seal, as Master of the Horse, as Master of the Wardrobe, as Lord Chamberlain, as Lord President of the Council and as Lord Privy Seal once more. So consummate a courtier would have been an invaluable friend for Fielding, had he lived.

Some may find it disturbing to find Fielding locked so tightly into the power structure. Certainly Battestin's findings serve to establish beyond doubt the extent of his dependence upon the Duke of Bedford. From early in 1748 (when the post of High Steward was perhaps granted him) there are signs of repeated favours asked and—generally—granted. There are letters to the agent Butcher from Twickenham, where Mary lay sheltered, speaking of various unspecified acts of kindness by the Duke. Through 1750 and 1751 we get further hints, and further promises of Fielding's intention to preserve the peace. (A recurrent strain, too, is the mention of gout: 'my feet are so tender I am not yet able to walk'.) Obscure as some of the letters are, it is apparent that Fielding saw it as his duty to promote the Duke's interests in and out of season. Whether or not this ever ran to anything like partiality in his conduct on the bench, we cannot be sure. It is not very comforting to find that he presided over electoral feasts at inns around Bow Street and Drury Lane during the Westminster contest, when a large number of voters were treated to a Hogarthian repast in order to strengthen their attachment to the Trentham cause. We should remember that a system of client and patron ran through the whole of national life, not just party politics; and men who were too scrupulous to touch bribery were unlikely to progress far in any walk of business. But this would not, even by the standards of the time, justify corrupt practices on the bench. It may well be that Fielding was innocent of the charges levelled against him by the opposition in 1749, but it would be untrue to say that we can confidently acquit him of malpractice.

There were isolated disturbances during 1750, but nothing to compare with the election or the Penlez affair—or, for that matter, with the Wilkes and Gordon riots which John Fielding was to encounter as a magistrate. In May, Fielding wrote to Bedford promising to do the utmost in his power to preserve the peace. A few months later, on 25 November, he sent a message to a lawyer friend regarding an alleged conspiracy to assassinate the Lord Chancellor. Hardwicke had suppressed three gaming-houses, and information was laid that the keepers had devised a plot to revenge themselves on his lordship. In his letter Fielding announces the progress of his enquiries:

Their characters are such that perhaps three more likely men could not be found in the kingdom for the hellish purpose mentioned in the letter. As the particulars are many and the affair of such importance I beg to see you punctually at six this evening when I will be alone to receive you . . .

Such threats were commoner in the period than might be supposed, but of course they seldom came anywhere near fulfilment. Lord Hardwicke lived safely for another fourteen years, but it may not be that Fielding's detective work had anything to do with that.

As a magistrate he remained firm and attentive to his office. He made several small advances in the realm of administration and staffing. At the start of 1751 he wrote to the Duke of Newcastle, to get one of the local constables appointed gaoler of the New Prison at Clerkenwell. This time he was successful, and the keeper showed himself an excellent choice. Later in the same year John Fielding joined his half-brother on the Westminster bench: the steady deterioration in Henry's health made this a particularly desirable course. Meanwhile the elder brother drew up a set of guide-lines for the eighty constables in his service, and it was no doubt with his approval that Saunders Welch produced his *Observations on the Office of a Constable* (1754). Welch remained a tower of strength, his encyclopaedic knowledge of every nook and cranny in London often speeding the course of detection. By December 1753 Fielding was convinced of his suitability for appointment to the Commission of Peace, and he duly made this recommendation to Lord Hardwicke, citing Welch's 'universal good character' and 'the many eminent services he hath done the public'. The recommendation was followed, but not until after Fielding's death. It was in 1755 that Welch was appointed to the bench; around this time he took over as co-proprietor of the Universal Register Office along with his judicial colleague John Fielding.

There is a famous story of Welch effecting an arrest by climbing from the roof of a coach into the first-floor bedroom of a house off Covent Garden, and then dragging a highwayman by the hair out of the bed in which he lay. Fielding's physical incapacities ruled out such acts of heroism, but that does not mean that he was content to sit quietly in Bow Street. A newspaper account dating from June 1751 illustrates the point that his course of life was anything but placid:

Information having been given to Mr. Justice Fielding that a set of gamesters who had lately received a great defeat from that magistrate, had rallied again, and repaired their fortifications in a house fronting the Thames in Surrey Street, the said Justice resolved to attack them a second time, and, as several gamesters had before sallied out by the waterfront, a disposition was now made to attack them by land and water, for which purpose a constable with a party of guards to attack by land [was placed in position.] But notwithstanding all precautions of secrecy, the garrison had, by some of their spies, received previous notice and had entirely evacuated the place before it was visited by the constables, who, without any opposition the second time, made a total demolition of all tables and other apparatus for gaming.

All too often the object of such a raid, whether gambling den or thieves' kitchen, seems to have been vacated by the time that the officers arrived. The tradition of corrupt and amateurish detection was too well entrenched to vanish overnight. It is within the bounds of possibility that Fielding may himself have connived in an occasional tip-off, but we have no evidence of this.

Inevitably there was little time for Henry to pursue his literary career. After the pamphlet setting out his side of the Penlez affair, which appeared in November 1749, there is a gap for more than a year. Only one publication is listed in the bibliography for 1750, and that was the long-delayed publication of his early play *The Author's Farce* in its revised version. Whether or not he had anything to do with its appearance so late in the day, the sight of his play in print must have served to jog Fielding's memory. It took the hard-pressed Bow Street magistrate back to his days as a swaggering young man about town. It brought to his mind a time when his colleagues had been not brother John and Saunders Welch, but the Cibbers and Kitty Clive—when he owed his advancement not to the wealthy Duke of Bedford but to the suffrage of the town, especially in that cramped little theatre on the unfashionable side of the Haymarket.

Early in 1751 he broke his silence with *An Enquiry into the Causes of the Late Increase in Robbers*, published by Millar on 19 January at the price of half a crown. It is the most searching of all his social tracts, full of concrete and constructive ideas on all aspects of organised robbery in the metropolis. His eloquent denunciation of such social blights as the 'heroic' Tyburn carnival and the widespread addiction to gin has been quoted by social historians ever since. For example:

The day appointed by law for the thief's shame is the day of his glory in his own opinion. His procession to Tyburn, and his last moments there, are all triumphant, attended with the compassion of the meek and tender-hearted, and with the applause, admiration, and envy of all the bold and hardened. His behaviour in his present condition, not the crimes, however atrocious soever, which brought him to it, are the subject of contemplation. And if he hath sense enough to temper his boldness with any degree of decency, his death is spoken of by many with honour, by most with pity, and by all with approbation.

'The great cause of this evil', Fielding concludes, 'is the frequency of executions. . . . The different effects which executions produce in the minds of the spectators in the country, where they are rare, and in London, where they are common, will convince us by experience.' This is a good example of Fielding's direct, masculine prose—balanced without any mechanical quality, clear but never insipid.

The unregulated sale of spirits had for many years been a cause of major concern. Fifteen years earlier Walpole had introduced what Dorothy George terms 'a heroic remedy', but the provisions of this act proved ineffectual. Another attempt was made in 1743, replacing a policy of virtual prohibition with one of officially licensed outlets. The results were little better. A parliamentary committee was now set up to see if more effective controls could be brought in, and the outcome was a new Act in 1751. Fielding's powerful advocacy had played a major part in clearing the ground for the new measure, which at last began to make some inroads into the consumption of cheap and lethal spirits.

Fielding's general outlook on crime was realistic but also compassionate. He attempts to explore the etiology of deviant behaviour, finding the roots of evil in institutions such as gaming-houses. He goes on to illustrate the connection of crime with poverty—a trite message today, perhaps, but one which bore repetition in 1751. He distinguishes between the merely idle and those who are genuinely unable to work through physical or mental incapacity—we should recall that such people were more commonly encountered in those days, when hereditary ailments and infant malnutrition produced many crippled bodies and impaired minds. He criticises the appalling administration of the poor laws. The mechanics of justice are equally subjected to careful scrutiny, with several helpful suggestions on how the conviction of professional criminals might be better achieved. All in all, Fielding combines as few writers have been able to do the highest moral aspirations with a hardheaded sense of concrete possibilities. There are signs that several measures apart from the Gin Act were influenced in content and even drafting by the tract. This is the case most notably with regard to 'An Act for Preventing the Horrid Crime of Murder', which went through Parliament in 1752; and with regard to its immediate predecessor in the statute-book, the Disorderly Houses Act. Other bills dealing with the poor and proposing an enlightened kind of workhouse system were dropped in the Commons in the face of organised opposition, and they too owed their inspiration to Fielding.

The spirit of the *Enquiry* is very much the same as that informing Fielding's magistracy. We learn a year later of a typical act of administering the law: 'Several wretches being apprehended the night before by Mr. Welch, were brought before Mr. Fielding and Mr. Errington: when one who was in a dreadful condition from the itch was recommended to the overseers [parish officers who administered the poor law]; another, who appeared guilty of no crime but poverty, had money given to her to enable her to follow her trade in the market.' A poor woman with three children was discharged against the strict letter of the law, 'the evidence not being positive'.

Not everyone approved of such judicial leniency, even though Fielding reserved it for cases of genuine hardship. There was more unanimity about the merits of his *Enquiry*. Even Horace Walpole—who had never been a friend of Fielding—was moved to speak of the 'admirable treatise' written by the Bow Street magistrate. The *Monthly Review* gave the tract a warm welcome; and after years of opposition Fielding was beginning to hear the unaccustomed sound of applause. A few weeks after the *Enquiry* came a slighter effort, that is a pamphlet describing the operations of the Universal Register Office. The preface is by John Fielding, but the main text has always been attributed to Henry. To tell the truth, the threepenny pamphlet is not much different from what we call today promotional literature, with some irony attaching itself to the noun. It is strange for us to think that a great creative artist could—in a period not so very remote from our own—move so easily into the rhetoric of commerce.

In April 1751 we can get one of our rare personal glimpses of Fielding. A clergyman named Richard Hurd—later to become a bishop and to be offered the see of Canterbury—was invited to dinner with Ralph Allen; in whom he found 'good sense in conjunction with the plainest manners'. On the same occasion he had been introduced to another guest: 'Mr. Fielding, a poor, emaciated, worn-out rake, whose gout and infirmities have got the better even of his buffoonery.' Even the better-disposed Edward Moore was inclined to attribute Fielding's declining state to the rash life he had led: 'Fielding continues to be visited for his sins so as to be wheeled about from room to room. . . . You will be pleased to note that Fielding is a wit, that his disorder is gout, and intemperance the cause.' Both these quotations come from private correspondence; no doubt they reflect what many people were saying more or less openly. Gout is now a faintly comic complaint; at that time it was often seen as the just reward of intemperance.

The amenities of Bath provided the sick man with a welcome respite from his ill-paid struggles with the misery and squalor of outcast London. He had not yet acquired his country retreat at Ealing, and it was all the more necessary for him to escape occasionally to the company of Allen. Bath was a place where people frequently went to die, as the tablets bearing distinguished names in the Abbey so clearly testify. Half the great composers seem to have died in Vienna, and half the élite of the English nation expired at this period in a town built around hospitals, pump-rooms and apothecaries' shops. It was a centre for the chair-borne; all the amusements were sedentary, and even young people had to observe a protocol suited to the aged and incapacitated. Some of the walking wounded could at least explain their limp by reference to a military career—there was old Field-Marshal Wade,* a veteran of both campaigns against the Jacobites and a friend of Allen's, who installed himself in a fashionably Palladian house in the Abbey Churchyard and perambulated gently round the streets until he died in 1748. Allen promptly erected a statue of him in the grounds at Prior Park, dressed in full Roman regalia. But Henry Fielding had elected to follow another path from that of his father, the general, and his ailing condition could argue no heroic past. He probably expected that he would breathe his last here. His sister Sarah was to do so, and although she was buried up the hill at Charlcombe (where her brother had married Charlotte, long ago, in such mysterious circumstances), she was to be accorded a memorial tablet in the Abbey.

The tradition is that both Henry and Sarah lived at various times in the lodge at Widcombe manor. Widcombe House survives today, next to the church of St Thomas à Becket, in a rustic hamlet somehow preserved amid the busy clatter of modern Bath. It was rebuilt around 1727 in a warm gold stone, its facade elegant with seven bays and four Ionic pilasters, gazing up with no undue humility at Prior Park, built on the same axis half a mile away and three hundred feet higher on Combe Down. The lodge stands just behind, a trim two-storey building. There is no documentary proof that Henry actually stayed in the lodge (despite a plaque on the wall to this effect), but the idea is plausible. Allen's brother-in-law, Philip Bennet, lived in the manor house at this date, and if Fielding was to dine with his patron it would have been no kindness to impose anything but the shortest coach journey on his crippled limbs. It was an ideal setting, with its calm beauty and mellow architecture. Even today Widcombe breathes an air of seclusion, perhaps privilege—the very opposite of what Fielding knew in

---

*There used to be a tale that Allen's first wife was an illegitimate daughter of Wade, but it is probably without substance.

the tall, narrow house at Bow Street, surrounded as he was there by the stench and bustle of the courtroom. At least he could be sure that his hideaway in Bath would not be besieged by an angry mob of sailors.

Somehow Fielding found the inner resource to complete his last novel, *Amelia*. In contrast to the situation with *Tom Jones*, nobody seems to have known that he was engaged in this work. It has generally been assumed that most of the writing dates from 1751 and in the absence of contrary evidence this is a fair assumption. The work appeared in four duodecimo volumes on 19 December 1751, at a price of twelve shillings for the set. The dedication, to Ralph Allen, is dated a few days earlier. This time Andrew Millar paid £800 for the manuscript, a very considerable sum which meant that he needed to sell a large number of copies. He embarked on an aggressive advertising campaign, and managed to convince the book trade (as well as the reading public) that there were not enough copies to satisfy demand. The original printing is said to have been 5,000, all allegedly snapped up on the very first day. One of Millar's devices was to assert that he had been obliged to employ four printers to set up the type—that was not anything special for a long work—and could not get it bound in time: therefore he would sell the unbound sheets at 10s 6d. The trick was to make some orthodox publishing procedures seem to indicate the existence of a runaway best-seller. By January, according to the printer's ledgers, a further 3,000 copies were being set in type. That would suggest that Millar's publicity had served its turn, and that the public eagerly bought copies as fast as they could be produced.

And yet, from the very beginning, *Amelia* disappointed its readers. Right up to the present there is a tradition of disparagement. The loss of Fielding's exuberant comedy is particularly regretted. Again, some people find the solemn moralising of Dr Harrison, the good clergyman, pale stuff beside the human depth of Parson Adams. And instead of the likeable if indiscreet Tom Jones, we have a hero, Booth, who seems to bear a good deal of responsibility for his own misfortunes—and who causes his wife untold anguish. *Amelia* is a sombre, one-key novel, set with claustrophobic intensity within the shabbier purlieus of the inner city: even the high life of masquerades and oratorios has an air of stale debauchery. Fielding's dedication to Allen speaks of a design 'to promote the cause of virtue, and to expose some of the most glaring evils, as well public as private, which at present infest the country'. There is no attempt to keep at arm's length the reforming zeal which shone through Fielding's social pamphlets at this period of his life. This is bound to disappoint those who enjoyed *Tom Jones* for its breezy fun and rapscallion antics.

It is noteworthy that even scenes with comic potential are now imbued with a certain earnest or evangelical air. A good case in point is the confrontation between two doctors which appears early in Book V. Significantly perhaps, this chapter was omitted in Murphy's collected edition and in succeeding texts. It describes the efforts to cure Amelia's infant daughter of a fever. Ranged on one side is a self-important physician, backed by an apothecary; this individual relies on textbook prescriptions, employs a 'tremendous apparatus of phials and galleypots', arranged 'in battle-array all over the room', and recommends hourly doses of powders and draughts. Against him is placed Fielding's doctor Thompson, unpopular with the 'regular' profession as a quack. Needless to say it is the unorthodox regimen proposed by Thompson which works: after blooding and 'a cooling physic', the little girl is restored to full health within three days, much to Amelia's relief.

There are ample opportunities here for Fielding's mordant exposure of professional jealousy. But the rival physician and Arsenic, the apothecary, are seen as unpleasant rather than as funny or even grotesque. They lack the absurd inflation which Fielding had pumped into his earlier satiric characters: this can be seen in the exchange when Amelia's husband seeks Booth's permission to get a second opinion. The doctor asks Arsenic who is to be called to supply this opinion. 'What do you think of Dr Dosewell?' the apothecary replies.

'Nobody better,' cries the physician.—'I should have no objection to the gentleman,' answered Booth, 'but another hath been recommended to my wife.' He then mentioned the physician for whom they had just before sent. 'Who, sir?' cries the doctor, dropping his pen; and when Booth repeated the name of Thompson, 'Excuse me, sir,' cries the doctor hastily, 'I shall not meet him.'—'Why so, sir?' answered Booth. 'I will not meet him,' replied the doctor. 'Shall I meet a man who pretends to know more than the whole College, and would overturn the whole method of practice, which is so well established, and from which no one person hath pretended to deviate?' 'Indeed, sir,' cries the apothecary, 'you do not know what you are about, asking your pardon; why, he kills everybody he comes near.' 'That is not true,' said Mrs. Ellison. 'I have been his patient twice, and I am alive yet.' 'You have had good luck, then, madam,' answered the apothecary, 'for he kills everybody he comes near.' 'Nay, I know above a dozen others of my own acquaintance,' replied Mrs. Ellison, 'who have all been cured by him.' 'That may be, madam,' cries Arsenic; 'but he kills everybody for all that—why, madam, did you never hear of Mr.——? I can't think of the gentleman's name, though he was a man of great fashion; but everybody knows whom I mean.' 'Everybody, indeed, must know whom you mean,' answered Mrs. Ellison; 'for I never heard but of one, and that many years ago.'

Something of the old élan has disappeared. Maybe Fielding was tired: maybe he did not find it so easy to laugh away the cruelties and pomposity of a self-protective code among such a powerful group in society.

Amelia opens with a courtroom scene, and the entire novel never strays far from images of captivity. The presiding magistrate is Mr Thrasher, a trading justice of the worst kind. A motley collection of human flotsam is brought before Thrasher by the constable Mr Gotobed—indolent, doubtless, in all other branches of his duty. Several hapless wretches appear in the dock before we come to 'a young fellow, whose name was Booth', charged with beating the watchman in the execution of his duty and breaking his lantern. The delinquents, as the narrator calls them, are duly despatched to prison; the justice and the constable adjourn to a neighbouring alehouse. It turns out that Booth is the principal male character, and that his offence was to come to the aid of a stranger who had been assaulted in the street. The assailants are able to buy their way out of custody, whilst Booth and the victim of this assault are sent for trial. The episode sets the tone for much of the novel. Corrupt officers, shortage of money, violence unpunished—these are to be seen again. Booth is himself a feckless and inadequate character. Fielding had taken a daring step in moving from courtship—the familiar area of fiction—to the married state. (This was a point picked up by John Cleland, of *Fanny Hill*, in his admiring review.) He increased the risk of disappointing his public by making the husband apparently unworthy of his wife, the long-suffering Amelia. Even at the end of the book, it is a bequest to Amelia (fraudently concealed up till then) which permits escape from the perils of London. The family can now leave the capital, which has seemed little more than a forest of gaols and spunging-houses. The house they inherit is evidently in Wiltshire, and we are told that Booth is content to stay there permanently: 'He went to London and paid all his debts of honour; after which, and a stay of two days only, he returned into the country, and hath never since been thirty miles from home.'

This seems unconvincing as it applies to the fictional character Billy Booth. It makes more sense in terms of Henry Fielding, for the happy ending enacts a movement almost directly contrary to his own life history. It is hard not to read the dénouement as a form of wish-fulfilment. This is not to say that the story is purely autobiographical, as many contemporaries assumed. Lady Mary Wortley Montagu, for one, wrote to her daughter:

H. Fielding has given a true picture of himself and his first wife in the characters of Mr. and Mrs. Booth (some compliment to his own figure excepted) and I am persuaded several of the incidents he mentions are real matters of fact. I wonder he does not perceive Tom Jones and Mr. Booth are sorry scoundrels.

Likewise Samuel Richardson was confident that he could trace a real-life basis for the book:

Booth, in his last piece, again himself; Amelia, even to her noselessness, is again his first wife. His brawls, his jars, his gaols, his spunging-houses, are all drawn from what he has seen and known. As I said . . . he has little or no invention; and admirably do you observe, that by several strokes in his Amelia he designed to be good, but knew not how, and lost his genius, low humour, in the attempt.

This last testimony is weakened by the admission (made in the same letter to a lady hanger-on) that Richardson had only read the first volume of the novel, i.e., the opening quarter of the text. It should also be recalled that Lady Mary had not seen her cousin in the last fifteen years of his life: she was abroad for half the duration of his marriage to Charlotte.

It is true, of course, that the novel centres round St Martin in the Fields parish, so long familiar to the novelist. An important series of events occurs when the couple take up residence with an unscrupulous woman called Mrs Ellison in Spring Gardens—as we have seen, the Fieldings lived in that street during the later stages of their marriage, when Henry was struggling to get ahead both as a barrister and as a writer. Nevertheless, the novel is far from bare transcription of fact; all kinds of details fail to tally if we try to make the story a disguised autobiography. Nor can Booth, the half-pay officer, stand directly for Fielding, who consciously rejected the military career which his father had followed. Insofar as the character represents aspects of Fielding's nature, it unduly emphasises the weak and self-indulgent side. Even Fielding's admirers were impatient with him for depicting Booth as a man so morally feeble. The bluestocking Catherine Talbot had been hoping the Bishop of Gloucester would read the book aloud to her, but a cold forced him to substitute a silent reading—however, Elizabeth Carter, Miss Talbot's friend, thought a cold was sufficient excuse for this dereliction of duty. Miss Talbot had to read the book for herself, and she greatly enjoyed it; but she added a caveat that would be echoed by many of the audience: 'Amelia makes an excellent wife, but why did she marry Booth?'

5

The muted critical response which greeted *Amelia* disappointed Fielding. But he had too many urgent concerns to be able to sit about feeling gloomy. (He had £800, too, which was even more of a compensation.) There was the usual variety of human problems to investigate at Bow Street. Cross tells us of one representative case:

One morning he was perplexed when Mary Macculloch and Jane Macculloch were arraigned before him for beating Elizabeth Macculloch, all of whom claimed the same man for husband. As none of the three wives had any evidence of her marriage, he decided that Elizabeth, who seemed to have known the man first, possessed the best right to him. The second and third wives, by consenting to the compromise, escaped Bridewell.

If not exactly a judgment of Paris, it was a tricky problem of where to bestow the apple of discord. Fielding's judgment reflects a rough common sense which he needed in his job, much more than any abstruse learning (a fact his critics chose to ignore).

He kept up a range of charitable activities, serving as governor of a lying-in hospital and organising collections for unfortunates, such as a baker whose premises had been burnt to the ground. He put a notice regularly in his own paper, the *Covent Garden Journal*, advising people who had suffered at the hands of thieves and burglars to come to Bow Street and report their loss, when he would actively pursue the malefactors. According to Arthur Murphy, he now enjoyed an income of some four or five hundred pounds a year: some way above destitution, but far below the appropriate rate for his responsible and demanding occupation. Of course, the expectation had always been that people in his position would draw the largest share of their income from extortion. Fielding tells us in the *Journal of a Voyage to Lisbon* that a predecessor 'used to boast that he made one thousand pounds a year in his office'; but he adds that even a very great rogue would find it hard to make the post so very lucrative.

The Covent-Garden Journal, the last of Fielding's ventures into periodical writing, is perhaps the best known. It follows very much the plan as before, but the density of topical politics decreases in its leading articles. Its appearance was foreshadowed in the press in November 1751, but the first issue was delayed until 4 January—the second volume of *Amelia* carried a short trailer for the new journal. Thereafter the paper came out on Tuesdays and Saturdays for six months; after which it was published every Saturday until 25 November. The entire series comprised seventy-two issues, at threepence each. Fielding is thought to have had some assistance: newspaper items, to which the usual ironic notes were added, owed their presence to a vigilant collaborator. This unidentified figure is often said to have been our old friend William Young, the original of Parson Adams: it is likely enough, but I do not know any firm evidence by which to break Young's cover. Court-room information was apparently supplied by the Bow Street clerk, Joshua Brogden. Finally, biographers have suggested that Arthur Murphy, an ambitious young Irish journalist, may have contributed to the paper: but this is an unnecessary speculation. Murphy would almost certainly have managed to let us know in the course of his own life of Fielding, published in 1762, if that had been the case.

The *Journal* made its entrance under curious auspieces. It happened that the Universal Register Office was experiencing difficulty in getting advertisements accepted in the press. This was the more serious, because (as mentioned in the earlier part of this chapter) the Office had attracted rivals. In particular, the Public Register Office just along from Covent Garden market threatened to take a fair amount of business away from the Universal. It had been set up by a young man called D'Halluin, who had been temporarily employed as a clerk by the Fieldings. He himself claimed that there were no business secrets to be learnt, because the Universal was too inefficient to justify any sort of commercial espionage; but the proprietors of the Universal, as one would expect, felt differently. *The Covent-Garden Journal* was first and foremost an organ of publicity on behalf of the office. In due course the Public replied with its own house periodical, named the *Drury-Lane Journal*. Its editor was Bonnell Thornton, a bright young university wit who numbered the eccentric Cambridge poet Christopher Smart among his friends. Thornton was a writer of some ability, and his presence was enough to spur Fielding on to some of his liveliest journalism.

This time Fielding—ever inventive in these matters—chose the persona of 'Sir Alexander Drawcansir, Knight, Censor of Great Britiain'. (Drawcansir was the hero of the burlesque play *The Rehearsal*, which Fielding had imitated years before in *Tom Thumb*.) The name suggests a blustering, devil-may-care attitude, and indeed Fielding had reached a time in life when he no longer felt much call to disguise his prejudices. With a fine self-confidence he parodies, pontificates, corrects the taste of the town. *The Jacobite's Journal* had contained a fair amount of material concerned with the drama: Garrick and the reliable actor Billy Mills had been praised, whilst John Rich and the impudent mimic Samuel Foote had been given less favourable attention. But literary criticism as such was a major constituent of the new organ as it had not been in the earlier ventures. On a number of occasions Fielding returns to the theme of wit and humour, attempting to erect a theory of comedy which would distinguish it from mere mindless levity. But it would be misleading to present the contents as though Fielding were writing for some remote academic public. He quickly found himself embroiled in a number of personal squabbles, not only with Thornton but also with the quack 'Sir' John Hill, and the novelist, Tobias Smollett. (There are even one or two blows in the direction of Colley Cibber, a harmless octogenarian by now.)

Hill was a miscellaneous writer who had come to prominence as an apothecary in the Covent Garden area and as a fearless critic of all and sundry—Smart, Garrick, the Royal Society, and at this moment Fielding, whom he portrayed as 'the worshipful Mr. Justice Feeler'. Hill ran a column in a newspaper under the heading of 'the Inspector', and Fielding retorted by describing him as a leader of the Grub Street forces, 'his Lowness the Prince of Billingsgate'. In years to come Hill was to acquire the Swedish order of Vasa, and to go on to wilder eccentricities of behaviour. In 1752 he appeared to be a hack of a familiar kind, and Fielding did not scruple to bandy opprobious epithets with him.

As for Smollett, he had convinced himself that Fielding had plagiarised many of his most successful ideas for his fiction from *Roderick Random*, that is Smollett's first novel published in 1748. It is impossible to believe that Fielding could thoroughly revise *Tom Jones* in such a way as to introduce the character of Partridge, within months of the appearance of *Roderick Random*: but that is apparently where Smollett thought Fielding found his model, in the shape of Roderick's servant Strap. We cannot enter here into all the complicated literary disputes then raging in London, which involved Fielding, Smollett, and Hill in different ways. It is enough to say that a satire on 'Habbakkuk Hilding, Justice, Dealer and Chapman', which appeared in the bookshops during January 1752, was universally supposed to be the work of Smollett. The attribution is now treated with some caution by scholars, but Fielding had less anxiety about covering himself from possible error. He abstained from any reply in the *Journal*, not because he doubted Smollett's authorship but rather because he did not wish to give further currency to the 'Habbakkuk Hilding' pamphlet, which contains some shrewd thrusts against Fielding and George Lyttelton. The battle with Grub Street went on in Drawcansir's lively columns, and Fielding again showed himself capable of enduring the most libellous abuse without turning a hair. A thin skin or an excess of *amour propre* was no fit equipment for the Augustan man of letters.

As the *Journal* drew towards its close, in November, a brief theatrical storm blew up. Garrick and Macklin, formerly in harness, had now gone into opposition to one another, at Drury Lane and Covent Garden theatres respectively. During April, Macklin had put on a comedy called *Pasquin Turned Drawcansir*. It was not, as the title might suggest, a satire on Fielding, but rather a critique of fashionable life much in the spirit of Sir Alexander Drawcansir's denunciations of vice. The play failed and not long afterwards Macklin went into temporary retirement. There now developed a theatrical war between Garrick and John Rich. At Drury Lane the talented actor Henry Woodward presented a skilful mimicry of Rich's ropedancing and animal performers. Hostilities reached such a pitch that on 9 November an attempt was made to interrupt the show at Drury Lane, and an unseemly scuffle broke out. There was talk of a duel; the newspapers took up the story; and Woodward swore an affidavit before Mr Justice Fielding concerning his part in the disturbance. A few days later the *Covent-Garden Journal*, in its penultimate issue, presented an amusing description of this dramatic dispute. Dr John Hill had inevitably had *his* say, on the side of the Covent Garden party, and this provided Fielding with a lever with which to relate the quarrel to his running battle with Grub Street. A week later came a further playful assault upon: 'John Hill, Doc. Soc. Burg. etc., alias Hill the Apothecary, alias Jack the Herb-gatherer, alias Player-Jack, alias Hilly-Pilly, alias Silly-Hilly, alias Jack the Trumpeter, alias Jack the Spectre of Great Britain.' After that Fielding laid down his paper. It was to be his final act as a journalist.

Two minor items belong to the same year. The first is a short collection of notorious murders entitled *Examples of the Interposition of Providence in the Detection and Punishment of Murder*. The message is simply 'murder will out'. In form, the work harks back to seventeenth-century compilations which aimed to demonstrate the workings of providence in human affairs— a genre now seen to have cast its influence upon *Robinson Crusoe*. The pamphlet was priced at one shilling a copy, but there was a reduced rate for bulk orders. We learn that an army colonel was distributing copies to his troops, whilst Fielding handed them out to offenders who came before him at Bow Street. A young man whom he had just committed to Newgate on a charge of slitting his wife's throat made a pathetic appeal to be given a copy of the work. It sounds like a timely reformation.

The other item was a proposal to translate the whole works of Lucian, Fielding's perennial favourite among ancient authors. Predictably he was to have the collaboration of that worthy scholar Mr William Young. None of the enterprises in which Fielding and Young worked together enjoyed any lasting success, and this was another venture which failed to get off the ground. An eloquent puff had appeared in the *Covent-Garden Journal* no. 52: Lucian is described as 'the father of true humour' and his ablest follower Swift is said to be 'second to his original'. The 'superiority of genius' for which Lucian is distinguished happily consorts with the abundant satiric materials which fell in his way. Fielding even indicates that he himself 'formed his style upon that very author' (Lucian). The article shows such a warm and exuberant response to the Greek author that we can only regret the demise of this enterprise.

Four exceedingly busy years had now elapsed since Fielding's appointment to the bench. He had managed to crowd into this space a major novel, a sparkling periodical, and some important tracts on social questions. But time was running out.

Gin Lane by Hogarth (1751)

Opposite above The mob destroying the Star Tavern in the Strand, during the Penlez riots of 1749

Opposite below Plate 4 of *The Rake's Progress* by Hogarth (1735), showing the rake arrested for debt as he makes his way to the court of St James's

Above The Hercules Pillar inn, Hyde Park Corner, in 1756

Below The royal docks at Deptford early in the eighteenth century

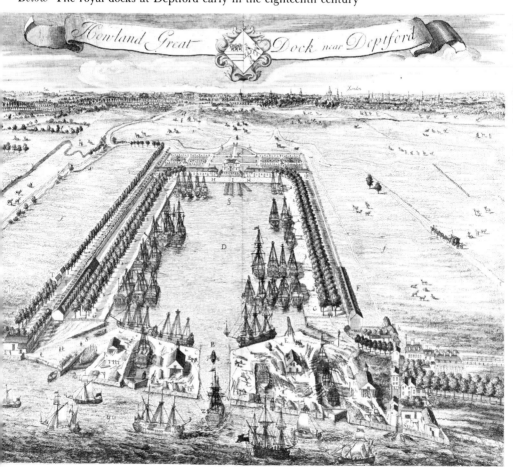

Above The monument to
Fielding in the British
Cemetery at Lisbon

Left Bust of Fielding carved
after his death

SEVEN

The Final Journey

1753-54

I

Fielding had grown up in the country, and he was to spend some of his last days—the pitifully few remaining—at a rural nook just outside London. During the summer of 1752 he acquired a farmhouse on the Uxbridge road, known as Fordhook. It was situated on the north side of the road, between Ealing and Acton. In the middle of the eighteenth century London effectively extended no further west than Hyde Park Corner. Here stood the inn called the Hercules Pillars (a sign traditionally associated with the boundaries of a city); it was much used by West Country carriers, and Fielding knew it well, as a scene in *Tom Jones*, XVI. ii, makes clear. When the traveller drove past the inn's imposing portico—or when he emerged from its comfortable interior—he proceeded along the Knightsbridge turnpike in the direction of villages such as Brompton and Kensington. Past Hammersmith and Chiswick the country opened out into what was considered a particularly healthy district. According to Fielding, it was 'guarded from the smells and smokes of London by its distance; which last is not the fate of Kensington, when the wind blows from any corner of the east'.

Here, no more than eight miles from Bow Street, Fielding could relax in peaceful surroundings. His house was rated at £70 a year; there was a small portion of land attached, but Fielding was now too stricken in health even to pose as a gentleman farmer. He had congenial friends not too far off, luckily. William Hogarth had settled three years earlier in a redbrick house down in Chiswick, not far from the river. Unlike Fielding's, the painter's home still survives, and he has even given his name to a roundabout on the Chiswick High Road. Close at hand, too, was the home of James Ralph, Fielding's old collaborator on *The Champion*. Ralph had gone through some unsuccessful years; now he was trying to retain the patronage of the Duke of Bedford and of Bubb Dodington, both of whom had gone into the opposition following the death of Frederick, Prince of Wales, in 1751. Ralph was living in Gunnersbury, a short step away even for the crippled Fielding (who was increasingly dependent upon chairs and bearers). Dodington himself had built a flashy riverside villa at Hammersmith, where Henry sometimes broke his journey to town. We know from Dodington's diary that Fielding dined with his old patron several times in 1752, once in company with the quack Thompson, who was house physician to Bubb. A final contact within reasonable range was David Garrick, when he came to live in the manor house at Hampton in January 1754; but these theatrical gatherings were of sadly short duration.

It was evident to all by now that the ministrations of Dr Thompson had proved futile. The praise accorded to this plausible gentleman in *Amelia* was wearing very thin. In the second edition the paean was omitted, either on grounds of taste or because of medical doubts. Fielding was placing more reliance on the royal surgeon, John Ranby, who was in time to acquire the house at Fordhook. But he was willing to receive a second opinion from fringe operators, and late in 1752 he began to take a nostrum called the Duke of Portland's medicine, made up of powdered roots. Continual dosing allowed him to persevere with his work on the bench, although he could not deceive himself with the illusion that he would ever be cured completely.

We can be sure of this fact from a moving passage in his *Proposal for making an Effectual Provision for the Poor*, which came out in January 1753: Fielding refers to the 'short remainder of life' left to him. The proposal had been submitted to the prime minister, Henry Pelham, in the previous November. Now it appeared as a tract of ninety pages, under the imprint of Andrew Millar, with a dedication to Pelham. The book criticises existing efforts to deal with the problem of poverty, and makes a large number of constructive suggestions towards remedying the situation. Early in the text we are given scenes of misery in outcast London foreshadowing Mayhew with their graphic depiction of 'hunger, cold, nakedness, and filth'—Fielding does not particularise as the Victorian writer would do, but he leaves the reader in no doubt of the social conditions prevailing in the poorer parts of the city.

At one time Fielding had believed that the administration of the law was largely to blame for the distress he saw around him. Now he had concluded that the poor laws were inherently defective, and that a radical overhaul of the statute-book was necessary if things were to improve. As with the *Enquiry* two years before, Fielding emphasises the scale of misery in the capital, arguing that few people—especially of 'the better sort'—had any idea of just how enormous the problem had become. As he remarked:

The sufferings of the poor are indeed less observed than their misdeeds; not indeed from any want of compassion, but because they are less known; and this is the reason why they are so often mentioned with abhorrence and so seldom with pity. ... They starve and freeze and rot among themselves, but they beg, steal and rob among their betters.

It was charitable on his part to suppose that no 'want of compassion' entered into the matter. Whilst it is true that day-to-day experience with the derelicts of society gave men like Henry, John Fielding and Saunders Welch a particular insight into the circumstances of depressed London, it is also the case that most affluent people had evolved techniques for averting their eyes from the seamy side of life in the metropolis. It would be unreasonable to expect the Duke of Bedford (who owned half Covent Garden) to follow his client Fielding into the gin-shops of St Giles or the bagnios* of Russell Street. But even Samuel Richardson, who was not unaware of the squalor that clustered around his printing-house—witness the brothel in *Clarissa*—preferred to sit among his lady admirers down in Fulham. Actively to have combated the evils of urban existence would have meant, for Richardson, knowing too much about things he chose to ignore. A letter he wrote in 1752 outlines his position with regard to Fielding's 'continual lowness'. He even expostulated on the subject to Sarah: 'Had your brother, said I, been born in a stable, or been a runner at a spunging-house, we should have thought him a genius, and wished he had the advantage of a liberal education, and of being admitted into good company.' Fielding was not 'born in a stable', but his Christian principles admittedly did allow him to contemplate what went on in such surroundings.

The best known feature of the *Proposal* is the master-plan to erect a County House near the village of Acton. It would shelter more than five thousand inmates, and contain both a home for the industrious poor and a reformatory for minor offenders committed by the courts. The cost of the scheme was put at £100,000, and elaborate architectural designs were drawn up to give the project a more concrete basis. According to Fielding's calculations the County House would pay for itself in time through the activities of the industrious poor—industrious indeed, since they were to rise at four o'clock each morning, and work most of the day until a brief respite in the evening (lights out would be at nine o'clock). A more draconian regime was planned for the idle and incorrigible group.

Whether these tough, albeit fairly conceived, regulations would have worked, we have no means of knowing. The proposal never came to anything. Pelham was dead within little more than a year, and provision for the poor remained piecemeal, ill-coordinated, and heavily dependent on private charity. It is an irony that Hogarth was able to support philanthropic activity in the most practical manner through his association with the Foundling Hospital, whereas Fielding's most ambitious project for social welfare was destined to moulder away—a mere paper scheme, left 'on the

---

*A 'bagnio', literally a bathing-house, was universally employed to mean brothel. There was a conscious indirection about it, as when people today sometimes use the term massage-parlour in an allied context.

table' whilst conditions grew more desperate in the poorer regions of London. Fielding's proposal might not have succeeded in the aims he set himself, but it deserved serious attention. Meanwhile the Commons solemnly debated the bill to allow champagne to be imported in bottles (the wine had formerly been shipped in casks); and the world went on its way.

2

Two months later Fielding brought out another pamphlet, and its subject was even more topical. In fact, *A Clear State of the Case of Elizabeth Canning* published by Millar on or about 18 March 1753, concerned the most sensational news story for many years. A huge controversy flared up, and indeed the pamphlet appeared whilst many of the central issues were still unresolved, with London divided into violently opposed factions.

The gist of the case was this. An eighteen-year-old servant girl named Elizabeth Canning had gone missing on New Year's Day, apparently in the vicinity of her home and workplace (an alehouse) near the notorious Moorfields slum. She reappeared exactly a month later, stumbling back home in a dishevelled condition at ten o'clock on the night of 29 January. Her account was a lurid one. She stated that she had been waylaid on New Year's Day as she crossed Moorfields towards Bedlam gate. She was dragged away to a house of ill fame. Here an old procuress tried to get her consent to take up a life of prostitution. When she refused, Elizabeth was imprisoned in an attic, where she remained for the next twenty-eight days. Eventually she managed to pull out a couple of boards covering the window, and slipped through the narrow gap thus effected. She then made off and found her way home within six hours.

The narrative was garnished with some telling details—the assault outside the walls of Bedlam lunatic asylum, the 'tall, dark, swarthy' woman who kept the house where Elizabeth was imprisoned, the diet of bread and water varied by a single mince-pie she had been carrying with her. Her family had no doubt about the truth of her claims. A hue and cry began, in pursuit of a certain Mother Wells who kept a notorious house at Enfield Wash, ten miles north of London. The search was quickly narrowed down to this woman, because Elizabeth claimed to have seen the Hertford coach through a chink in the attic wall; because she said she had heard a name like 'Wills or Wells' spoken in the house; and because of the old woman's bad reputation. On 1 February a party set out for Enfield, made up of a kind of licenced vigilante group with a local headborough to deliver a warrant from the Middlesex magistrate. In due course Elizabeth was able to identify several of the occupants, notably the grotesquely ill-favoured gipsy named Mary Squires.

Curiously, she did not appear to recognise Mother Wells herself. Her description tallied with the contents of the house closely enough to satisfy the party of largely self-appointed investigators. Mother Wells and the others were taken before a magistrate at Edmonton. Only the two old women could be held, and the remaining occupants of the house were set free. Mary Squires was committed to the New Prison in Clerkenwell, charged with stealing Elizabeth's stays; whilst Susanna Wells was dispatched to the adjoining Bridewell for keeping a disorderly house.

This was the situation when Fielding became directly involved. On 6 February he was approached by one Salt, the solicitor acting for Elizabeth's family. After some discussion he agreed at Salt's request to take an information from the girl, that is to say a sworn statement. Despite pressure of business and great fatigue, he saw Elizabeth the next day—testimony to his indomitable will and humane feeling, since he had been planning to make a rare mid-week visit to his farm at Fordhook. After hearing Elizabeth's story, he issued a warrant for the arrest of the other occupants of the house at Enfield. Only two could be found, but one of them, a prostitute named Virtue Hall (with horrible infelicity), appeared to corroborate the entire story. The next step was to confront the two old women with Elizabeth and Virtue Hall, and this happened a week later. The prisoners were moved to Newgate to await trial at the Old Bailey.

Susanna Wells and Mary Squires duly appeared before the Lord Mayor on 21 February. Both Elizabeth herself and the prostitute gave evidence against them. For the defence, it was claimed that Mary Squires had been in Dorset at the time in question, and witnesses were brought to London to support this alibi. The result was predictable; both the accused were found guilty. Mary Squires was sentenced to death, whilst Mother Wells was given six months imprisonment in Newgate and ordered to be branded on the thumb. The discrepancy in these sentences may surprise people today.

For some reason Sir Crisp Gascoyne, who had presided in his capacity as Lord Mayor, harboured doubts as to the rightness of the jury's verdict. Such scrupulosity was not always shown where civic dignitaries acquired a legal function, but Gascoyne was a man of charitable inclinations and had served a distinguished term as Sheriff. He now instituted further enquiries, which culminated in a complete recantation by Virtue Hall. She had been, so she said, threatened into giving false evidence in court. Early in March the town was buzzing with rumours; Fielding's old adversary Dr John Hill took up the cause of the gipsy woman, and used his newspaper column to stir up feeling against Fielding. The affronted magistrate felt it necessary to explain his part in the affair, and so the *Clear State* appeared in vindication of the course he had taken. He reasserted his belief in the guilt of those convicted. Hill replied with a pamphlet in which he analysed Fielding's arguments with a brusque air of contempt; and other writers entered the fray.

At this juncture the law officers of the crown were asked to re-examine the case. They got little cooperation from the Canning family, and this strengthened suspicions that Salt had suborned witnesses prior to the hearing. Application was then made to Fielding, in order to obtain affidavits sworn by people who claimed, individually, to have seen Mary Squires at another place during the critical period. Fielding himself had not taken these statements, but he assured the Duke of Newcastle that he would try to obtain them. On 27 April he wrote to the Duke a second time (both letters were directed from Ealing, i.e., Fordhook) reporting on these efforts. He obviously wished to disengage himself utterly from the Canning party, whose motives he now regarded with the utmost suspicion.

Soon afterwards the law officers made their report, with the dual consequence that Mary Squires was pardoned and set free while Elizabeth Canning was to be charged with perjury. It took another year before she came to trial at the Old Bailey, before Lord Chief Justice Ryder and sixteen other judges. She was sentenced to transportation for a term of seven years. Early in August she was shipped to Philadelphia on board the *Myrtilla*, Captain Budden. A pamphlet reported her fortunes when she reached Connecticut: *Virtue Triumphant, or Elizabeth Canning in America* (1757). By this date she was married, to a silly young man named John Treat. Nobody knows for sure whether or not she returned to England for a spell, as she could legally do from 1761. What is certain is that she died in Connecticut in 1773, aged about thirty-eight. The local newspaper reported this event laconically: 'Last week died very suddenly ... Mrs. Elizabeth Treat, wife of Mr. Treat, formerly the famous Elizabeth Canning.' The story would not lie down.

What was the truth of Elizabeth's alleged abduction? It is unlikely we shall ever be able to say with any certainty exactly what happened. The mystery is as deep as it ever was; the questions which divided people in 1753 have not been cleared up by the passage of years, and a book-length investigation conducted in 1947 proposes one rather far-fetched solution in a deliberately teasing way. Elizabeth may possibly have told some of the truth, but she emphatically cannot have told the whole truth. I do not think that she is very likely to have suffered from the abnormal psychological condition suggested by Lillian de la Torre: but this can only be a guess.

Fielding did not come out of the affair entirely unscathed. He had apparently been taken in by Elizabeth's innocent demeanour. She was said not to be particularly pretty, with her face marred by smallpox and her eyelashes pale almost to invisibility; but a girl of eighteen could reach the heart of a middle-aged man like Fielding without an excess of personal charms. His trusting nature had been more culpably in evidence when he allowed the solicitor Salt to take the wretched Virtue Hall's statement outside his own hearing when the girl came to Bow Street on 7 February. There were other minor improprieties in his conduct of the case, though nothing amounting to real dereliction of duty. On the other hand, we have come to expect the highest qualities from Fielding's magistracy, and we look to him for sound common sense on all occasions. It is some defence, perhaps, that he was in such bad health and desperately needing a break from the taxing routine of Bow Street. Certainly he was unlucky that one of his relatively few known lapses should have occurred in connection with a case that dominated the public's mind for many weeks and months. As with the Penlez episode, the story indicates just how sensitive and exposed a position Fielding occupied.

3

The rest of that year, 1753, witnessed other dramatic events. Most of the Bow Street calendar involved similarly inadequate and desperate people, whom Fielding treated with discriminating care. We get further evidence of his lenience towards genuinely hard cases: one infected woman, charged with stealing blankets, was dispatched not to gaol but to hospital.* However, a crime wave in the summer called for strong action against hardened offenders who were terrorising the shopkeepers in certain quarters of London and attempting to set up a protection system. It was not unknown for Fielding to be threatened whilst hearing a complaint at his court, and yet whenever the authorities were looking for positive action against the underworld it was to Fielding they invariably turned. As we have seen, he was trying to get Saunders Welch deputed to the bench of magistrates as a further bulwark against organised crime. And now, his health more or less broken, he was required to redouble his efforts.

He had been planning, early in August, to spend at least a month in Bath, on Dr Ranby's advice. However, his much needed vacation was abruptly prevented. The Duke of Newcastle, worried by a mounting series of gang murders, summoned Fielding to ask him for the best means of suppressing the wave of killings, which had already resulted in five deaths within the space of a single week. Fielding described himself as 'lame' and 'very ill

---

*Another story, dating from the previous spring, concerns a poor girl from the East End who had come all the way up to Covent Garden theatre to see Rich's *Harlequin Sorcerer*. Whilst waiting in a queue to get into the playhouse, she was robbed of fourteen shillings—and also of the chance to see the performance. When she made her complaint at Bow Street, Fielding did what he could to make restitution—that is, he gave her a free pass to the gallery. It is the kind of humane remedy for which he was famous.

with the great fatigues I had lately undergone'—understandably he tried to get out of the interview. However, the summons was repeated, and he duly presented himself at Lincoln's Inn Fields. As it turned out, the Duke was 'particularly engaged' and there was only a junior functionary to see Fielding. What was needed, he learnt, was a plan to put 'an immediate end' to the murders. Just one more small task, in fact, for the ill-paid justice of the peace.

Despite contracting a fever during this ungracious interview, Fielding set about doing as he was asked. Within four days he managed to produce a detailed programme to bring down the gangs involved. He asked for a sum of £600, much of it no doubt to be used to pay 'thief-takers'—not the old Wild-like crooks, but something much more like modern detectives. His plan was accepted and he obtained a first instalment of £200. According to his own account, within a few days 'the whole gang of cut-throats was entirely dispersed, seven of them were in actual custody, and the rest driven, some out of the town, and others out of the kingdom'. Known casualties include one of the thieves and one of the detective force. In the brief account he gives at the start of the *Voyage to Lisbon*, Fielding displays some understandable complacence about the results:

Meanwhile, amid all my fatigues and distresses, I had the satisfaction to find my endeavours had been attended with such success that this hellish society were almost utterly extirpated, and that, instead of reading of murders and street-robberies in the news almost every morning, there was, in the remaining part of the month of November, and in all December, not only no such thing as a murder, but not even a street-robbery committed. . . . In this entire freedom from street-robberies, during the dark months, no man will, I believe, scruple to acknowledge that the winter of 1753 stands unrivalled, during a course of many years; and this may possibly appear the more extraordinary to those who recollect the outrages with which it began.

The success of 'Mr F's plan' is supported by an account in the press on New Year's Day, 1754, which testifies to the general surprise people felt about the sudden fall in violent crime. Nor did the gangs find it easy to regroup their forces after this setback. Fielding's hope that the evil could be wiped out 'for ever' was surely over-optimistic, but he had laid the foundations of the first effective anti-crime squad.

It is obvious that this hectic activity must have taken its toll of his fragile health. He was, he says, 'in the opinion of all men, dying of a complication of disorders'. He had jaundice, dropsy and asthma together attacking a body 'so entirely emaciated that it had lost all its muscular flesh'. Urgent treatment was vital.

Mine was now no longer what was called a Bath case; nor, if it had been so, had I strength remaining to go thither, a ride of six miles only being attended with an intolerable fatigue. I now discharged my lodgings at Bath, which I had hitherto kept. I began in earnest to look on my case as desperate.

If he had not been forestalled by the Duke of Newcastle's intervention, he could at least have spent some tranquil days in familiar surroundings, and might have died among his own people. But nothing could save him now.

It happened to be a severe winter. Fielding survived 'the terrible six weeks' which succeeded Christmas, which 'put a lucky end, if they had known their own interests, to such numbers of aged and infirm valetudinarians, who might have gasped through two or three mild winters more'. He returned from the country to take up his duties in February. The effort caused another relapse, and early in March he was almost at the end of his strength. He was now receiving treatment from the most famous quack alive, Dr Joshua Ward. This remarkable man was known chiefly for his 'pill and drop', widely publicised and often suspected of operating on a rapid 'kill or cure' principle. Fielding defended Ward as one who had expanded a great deal of time and labour in improving his treatment, and who would omit no care in serving the patient 'without any expectation or desire of fee or reward'. Cynics would say that Ward had made his pile by this time.

Ward's remedies proving unavailing, Fielding eventually found it necessary to retire to Fordhook. He heard his last cases at Bow Street early in May, and then left his brother John to take over the formidable case-load. He now tried another much vaunted cure of the day, that is Bishop Berkeley's celebrated tar water. In his library was a copy of *Siris* (1744), in which the good bishop proclaimed the virtues of a universal medicine he had encountered in use among the Narragansett Indians of Rhode Island. Others shared Berkeley's faith that dropsy was one of the disorders which might be relieved by tar water. Even Elizabeth Carter and Catherine Talbot, bluestockings too busy ever to be ill, experimented with a course and found it did some good. Miss Carter had a nightmare of being 'sick in a land overrun with physicians, and not like Deal flowing with tar-water'. Fielding tried out the cure with less scientific detachment. He turned to Berkeley's medicine as he had tried Ward's drop and, more briefly, Booerhaave's milk diet—this last a course recommended by the greatest son of his own *alma mater*, Leyden. Slowly he began to feel some benefit from the tar water, and when he underwent the surgical trocar for a third time, late in May, there was less water to be tapped.

It was a dull, miserable month, as May so often proves to be in northern climates, and Fieldings' physicians began to think in terms of sending him abroad to seek warmer weather. The obvious places were in the South of

France, where Sterne and Smollett were to travel for the sake of their health, just a decade later. But there were no convenient sailings, and it was decided to make the destination Lisbon, a journey of some three weeks by merchant-man. Accordingly plans were set in motion to obtain an immediate passage. There could be no time to lose. One newspaper even printed a report of Fielding's death; unlike Mark Twain, he could not claim that the story was greatly exaggerated. It was very little short of the truth.

The last journey was also to form the basis of Fielding's final major work, *The Journal of a Voyage to Lisbon*, published a year after his death. It is one of his most appealing books, moving in its courage and unabated power of observation, and as rich in humanity as the best of his novels. Before he embarked on the trip he had time to bring out a revised edition of *Jonathan Wild*, an astonishing feat when one considers what Fielding had to endure that miserable winter of 1753/54. By a bitter irony, the inclement weather finally relented after Fielding had set out for the south, and it was a good harvest that autumn; but Henry spent his last hours on English soil in the midst of chill and despondency:

Wednesday, June 26, 1754. On this day the most melancholy sun I had ever beheld arose, and found me awake at my house at Fordhook. By the light of this sun I was, in my own opinion, last to behold and take leave of some of those creatures on whom I doted with a mother-like passion, guided by nature and passion, and uncured and unhardened by all the doctrine of that philosophical school where I had learned to bear pains and to despise death.

Until the coach arrived at his door, promptly at noon, he had eight further hours to 'suffer' rather than enjoy the 'company of my little ones'. It is a harrowing start to the narrative.

There were six in the party, whose passage to Lisbon cost Fielding £30 in all. Along with his wife and his sixteen-year-old daughter Harriet, there were a maid, a footman, and a lady companion—Margaret or 'Peggy' Collier, the old family friend of Henry and Sarah from their Salisbury days. Left behind were three young children, consigned to the care of old Mrs Daniel, Mary's mother. They were William, now aged six; Sophia, aged four; and the latest arrival, Allen (named of course after Ralph Allen), who was only a few months old. One other child, a girl named Louisa, had been born at Bow Street eighteen months before, but she had survived only to the next summer, and was buried at Hammersmith in May 1753. A bailiff was appointed to look after the farm at Fordbrook. John Fielding and Saunders Welch were to manage the legal and detective work centred on Bow Street. Also to remain in England were Sarah and the other Collier sister, Jane. No wonder there were so many fond farewells. Apart from his children, Henry would never again see his lone surviving sister, his loyal colleague and half-brother, or his trusted lieutenant in the fight against crime. The three infants were alone in their ignorance of the poignancy of this moment.

Saunders Welch and Jane Collier went along in the coach for the two-hour journey to Rotherhithe, as Henry took leave for ever of the city he had served so nobly. The last stage of the trip was made in a wherry, and then Fielding was hoisted aboard ship by a contraption of pulleys. Welch super-intended this cumbrous operation, whilst rows of sailors and watermen stood by to offer cruel jibes at the unfortunate man. As Fielding says, 'The total loss of limbs was apparent to all who saw me, and my face contained marks of a most diseased state, if not of death itself.' As soon as he was aboard, he settled to rest in his cabin, expecting a prompt departure. But the ship remained at anchor for a further four days, despite repeated promises from the master that the voyage was on the point of beginning. On the Friday, Fielding even had to get William Hunter, the eminent Scottish surgeon, to come out to Rotherhithe from his home at Covent Garden to perform a trocar. Ten quarts of water were tapped.

Finally on Sunday morning, 30 June, the *Queen of Portugal* set sail, and made her way down river towards Gravesend, by the royal dockyards at Deptford and Woolwich, past the stately domes of Greenwich Hospital. Fielding comments in his narrative on the warships then under construction in the yards, and of course the Seven Years War—which began only a year or so later—was to test England's sea power to the limits. Eventually the ship weighed anchor at Gravesend, where Welch and Jane Collier took their leave and set off back to London by post-chaise. Henry made an attempt to get some relief for his wife, who was suffering from severe toothache, but the surgeon whom he called was unable to perform the extraction.

After a further day's delay, the ship set out again in the evening of 1 July. The wind was set obstinately in the wrong quarter, and for some days the ship lay at anchor off Deal, home of Fielding's great admirer Elizabeth Carter. It took until 12 July to get as far as the Isle of Wight, where Fielding was encouraged by his wife to go ashore at Ryde. He himself wrote to John, back at Bow Street, describing progress so far: 'Our voyage hath proved fruitful in adventures all which being to be written in the book, you must postpone your curiosity.' He added that the captain was recognised as 'a most able and experienced seaman, to whom other captains seem to pay such deference that they attend and watch his motions, and think themselves only safe when they act under his direction and example'. In view of some of the treatment his party received, this was a generous estimate. Richard Veal, the seventy-year-old former pirate who commanded the *Queen of Portugal*, had postponed sailing chiefly for the sake of a couple of additional paying passengers; and throughout the voyage he made it clear that he placed his own interests ahead of those of the dying man. His adventurous career had included a spell of two years as a slave of the Moors, following capture by Barbary corsairs—an ever-present danger for the imprudent seaman at this period. He had later brought a treasure of thirty thousand Spanish dollars from Lisbon to London unscathed, and no doubt considered his present assignment a voyage of little consequence.

Not until the afternoon of Thursday 18 July did the wind change sufficiently for Captain Veal to give the order to leave the anchorage off Ryde. This gave Fielding the opportunity to make the acquaintance of a grasping landlady named Mrs Francis, and to give us some brilliant sketches of boarding-house existence. At long last the *Queen of Portugal* could set sail. Off Spithead there was another distraction when the captain received a visit from his nephew, an army lieutenant just returned from Gibraltar. The contrast between the uncle—crafty, self-important and aloof—and the easy-going young coxcomb of a nephew is drawn with the utmost economy. Some of the writing in the *Journal* belies its tragic occasion: Fielding's pen moves with all the old vivacity and comic insight. In particular, Captain Veal emerges as a rich and complex character, now browbeating his passengers, now sagely predicting the course of the weather, now dressing himself up in scarlet finery to visit a local squire. Almost a week was spent anchored at Brixham; Henry wrote once more to his brother John, and sent back to London two hogsheads of local cider, to be shared out between John, Andrew Millar, Saunders Welch and William Hunter. Another stop was made off Dartmouth, where Fielding took his last glimpses of the English mainland. The ship headed out into the open sea, and within two days sailed past the Lizard and Ushant into the Bay of Biscay.

The travellers had almost reached Cape Finisterre when beset by a calm, immediately succeeded by a storm from the south-west which threatened to blow them as far as Newfoundland. However, the wind abated as quickly as it had risen, and on 6 August the *Queen of Portugal* sailed safely into the River Tagus. She cast anchor in the port of Lisbon late that night, and the following day Fielding's party disembarked. 'About seven in the evening', the *Journal* tells us, 'I got into a chaise on shore, and was driven through the nastiest city in the world.' The travellers repaired to a coffee-house with a fine view towards the river and the sea, and ordered a good supper, 'for which we were as well charged as if the bill had been made on the Bath Road, between Newbury and London'. Thus, with resolution and even some gaiety, Fielding entered the brief final scene of his life.

He had brought with him some recently published essays by the free-thinking philosopher, Henry St John, Viscount Bolingbroke. These sceptical reflections had been published by a minor writer called David Mallet, once leagued in the opposition to Walpole with the satirical dramatist Henry

Fielding. The reaction of pious people to the essays is summed up in Dr Johnson's splendid outburst, reported by Boswell under 6 March 1754:

Sir, he [Bolingbroke] was a scoundrel and a coward: a scoundrel for charging a blunderbuss against religion and morality; a coward, because he had not resolution to fire it off himself, but left half a crown to a beggarly Scotchman, to draw the trigger after his death!

Fielding's own fragmentary comments on Bolingbroke were published together with the *Journal* the next year. Whilst at Lisbon, he had time only to supply an introductory section for the *Journal*, which seems to have been written up in instalments as the voyage progressed. If he had hoped to complete some major literary undertaking whilst taking the 'cure' in Portugal, he was to be disappointed in this last wish.

We know all too little of those final weeks. A letter to John, written in considerable distress, gives us some indication of events up to the beginning of September. Unfortunately some portions of the letter have been lost, and others are so damaged as to be illegible. What emerges is that Mary was ill from the time of their arrival; that she wanted to return to England, despite some signs of improvement in the health of her husband; and that Margaret Collier had been angling for a man of her own, that is an English clergyman named John Williamson. There were problems with both of the servants: the footman William had made straight back for London in the *Queen of Portugal*, taking with him some money belonging to his master. Adding to the comic opera situation was the maidservant Bell Ash, who had pursued Captain Veal to England in the conviction that he was about to marry her. Fielding naturally treated this expectation with scepticism; he asked his half-brother to see that Bell was provided with a new post through the Universal Register Office. The family was now attended by a black slave, probably a West African, together with his wife. They were living in a villa in the suburb of Junqueira; the district was both less expensive and less noisy than the centre of Lisbon. Instead of living expenses running to three pounds a day (as he incurred on arrival) he was able to get by on something like a pound a week. The rent for this villa was nine *moidores*, just over twelve pounds, per year—a tenure far beyond Fielding's life expectancy.

Characteristically, the letter includes warm tributes to new friends he had made in Lisbon, as well as gifts to old acquaintances back in England. Even Arthur Collier, the brother of Margaret and Jane who caused Henry to incur a legal obligation of £400, was to receive a present. As for his own needs, Fielding asked for a new hat and wig to be ordered from his usual suppliers in London. His health seemed to be on the mend; his tailor was to make a new coat rather broader in the shoulders, and this has been taken to mean that he was starting to put on flesh after the long wasting disease. The last words are these: 'God bless you and yours H. Ffielding.'

It may be that Fielding unconsciously exaggerated the turn for the better in his health. Perhaps he was simply trying to shield his friends at home from the truth. The final letter shows signs of incoherence, and he may not have realised how near the end was. It took just a month more before his brave spirit succumbed. He died on 8 October, aged forty-seven.

His body was taken to the British cemetery, laid out by the merchants earlier in the century, among the avenues of cypress trees. Subsequently the tomb fell into neglect, and it was only in 1830 that an elaborate monument was erected. Several Latin inscriptions were cut in the marble: one laments that Britannia should not be able to enfold her son within her bosom; another eulogises Fielding as one who, sprung from the soil of Somerset '*apud Glastoniam*', served humanity as a writer and as a philanthropist. The setting is a strange one in which to find the tomb of this most English of authors, a place of luxuriant southern foliage, with the graves of obscure merchants in the wine trade surrounding his memorial. Here George Borrow came almost a century after Fielding's death, and kissed the cold slab, commemorating 'the most singular genius which Britain ever produced'.

If he had survived, Fielding would obviously have wintered in Lisbon, and in all likelihood he would have stayed on through the following summer. Both Sterne and Smollett followed this course. If so, he would have completed his first year's lease at Junqueira in September 1755. That takes us within weeks of the shattering events of 1 November, when an earthquake destroyed most of Lisbon within eight minutes. Out of a population of 300,000, at least a tenth were killed. Pangloss was able to give Candide a sufficient explanation for the event. Henry Fielding, wiser as well as more compassionate, could have dramatised for us this remarkable day, which sent shock-waves through the entire nervous system of Europe. But he was already in his grave, up on the hillside among laurels and geraniums.

4

There is little more which needs to be told. Mary Fielding, her daughter and her friend Margaret Collier soon returned to England. Margaret had witnessed the dead man's will, drawn up in evident haste during his final illness. The widow and her four surviving children were naturally principal beneficiaries. We do not know the value of the estate: it was just enough to clear all debts, but the surplus is unlikely to have provided any large annuity. Ralph Allen was named as executor but in fact renounced administration in favour of John Fielding. Instead, Allen made an annual contribution to the education of the growing family. When he died in 1764, his legacies in cash amounted to more than £60,000, which included bequests to Mary Fielding, to Harriet, William and Allen (the only living children), and to Henry's sister Sarah. Shares in the Universal Register Office were divided between Mary and her daughters, but they cannot have brought in a large income. Henry's own impressive library was auctioned in February 1755, and brought in the considerable sum of £650, that is an average of about 10s per volume.

The subsequent history of these various members of the family can be briefly stated. Mary lived on until 1802, when she died at her son's home in Canterbury, having reached her eighties. Harriet became companion to the scandalous Elizabeth Chudleigh, celebrated for scrapes in high society and ultimately for a bigamous marriage to the Duke of Kingston. In 1766 Harriet herself married a military engineer named James Gabriel Montresor. He was a widower aged sixty-four at the time, but it was Harriet who died within a few months; he endured to find a third wife. As for the sons, the elder, William, went into the law and followed in his father's footsteps when he became a Westminster magistrate: he died in 1820.* The younger boy, Allen, entered the church and was Vicar of St Stephen's, Canterbury. He died in 1823, loved and respected for his equable nature.

When Allen Fielding married in 1783 his bride was the adopted daughter of John Fielding. The novelist's half-brother had enjoyed a distinguished career on the bench. He had further extended the detective system which Henry had introduced, and he played a notable part in the life of the capital for a further quarter of a century. For these services he was knighted in 1761. On two occasions he had to face problems comparable to those undergone by his brother in the Penlez episode: in 1768, during the Wilkite disturbances, and in 1780, when the Gordon rioters actually smashed his office in Bow Street. A few weeks later he was dead. Sarah continued her career as a writer under the patronage of Ralph Allen, settling in Bath with an occasional visit to London. She survived her brother by fourteen years; at her death in April 1768 she was buried in Charlcombe church, where long before Henry

---

*In 1757 Mary wrote to the Duke of Bedford, asking his help in getting her son William elected to Charterhouse. In fact he went to Eton, like his father. The letter reveals that Mrs Fielding had settled in Theobald's Row; she mentions Saunders Welch as willing to transmit any message. In 1770 William Fielding himself wrote to the Duke, requesting the same favour Henry had solicited twenty-two years earlier—that is, help in obtaining a property qualification for the Middlesex magistracy. As far as we can tell, the result was negative this time; in any case, the Duke died a year after. An accompanying document from Sir John Fielding refers to mysterious 'family broils' between Mary and himself during the winding up of Henry's estate. This is scarcely surprising, because (on John's own admission) Henry's affairs were 'left in a very bad state for his family, there being scarce sufficient for the creditors'.

and Charlotte had taken the sacraments on the occasion of their runaway marriage.

Among Fielding's friends, we have seen that Ralph Allen lived on in continuing prosperity until 1764. George Lyttelton was made a peer and died in 1773, just in time to earn the last place in Johnson's *Lives of the Poets*—only the deceased were admitted to that collection. Andrew Millar enjoyed further success in publishing with works of history proving particularly remunerative (he was able to give £3,400 to the forgotten writer William Robertson for a study of the Emperor Charles V). Not for nothing did Dr Johnson observe, 'I respect Millar, Sir; he has raised the price of literature.' David Garrick remained at the pinnacle of his profession up to his death in 1779. A year previously he had arranged for the production of a long lost play by Fielding; although he was no longer performing on the stage, he remained an elder statesman among theatrical personalities at Drury Lane, where Sheridan was now manager. *The Good Natured Man* was put on, extensively revised by Garrick, late in 1778, which brought it into direct competition with *The School for Scandal*. It enjoyed moderate success, which is perhaps as much as Sheridan wished for it.

William Hogarth, who had known Fielding for twenty years, must have been one of those most affected by Henry's death. In 1762, when Arthur Murphy was bringing out the first collected edition of the *Works*, Andrew Millar decided that a portrait was needed to set at the head of Volume I. A sketch was thereupon made by Hogarth; obviously the study is chiefly based on memory, but different stories have attached themselves to its origins. Murphy says that a lady (thought to be Margaret Collier) supplied the artist with a silhouette in paper of Fielding's profile, which served as the basis of Hogarth's pen-and-ink drawing. It may or may not be true. What is certain is that this remains the only authentic portrait we have, surprisingly so in view of Fielding's fame and the cult of portraiture in mid-Georgian England. It represents Fielding in his later years: the eyes remain dark and keen, but the heavy jaw sags under a toothless mouth, and there is a slightly bloated look about the nose and its widely dilated nostrils.

Many tributes to Fielding appeared after his untimely passing. The most notable is that of Lady Mary Wortley Montagu, who had known him first when he was in the full bloom of youth, and who admired his qualities without attempting to palliate his 'continued indiscretion'. When she learnt of her cousin's decease, almost a year after the event, she wrote to her daughter:

I am sorry for H. Fielding's death, not only as I shall read no more of his writings, but I believe he lost more than others, as no man enjoyed life more than he did, though few had less reason to do so, the highest of his preferment being raking in the lowest sinks of vice and misery. . . . His happy constitution (even when he had, with great pains, half demolished it) made him forget everything when he was before a venison pasty or over a flask of champagne, and I am persuaded he has known more happy moments than any prince upon earth. His natural spirits gave him rapture with his cookmaid, and cheerfulness when he was fluxing in a garret. There was a great similitude between his character and that of Sir Richard Steele. He had the advantage both in learning and, in my opinion, genius. They both agreed in wanting money in spite of all their friends, and would have wanted it if their hereditary lands had been as extensive as their imagination, yet each of them so formed for happiness, it is a pity they were not immortal.

More elaborate and finished elegies were composed, but this is the most convincing from a human point of view. Lady Mary had written on her copy of *Tom Jones* '*ne plus ultra*', and affection clearly outweighs all other elements in her response.

Today we know a good deal about Fielding's life of which Lady Mary must have been ignorant—especially as regards his work of 'raking in the lowest sinks of vice and misery' whilst a London magistrate. But the new evidence simply confirms the picture of a dedicated, charitable and thoroughly good man. His weaknesses have always been obvious to the most casual observer; if intemperance was the cause of his physical breakdown (and we have no positive medical evidence of this), then the price he paid was a high one. His virtues are equally apparent, to anyone who savours warm, direct and spontaneous feeling. Above all, his immense fund of humour pervades his biography as it does his books. In his own day writers were often figures of menace—witness the terrible Swift or the overpowering Johnson. In this century the great masters of literature have been impossibly distant, wringing their art from neurosis and despair. Fielding reminds us that a sane and humane outlook can also be a true and profound one.

An Inheritance Reclaimed

It is easy, in a certain frame of mind, to imbue Fielding's life history with a sense of disappointment or anti-climax. The heir of the Habsburgs (as he thought), he retained all the swagger of an aristocrat without having the means to support such an outlook. Sometimes one feels that he might have been happier as a country gentleman living privately in some easygoing corner of Georgian England. One pictures him perhaps at Salisbury, engaged in amiable philosophic discussion with James Harris as the two men perambulate round the spacious cathedral close. Or rusticating in Dorset, with his books and his wine, his children busy with their games among streams and meadows.

But it is all delusion. The contemplative, bookish, learned Fielding existed all right; but he was only half of the full man. There was an equally powerful urge in him towards active involvement with the world. The drives which led him to become a professional playwright were later to impel him toward the seamiest area of life that his legal vocation could offer. In both capacities he displayed practical philanthropy: as a dramatist, in the benefit performances he arranged, and then more seriously as a magistrate, in the efforts towards penal reform he instituted. He had been a scholar among hack writers, and then he became a bohemian among his learned brethren of the gown.

Of course it is a terrible shame that he had so little time in which to achieve what he wanted. The tragic brevity of his life can be enforced by a few simple comparisons. Among the men and women he encountered, even the most senior group survived him. Colley Cibber, Handel, Richardson, Beau Nash, Lady Mary Wortley Montagu, John Rich, Ralph Allen, Bubb Dodington—all were fifteen, twenty, twenty-five, thirty, even thirty-five years old when Fielding was born, yet they outlasted him. When the young writer began his career, George II had ascended the English throne, already a middle-aged man; he still had several years of active life before him when Fielding's career was cut short. Hogarth, ten years older, survived Fielding by almost a decade. The actor Charles Macklin, who was about seven when Henry was born, came within three years of witnessing the start of the nineteenth century. Abroad, there was the greatest Italian dramatist of the day, Carlo Goldoni, who entered the world just two months prior to

Fielding; he observed the French Revolution at first hand and was even voted a pension by the National Convention. The greatest comic genius in France during Fielding's time, Voltaire, was just reaching his teens when the English writer was born; he still had almost a quarter of a century of valiant service to perform in October 1754. Finally, consider Henry Fielding's own English contemporaries. His cousin Henry Gould went on to reach the age of eighty-four; Kitty Clive lived till seventy-four; William Pitt till seventy; Thomas Arne till sixty-eight; George Lyttelton till sixty-four; Andrew Millar till sixty-one. Even the ailing James Ralph attained his later fifties, and Theophilus Cibber was fifty-five when (wretched and absurd to the end) he was drowned whilst crossing the Irish Sea. Dr John Ranby took up residence at Fordhook and could enjoy it until his three score years and ten were complete. It is worth adding that neither Defoe nor Richardson had even begun to write novels when they were forty-seven. Laurence Sterne and Tobias Smollett, a pair of valetudinarians who made invalidism into a way of life, each had a lifespan longer than Fielding's.

It is idle, I know, to lament such things. I have instanced these facts only to emphasise what Fielding *did* achieve in the pitifully short time which was allowed to him. As an artist and as a man, he drank down experience to the full. His books are unrivalled in the density of their social coverage. Martin Battestin says of his fictional world that, 'like Joyce's Dublin, it is populated both by characters of the author's imagination and by living people of his own acquaintance—by inn-keepers and dancing-masters, actors and attorneys, doctors and divines, coachmen and mantua-makers.' In the same way, his humanity on the bench was informed by the range of his contacts and the wealth of his stored insights about people. In the words of his great friend James Harris:

Had his *life* been *less irregular* (for irregular it was, and spent in a promiscuous intercourse with persons of all ranks) his *pictures* of *human kind* had neither been so *various*, nor so *natural*.

Had he possessed less of *literature*, he could not have infused such a spirit of *classical elegance*.

Had his genius been less fertile in *wit* and *humour*, he could not have maintained that *uninterrupted pleasantry*, which never suffers his reader to feel fatigue.

Perhaps, after all, Henry Fielding did come into his inheritance. It was not the world he had glimpsed from Glastonbury, a settled and prosperous shire with rivers meandering placidly to the sea. Or the prospect from Eton College, a stable and ordered society; or the vista from Prior Park, with classical Bath receding into the distance; or even the view from Old Sarum, history without any present tense, a remnant of political archaeology that stood aloof and isolated. Fielding's Salisbury was the bustling Georgian town itself, gracious beneath the great cathedral spire and yet full of life and energy. He needed the still places, but he was most himself on the busy highway and in the haunts of men and women. So he transmits to us a vision of confused and raucous human life, tolerantly observed from a garret, the breakfast-parlour of an inn, or the ground floor of Bow Street courthouse.

FAMILY TREE

BIOGRAPHIC INDEX

READING LIST

GENERAL INDEX

The Fielding Family Tree

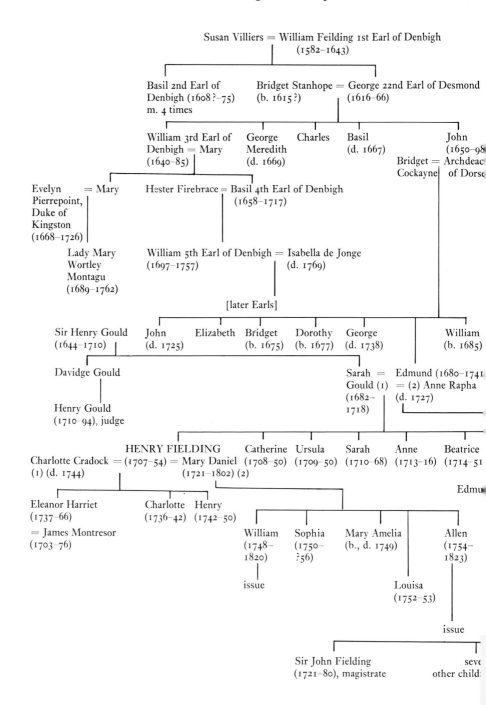

Susan Villiers = William Feilding 1st Earl of Denbigh
(1582–1643)

Basil 2nd Earl of Denbigh (1608?–75) m. 4 times

Bridget Stanhope (b. 1615?) = George 22nd Earl of Desmond (1616–66)

William 3rd Earl of Denbigh = Mary (1640–85)

George Meredith (d. 1669)

Charles

Basil (d. 1667)

John (1650–98)
Bridget Cockayne = Archdeac of Dorse

Evelyn Pierrepoint, Duke of Kingston (1668–1726) = Mary

Hester Firebrace = Basil 4th Earl of Denbigh (1658–1717)

Lady Mary Wortley Montagu (1689–1762)

William 5th Earl of Denbigh (1697–1757) = Isabella de Jonge (d. 1769)

[later Earls]

Sir Henry Gould (1644–1710)

John (d. 1725)

Elizabeth

Bridget (b. 1675)

Dorothy (b. 1677)

George (d. 1738)

William (b. 1685)

Davidge Gould

Sarah Gould (1) (1682–1718) = Edmund (1680–1741) = (2) Anne Rapha (d. 1727)

Henry Gould (1710–94), judge

Charlotte Cradock (1) (d. 1744) = HENRY FIELDING (1707–54) = Mary Daniel (1721–1802) (2)

Catherine (1708–50)

Ursula (1709–50)

Sarah (1710–68)

Anne (1713–16)

Beatrice (1714–51)

Edmu

Eleanor Harriet (1737–66) = James Montresor (1703–76)

Charlotte (1736–42)

Henry (1742–50)

William (1748–1820)

Sophia (1750–?56)

Mary Amelia (b., d. 1749)

Allen (1754–1823)

issue

Louisa (1752–53)

issue

Sir John Fielding (1721–80), magistrate

seve other child

Biographic Index

Entries are confined to persons who played a substantial part
in Fielding's life or who affected his work in some degree.
For all other figures, see the General Index.

Sub = subscribed to Fielding's *Miscellanies* (1743).

ALLEN, RALPH (1694–1764). Postal reformer and entrepreneur, whose home at
Prior Park F often visited: friend of Pope: dedicatee of *Amelia* and patron of
Sarah Fielding.

ARNE, THOMAS AUGUSTINE (1710–78). Composer. F's schoolfellow at
Eton: supplied music for some of his plays. Brother of Susanna Cibber (*q.v.*).

BEDFORD, JOHN RUSSELL, fourth Duke of (1710–71). Politician: member of
opposition to Walpole, later joined Pelham administration. Helped to obtain
F's post as magistrate. *Sub.*

CARTER, ELIZABETH (1717–1806). Translator; learned lady of Deal, friend
of Richardson and of Samuel Johnson; also admired F's novels.

CHARKE, CHARLOTTE (1713–60). Actress: daughter of Colley Cibber, who
performed in several plays by F.

CHESTERFIELD, PHILIP DORMER STANHOPE, fourth Earl of (1694–73).
Politician and writer; minister and later member of the Patriot opposition. Led
the attack on the theatrical Licensing Act. *Sub.*

CIBBER, COLLEY (1671–1757). Playwright, theatrical manager, poet laureate.
Author of *Apology* for his own life (1740). A frequent butt of the satirists,
including F. Engaged in a famous quarrel with Pope.

CIBBER, SUSANNA (1714–66). Singer and actress: *née* Arne. Married Theophilus Cibber. At the centre of the William Sloper episode.

CIBBER, THEOPHILUS (1703–58). Actor; son of Colley Cibber. Much involved
in London theatrical disputes during the 1730s, and satirised by F on several
occasions. Putative author of *Lives of the Poets* (1753).

CLIVE, CATHERINE (1711–85). Known as 'Kitty' Clive: *née* Raftor. Actress
and singer who starred in many of F's plays. *Sub.*

COLLIER, ARTHUR, JANE, and MARGARET. Children of the philosopher
Arthur Collier (1680–1732); the family resided at Salisbury and were friends of
Henry and Sarah Fielding. Margaret accompanied F on his final journey to
Lisbon.

CRADOCK, CHARLOTTE (d. 1744). F's first wife; a Salisbury beauty, whom
he married in 1734; in part the model for Sophia and Amelia in F's fiction.

DANIEL, MARY (1721–1802). F's second wife; formerly a family servant who kept house after Charlotte's death. Married F in 1747 and bore him several children.

DE VEIL, THOMAS (1684–1746). Magistrate who helped to destroy criminal gangs in London during the 1730s and 1740s; F's predecessor at Bow Street.

DODINGTON, GEORGE BUBB (1691–1762). Politician and patron, who held office under Pelham. A long-time supporter of F's work. *Sub.*

FIELDING, EDMUND (1680–1741). General: F's mercurial and imprudent father.

FIELDING, JOHN (1721–80). F's half-brother. Succeeded in the magistracy at Bow Street. Continued the policies of building up a detective force and seeking out the causes of crime.

FIELDING, SARAH (1710–68). F's favourite sister; novelist, author of *David Simple* (1744); a friend of Ralph Allen.

FREDERICK, Prince of Wales (1707–51). Son of George II and heir to the throne; titular head of opposition groups in the era of Walpole and then of Pelham. *Sub.*

GARRICK, DAVID (1717–79). The greatest actor of the age; member of the Johnson circle. Collaborated with F on dramatic work and earned his warm admiration. *Sub.*

GEORGE II, King of England (1683–1760). Succeeded to the throne in 1727. Together with his wife Caroline, gave support to Walpole right up to the fall of the premier. Ironically celebrated in Pope's 'Epistle to Augustus' (1737).

GIFFARD, HENRY (1694–1772). Actor-manager and dramatist, who gave F some of his first opportunities in the theatre.

GOULD, HENRY (1710–94). F's worthy and successful cousin. Studied at the Middle Temple, later a K.C. and a judge. *Sub.*

HANBURY WILLIAMS, CHARLES (1708–59). Eton schoolmate of F; diplomat and writer, K.B. (1744); receives favourable mention from F on several occasions. *Sub.*

HANDEL, GEORGE FREDERICK (1685–1759). The great composer. Active in London musical and theatrical life throughout F's lifetime.

HARDWICKE, PHILIP YORKE, first Earl of (1690–1764). Lord Chancellor; presided over trials of Jacobite lords. F helped to scotch an assassination attempt.

HARRIS, JAMES (1709–80). One of F's most durable friendships; writer and political placeman, author of *Hermes* (1751), and engaged in an extensive correspondence with F (still unpublished). *Sub.*

HEIDEGGER, JOHN JAMES (?1659–1749). Impresario; at various times joined with Handel to promote opera in London. Best known as a pioneer of the taste for masquerades. Figures in F's poem *The Masquerade* and elsewhere in the works.

HERVEY, JOHN, first Baron (1696–1743). Politician and memoir-writer, satirised by Pope as 'Sporus'. An adherent of Walpole. Appears as 'Miss Fanny' in *Shamela* and possibly as Beau Didapper in *Joseph Andrews*.

HENLEY, JOHN (1692–1756). Eccentric preacher and journalist; frequent target of the wits, and regularly an object of satire for F, especially in his plays

HILL, JOHN (?1716–65). Quack and miscellaneous writer, who entered into several disputes with F towards the end of the latter's life. A specialist in popular treatments of scientific and medical topics.

HOGARTH, WILLIAM (1697–1762). Painter and caricaturist. Had close personal and artistic ties with F for more than twenty years, and received many warm tributes from his friend.

HUNTER, WILLIAM (1718–83). Anatomist and surgeon; brother of another great medical pioneer John Hunter (1728–93). Treated F just before he set out on his final voyage. He lived in the Great Piazza of Covent Garden.

LYTTELTON, GEORGE (1709–73). A lifelong friend of F from their meeting as schoolboys at Eton. Politician, patron, and poet; dedicatee of *Tom Jones*; leading member of opposition to Walpole and later a Lord of the Treasury during Pelham administration. *Sub.*

MACKLIN, CHARLES (?1700–97). Actor, manager, and playwright. Created many roles in F's comedies in the 1730s.

MILLAR, ANDREW (1707–68). Bookseller who published most of F's later works including the novels; also issued work by Johnson, Thomson and Hume. *Sub.*

MONTAGU, Lady MARY WORTLEY (1689–1762). Lady of letters who wrote poems, essays, and some notable personal correspondence. F's cousin who gave him early encouragement. Retired to Italy in 1739. Friend of Hervey, and also at one time of Pope, with whom she subsequently quarrelled.

MURPHY, ARTHUR (1727–1805). F's first biographer in 1762; later wrote on Garrick and Johnson. Dramatic critic and journalist.

NASH, RICHARD (1674–1762). 'King of Bath' during F's sojourns in the city. Receives glancing mention in *Tom Jones* and elsewhere. A colleague of Ralph Allen in several civic enterprises.

NEWCASTLE, THOMAS PELHAM-HOLLES, first Duke of (1693–1768). Politician and courtier, who held high office throughout the administrations of Walpole and then of his brother Henry Pelham. Authorised F to crush the gangs of street-robbers terrorising London in 1753. *Sub.*

PELHAM, HENRY (1696–1754). A principal lieutenant of Walpole who came to the head of the ministry after the latter's death. Received F's loyal support throughout his period in office. Younger brother of the Duke of Newcastle.

PITT, WILLIAM (1708–78). 'Pitt the Elder', made Earl of Chatham in 1766. At Eton with F; subsequently a major figure in the Patriot opposition. After F's death attained power and spectacular success for a time. MP for Old Sarum with Lyttelton, and a frequent visitor to Bath; helped to promote *Tom Jones*. *Sub.*

POPE, ALEXANDER (1688–1744). Poet; member of the Scriblerus group of satirists along with Swift and John Gay. Provided a model for F's early work, and in turn used aspects of F's dramatic technique in his 'new' *Dunciad* of 1742. A close friend of Ralph Allen and may well have met F at Prior Park.

RALPH, JAMES (?1705–62). Miscellaneous writer, who worked with F on *The Champion*, and was involved in the London theatre during F's years as a dramatist. Later on wrote for Pelham and for Dodington.

RANBY, JOHN (?1703–73). Serjeant-surgeon to George II: treated Walpole and became engaged in pamphlet war; later attempted to cure F's gout and received warm tributes in *Amelia* and elsewhere. Took over F's country house at Fordhook after his death. *Sub*.

RICH, JOHN (1692–1761). Theatrical impresario, who made Covent Garden playhouse the home of pantomime, farce and harlequinade. Much involved with F during the 1730s. Lived in the Great Piazza, close to the theatre.

RICHARDSON, SAMUEL (1689–1761). Printer and novelist. His hugely successful *Pamela* (1740–41) inspired F's *Shamela* and *Joseph Andrews*. Richardson's next work *Clarissa* (1747–48) earned F's unstinting admiration, but Richardson remained cool and resentful towards his rival.

SMOLLETT, TOBIAS (1721–71). Novelist; believed that F had plagiarised his book *Roderick Random* (1748), and was the probable author of an attack published in 1752.

SWIFT, JONATHAN (1667–1745). F's much admired predecessor in satire, whose work he repeatedly instanced as the true fount of English humour. A member of the Scriblerus group together with Pope and John Gay.

THOMPSON, THOMAS (d. 1763). A well-known practitioner of fringe medicine, who treated Pope and the Prince of Wales. In the 1740s he became physician both to Dodington and to F. Unsuccessful in his ministrations in the case of F.

WADE, GEORGE (1673–1748). Field-marshal; took part in both campaigns against Jacobites, and built roads and forts in Scotland after the 1715 rising. MP for Hindon; lived in Bath, where he became a friend of Ralph Allen. Praised by F in *Jacobite's Journal*.

WALPOLE, HORACE (1717–97). Subsequently fourth Earl of Orford. Letter-writer, author of *The Castle of Otranto*, and creator of Strawberry Hill. Son of Robert Walpole. Hostile towards F and the source of some damaging anecdotes.

WALPOLE, ROBERT (1676–1745). Subsequently first Earl of Orford. Dominated national politics from 1721 to 1742. F originally joined the opposition to Walpole, and his work of the 1730s contains repeated thrusts at the prime minister, as does *Jonathan Wild*. Shortly before Walpole's fall F came over to his side, probably impelled in part by a bribe from the government. *Sub*.

WALTER, PETER (?1664–1746). Dorset landowner, in the vicinity of F's boyhood home at East Stour. A financial operator and extortionate agent who lent money at high interest. Characterised by F as 'Peter Pounce' in *Joseph Andrews*.

WARD, JOSHUA (1685–1761). Quack doctor, famous for his 'drop', who treated F in his last illness.

WELCH, SAUNDERS (1711–84). High constable of Holborn, who was recruited by F to help fight crime and subsequently became a Westminster magistrate. Friend of Dr Johnson.

WILD, JONATHAN (1683–1725). The notorious thief-taker, satirised in *The Beggar's Opera* and then the basis for F's own sardonic novel (1743). Often seen as the criminal counterpart to Walpole.

YOUNG, WILLIAM (1702–57). A Dorset curate who is thought to have supplied many touches for the portrait of Parson Adams, by reason of his combination of learning and innocence. Collaborated with F on translations and on his journalistic ventures.

The average life-span for those listed is approximately sixty-nine years. (I have allowed thirty-five years for Charlotte Fielding, which may be a little on the high side.) This finding underlines the point I have tried to make in the Epilogue. Only two others among those listed had a shorter life-span than Henry Fielding; one was the Prince of Wales, and the other Jonathan Wild, whose term was abruptly curtailed at Tyburn.

Reading List

(Details given of editions of origin only. All places of
publication London except where otherwise stated)

Biography

Arthur Murphy, 'An Essay on the life and Genius of Henry Fielding esq', prefixed
to vol. 1 of the *Works* (1762). Vigorous but undependable.
Austin Dobson, *Fielding* (English Men of Letters series, 1883). Still one of the
more judicious treatments.
Wilbur L. Cross, *The History of Henry Fielding*, 3 vols (New Haven, 1918). Still
the best in the field.
F. Homes Dudden, *Henry Fielding: His Life, Works, and Times*, 2 vols (Oxford,
1952). To a large extent a paraphrase of Cross, with little independent material
of importance.

Editions

Works, originally 4 vols, ed. Arthur Murphy (1762).
Complete Works, ed. W. E. Henley, 16 vols (1903).
The first true scholarly edition is the new Wesleyan Edition, general editor W. B.
Coley, in progress; four volumes so far available including *Joseph Andrews*
(1967) and *Tom Jones* (1974). Henry Knight Miller is responsible for editing
the *Miscellanies*, vol 1 (1971); he is also the author of valuable *Essays on Fielding's
Miscellanies* (Princeton, 1961).

Criticism and Scholarship

The history of Fielding criticism can be followed in two good books: Ronald
Paulson and Thomas Lockwood (eds), *Henry Fielding: the Critical Heritage*
(1969), and C. J. Rawson, (ed.), *Henry Fielding: a Critical Anthology* (1973).
There are several casebooks on the novels, of which the collection edited by
Ronald Paulson in the Twentieth Century Views series (Englewood Cliffs, NJ,
1962) is the best.
Important recent criticism includes: Robert Alter, *Fielding and the Nature of the
Novel* (Cambridge, Mass., 1968); Glenn W. Hatfield, *Fielding and the Language
of Irony* (Chicago, 1968); and C. J. Rawson, *Henry Fielding and the Augustan
Ideal Under Stress* (1972), an especially lively study.

W. R. Irwin, *The Making of Jonathan Wild* (New York, 1941) may be supplemented by Gerald Howson, *Thief-Taker General* (1970), a life of the real Wild.
The Criticism of Henry Fielding, ed. Ioan Williams (1970) is a convenient collection of critical pronouncements.
Malvin R. Zirker, *Fielding's Social Pamphlets* (Berkeley and Los Angeles, 1966) discusses Fielding's views on legal and social issues.
There is no adequate study of the plays, though a French work, *Le Théatre de Fielding* by Jean Ducrocq (1975) is workmanlike. The most incisive criticism will be found in Ian Donaldson's excellent book *The World Upside Down* (Oxford, 1970).

Background

For the theatre, see the volumes of *The London Stage 1660–1800* (Carbondale, Ill. 1960–68 , esp. part 3 (1729–47), edited by Arthur H. Scouten. The same writer contributes valuably to *The Revels History of Drama in English*, vol. 5 (1976), which covers the period 1660–1750. John Loftis, *The Politics of Drama in Augustan England* (1963) is a sound discussion.
Ronald Paulson, *Hogarth : His Life, Art and Times* (New Haven, 1971), 2 vols, is an indispensable guide.
R. H. Barker, *Mr Cibber of Drury Lane* (New York, 1939) is a reliable study, as is Robert Halsband, *The Life of Lady Mary Wortley Montagu* (Oxford, 1956).
A. R. Humphreys, *The Augustan World* (1954) provides a readable introduction to ideas and tides of taste within the period of Fielding's lifetime. My own *Grub Street* (1972) considers the position of professional writers, whilst *The Augustan Vision* (1974) is a general survey designed to set literature in the context of political, social and intellectual change.
A thorough, provocative but regrettably uncompleted biography is J. H. Plumb's account of Robert Walpole, 2 vols (1956–60); the same author's book on *The First Four Georges* (1956) contains a highly personal reading of the character of George II.
Bertrand A. Goldgar, *Walpole and the Wits* (Lincoln, Nebraska, 1976) helps to locate Fielding's work within the context of the opposition to Walpole.
A controversial account of many aspects of crime in the period can be found in D. Hay, *et al.*, *Albion's Fatal Tree* (1975; Penguin edn 1977).
A classic study is that of M. Dorothy George, *London Life in the Eighteenth Century* (1925; Penguin edn 1966).
An ingenious, if not wholly convincing attempt to unravel the mystery of Elizabeth Canning is provided by Lillian de la Torre, *Elizabeth is Missing* (1947).
For Ralph Allen, see Benjamin Boyce, *The Benevolent Man* (Cambridge, Mass., 1967). Good on both Allen and Peter Walter is Howard Erskine-Hill, *The Social Milieu of Alexander Pope* (1975).

General Index

Page numbers in italics refer to illustrations. An asterisk preceding names indicates an entry in the Biographic Index, pp. 227–31